CAMBRIDGE STUDIES IN
MEDIEVAL LIFE AND THOUGHT
Edited by M. D. Knowles, Litt.D., F.B.A.
Fellow of Peterhouse and Regius Professor of Modern History in the
University of Cambridge

NEW SERIES VOL. VIII

WYCLIF AND
THE OXFORD SCHOOLS

WYCLIF

AND THE

OXFORD SCHOOLS

THE RELATION OF THE 'SUMMA DE ENTE' TO
SCHOLASTIC DEBATES AT OXFORD IN THE
LATER FOURTEENTH CENTURY

BY

J. A. ROBSON

formerly Fellow of Gonville and Caius College, Cambridge

CAMBRIDGE
AT THE UNIVERSITY PRESS
1961

PUBLISHED BY
THE SYNDICS OF THE CAMBRIDGE UNIVERSITY PRESS

Bentley House, 200 Euston Road, London, N.W.1
American Branch: 32 East 57th Street, New York 22, N.Y.
West African Office: P.O. Box 33, Ibadan, Nigeria

©

CAMBRIDGE UNIVERSITY PRESS

1961

Printed in Great Britain at the University Press, Cambridge
(Brooke Crutchley, University Printer)

FOR MAUREEN

CONTENTS

LIST OF ABBREVIATIONS

Lechler   *John Wycliffe and his English precursors* (London, 1884). English edn and trans. by P. Lorimer of G. Lechler, *Johann von Wicliff und die Vorgeschichte der Reformation*, 2 vols. (Leipzig, 1873).

Workman   H. B. Workman, *John Wyclif*, 2 vols. (Oxford, 1926).

AFH   *Archivum Franciscanum Historicum.*

AHDL   *Archives d'histoire doctrinale et littéraire.*

DNB   *Dictionary of National Biography.*

DTC   *Dictionnaire de théologie catholique.*

EHR   *English Historical Review.*

FZ   *Fasciculi Zizanorium*, ed. W. W. Shirley (Rolls Series, 1858).

OHS   *Oxford Historical Society.*

RTAM   *Recherches de théologie ancienne et médiévale.*

TRHS   *Transactions of the Royal Historical Society.*

WS   *Wyclif Society.*

PREFACE

W HEN in 1909 the Wyclif Society published Michael Dziewicki's edition of six tracts of the *Summa de Ente*, the Society's life was already drawing to a close. One further volume was published before the outbreak of the first world war; two more (one not of Wyclif's own writings) were issued in 1922. Two boxes of long-hand transcriptions in the library of Trinity College, Cambridge, show that work had begun on an edition of the remaining tracts of the *Summa*. In 1930 Professor S. H. Thomson, of the University of Colorado, planning to finish what the Wyclif Society had left incomplete, edited Book I, tracts 1–2; and between 1928 and 1937 he published a series of valuable papers, which greatly enlarged our knowledge of the manuscripts of Wyclif's philosophical treatises, especially those now in Central European libraries. As will be seen, I have drawn extensively on these studies. It is greatly to be hoped that Professor Thomson's other interests will permit him to complete the edition of the *Summa de Ente*, for which his own researches have paved the way. Such an edition will certainly resolve many uncertainties and correct many errors in this study. We shall then have the fundamental texts without which our judgements and assertions remain provisional.

Meanwhile there is room, I believe, for the present work, which is perhaps rather wider in scope, though far less profound in scholarship. It attempts to relate the broad lines of Wyclif's meta-physics and theology, as set out in the *Summa de Ente*, to their Oxford setting, by comparing the *Summa* with the writings of masters who were prominent in the university in Wyclif's early days, or by whom we know he was influenced. This approach is, of course, open to criticism. There is bound to be a temptation to seek like rather than unlike, to emphasise what Wyclif shared with other scholastics and not what is distinctive in his work. Such a bias (if it exists) has at least the merit of being the opposite of the usual; and in fact one of the values of studying the *Summa de Ente* is that it helps us to distinguish what is original in Wyclif's early philosophy. One part of this is a distinctive and personal elaboration of his own ideas, whilst the other part is best regarded as a contribution to a long debate on certain difficult problems, mainly theological, which preoccupied theologians at Oxford as in all Europe in the fourteenth century.

It is a pleasure to acknowledge the many courtesies and kindnesses I have received. Mr H. M. Adams, lately Librarian of Trinity College, Cambridge, agreed to deposit the manuscript of Wyclif's *Summa de Ente* in the University Library for a whole year, thus greatly easing my task. The Librarians of New College and Merton College, Oxford, and of Worcester Cathedral Chapter Library also permitted manuscripts in their charge to be deposited for my convenience either in Bodley or the Cambridge University Library. Members of the staff of these libraries, and many of those named below, aided me with manuscript problems. But none of them is to blame for any misreadings that occur; and he would be a bold student of scholastic contractions of the later Middle Ages who declared his decipherment to be quite faultless.

Of those who helped me whilst this book was prepared, I wish first to thank my parents for their support and continued interest. The Master and Fellows of Gonville and Caius College encouraged me first as scholar and research student and then as research fellow. In particular I would like to thank Mr Philip Grierson and Professor C. N. L. Brooke for their advice and friendship. Professor Brooke has also most kindly read the final draft and the proofs. He has been able to remove many errors; but neither he nor any other person is responsible for those that remain. The Warden and Fellows of Merton College, Oxford, gave me much pleasure by allowing me to pass a happy year in that society of which, many centuries ago, so many of the scholars touched on in the following pages were members. In particular I wish to thank the Librarian, Dr J. R. L. Highfield. To Professor Knowles I owe many debts of gratitude. He supervised my thesis; encouraged me when my interests turned to fresh woods and warmer climes, and when, like Richard FitzRalph, I felt weighed down by the 'vain croakings of the Schools'; and he has now agreed to include this study in his Series. At many points I have profited from conversations with Dr Gordon Leff. At Oxford Professor Ernest Jacob and Mr W. A. Pantin gave me much help and advice; and I hope I have benefited from the criticisms of Dr Walter Ullmann, Professor H. S. Offler and Professor C. R. Cheney. My wife compiled the index, and I am most grateful to her. The final draft of this book was prepared at University College, London; and I must thank the head of the Department of History, Professor R. A. Humphreys, for giving me time to complete it.

J.A.R.

DECEMBER 1959

INTRODUCTION

THE study of the life and writings of John Wyclif has seldom, until recently, been free from controversy or acrimony; and the changing attitudes which English historians have assumed towards him only reflect the succeeding changes in the outlook of English Protestantism. That Wyclif's name became a symbol of the revolt against Rome, the supposed harbinger and precursor of the Reformation, was in large part the result of the circumstances in which Foxe composed the first version of his *Acts and Monuments of the English Martyrs*. His work truncated by sudden flight to Strasbourg in 1554, Foxe was unable to prepare in exile the detailed history of the martyrs under Henry VIII, and was compelled to make Wyclif the centre of his book. His success was such that, for Continental as well as English writers, Wyclif began to eclipse even the Bohemian reformers as the John the Baptist of the Reformation.[1] Catholic apologists also came to accept this position; like Antoine Varillas, who began his history of the Reformation with Wyclif and with Hus.

Launched as a symbol of uncompromising Protestantism, Wyclif could not avoid being a figure of contention during the first great age of English historical scholarship at the end of the seventeenth century.[2] Among the Non-Jurors he was decidedly out of favour. Jeremy Collier, in his *Ecclesiastical History* published in 1708, cautiously described Wyclif's appearance in these words:

About this time John Wickliff a secular divine advanced several tenets which were looked on as novel and heterodox. Neither indeed, as they are represented, are they altogether defensible; some of them, to say nothing further, striking at the government and property of the church.

His final judgement, which avoided both the extravagant praise of Fuller and the bitter censure of the Laudian Peter Heylin, was

---

[1] J. F. Mozley, *John Foxe and his Book* (1940), pp. 118–19.
[2] For the historiography of Wyclif see Workman, I, 12–16.

'that though we may allow him some gold in his mine, it was not without a mixture of coarser ingredients'.[1]

Protestant low-church whiggery, flushed with the triumph of the Hanoverian settlement, came to the defence of Wyclif's memory in the person of John Lewis of Margate (1675–1747). A protégé of Archbishops Tenison and Wake, he composed refutations of Collier and Varillas ('infamous even amongst the Papists themselves for his want of even common honesty'), and lives of Wyclif, Pecock and Caxton. The *Dictionary of National Biography* condemns these 'tedious compilations', but allows that they 'contain the result of much original research', and Lewis deserves to be remembered with respect by students of Wyclif for making the first serious attempt to list the manuscripts of his works. The *History of the life and sufferings of the reverend and learned John Wicliffe D.D.*, a rejoinder to Varillas, appeared in 1720; a second posthumous edition, with a much enlarged list of Wyclif MSS., in 1820. Wyclif's own university, however, remained unaffected by such whiggish enthusiasms. Lewis himself, who had graduated from Exeter College in 1697, proceeded M.A. in 1712 from Corpus Christi College, Cambridge; and the subscribers' list for his edition of the Wycliffite Bible (1731), which includes several Cambridge colleges, contains no named representative from Oxford.

If the age of reason approved Wyclif as one of the great anticlericals, it was sure by the same token to abhor his scholasticism. Confirmed in its prejudices, the eighteenth century rejected what it certainly had not read. The most delightful expression of this distaste appears in the *Life* by William Gilpin (1765). Preceded by some vigorous stanzas ('The House of Superstition: a vision, by Thomas Denton M.A.'), Gilpin traces Wyclif's career as far as his entering Merton to study theology.

Thus prepared, he began next with divinity. The divinity of those times corresponded with the logic. What was farthest from reason, appeared most like truth: at least most worth a scholar's pursuit. In that age flourished those eminent doctors, who mutually compliment-

---

[1] Jeremy Collier, *An Ecclesiastical History of Great Britain* (ed. T. Lathbury, 1852), III, 136.

ing each other with sounding titles, the profound, the angelic, and the seraphic, drew upon themselves the reverence of their own times, and the contempt of all posterity. Wiclif's attention was a while engaged in this fashionable study.[1]

It was not until the mid-nineteenth century that the renewed vigour in medieval studies led scholars in England and Germany to a fresh interest in Wyclif's thought. Lechler's *Johann von Wiclif und die Vorgeschichte der Reformation* (1873) and Shirley's edition of the *Fasciculi Zizaniorum* (Rolls Series, 1858) mark the beginning of modern critical study, and have lost none of their value. English and German scholarship met in the foundation of the Wyclif Society by F. J. Furnivall in 1882. Over the following forty years, despite persisting lack of funds and support, the Society published over thirty volumes of the works of Wyclif. And no one who has had occasion to consult these editions can fail to give thanks to the scholars who laboured, as they so often and justly complained, on such crabbed and difficult manuscripts.

Wyclif's controversial works fared better, for several reasons, than the study of the treatises of his purely academic years. First, while the edition of his polemical tracts is complete, a number of philosophical treatises remain unprinted. These include about two-thirds of the *Summa de Ente*, an examination of which fills the central chapters of this study. The first world war interrupted the efforts of the Wyclif Society to publish the whole of the *Summa*; and the war was soon followed by the dissolution of the Society itself. Since then the only substantial addition to the corpus of texts has been S. H. Thomson's edition (1930) of the first two tracts of the *Summa*.

Moreover, the editors of the Wyclif Society were faced with two further difficulties. The first was lack of knowledge of the background to Wyclif's works. Only in comparatively recent years has an intensive publication of texts and monographs enabled us to trace the development of thought in the universities of the fourteenth century. It was hard, therefore, convincingly to relate Wyclif's philosophical opinions to the age in which he

[1] W. Gilpin, *The Lives of John Wicliff, and of the most eminent of his disciples, Lord Cobham, John Hus, Jerome of Prague and Zizca* (1765), pp. 3–4.

lived; and there is still need, as this study seeks to show, for further research into scholasticism at Oxford in the generation before Wyclif matriculated. The second difficulty was self-imposed. It was the determination of the Wyclif Society editors to prove their subject a major original philosopher. For them he was not merely a great scholastic; he was also a great Balliol man. (It was to Jowett that R. L. Poole dedicated 'this work of a former Master of his College'—his edition of the De civili dominio.) It is amusing and disturbing to read Dziewicki's attempt to prove Wyclif's logic superior to Ockham's and his opinion that, whilst his work has 'grave omissions' and his digressions 'go beyond all bounds', nevertheless 'without Occam's affectation of mathematical order, Wyclif had as much of the true philosophical spirit as he: and as for subtlety and originality, he perhaps had more'.[1]

Such exaggerated claims have failed to stand the test of time, and have positively harmed the cause for which the Wyclif Society so selflessly laboured. Discredited both as prophet of the Reformation and as scholastic, Wyclif's reputation has been greatly damaged; and recent historians have dwelt with measured severity, if not with relish, on the more obviously unattractive facets of his thought and character. Vanished is the picture of the Great Reformer; in his place stands an obstinate and rancorous pedagogue. Moreover Wyclif, like others of his contemporaries, has suffered for being a secular. There has been no religious order anxious to vindicate his name (as Ockham's reputation has been so brilliantly sustained by the Friars Minor). In consequence 'there is still room for a definitive examination of Wyclif's philosophical and theological position similar to existing studies of earlier English scholastics'.[2]

The following chapters are in no way definitive; but the times do now seem propitious for a fresh attempt. The loss of outworn and sentimental prejudices coincides with great advances in the study of late medieval thought; and the eirenic spirit has reached even the world of the schools (where it was often so sadly want-

---

[1] M. H. Dziewicki, ed., Johannis Wyclif tractatus de logica (WS, 1893), I, xi.
[2] M. D. Knowles, Religious Orders in England, II, 98 n. 3.

ing). Dom Paul de Vooght's recent study of the use of scriptural authority by theologians of the fourteenth century, *Les Sources de la doctrine chrétienne* (1954), not only gives Wyclif a section to himself, but almost makes him the hero of the work. And all modern investigations confirm that it is by a return to the earlier period in his career that we can know more fully the man and the world in which he lived. For the last decade of his life Wyclif was a figure of national controversy; for more than fifteen years before that he had been an Oxford don. This study is concerned only with these earlier years and with the philosophers and theologians whose writings influenced speculation in the Oxford of Wyclif's youth.

PART I
THE PRECURSORS OF WYCLIF

CHAPTER I

EARLY CAREER AND THE SCHOLASTIC BACKGROUND AT OXFORD

I

THIS study has a double purpose, to describe and illumine the scholastic career of John Wyclif[1] up to his inception as Master in Theology, and to relate his thought to the philosophical speculation in the Oxford of his day. Our first task, therefore, is to establish as far as possible a chronology of his progress in the academic life. But the certain and authoritative sources for these years are so few and so stark that they permit, and even encourage, an assessment de novo.[2] The printing of the relevant documents from the papal registers, and the clarification of the circumstances in which Wyclif was first appointed to and then ejected from the Warden-ship of Canterbury Hall, have banished most of the clouds which for so long encompassed his early life. But some questions remain.

In spite of the possibility that Wyclif belonged to the family of minor country gentry of that name, living in the North Riding,[3]

[1] Modern scholarly study begins with G. Lechler, *Johann von Wiclif und die Vorgeschichte der Reformation* (2 vols., 1873); references in the following to 'Lechler' are to the second English edn, *John Wycliffe and his English Precursors*, trans. P. Lorimer (1884). Research between *c.* 1880 and 1920 is synthesised by H. B. Workman, *John Wyclif* (2 vols., 1926). See also B. L. Manning in *Cam. Med. Hist.* VII, 486–507. Two notable character studies of Wyclif appear in K. B. McFarlane, *John Wycliffe and the Beginnings of English Non-conformity* (1952) and David Knowles, *Religious Orders in England*, II (1955), 98 ff.

For bibliographies of Wyclif see U. Chevalier, *Répertoire des sources historiques du moyen âge*, new edn (1907), II, 4762–6 (*s.v.* Wiclef); *Cam. Med. Hist.* VII, 900–7; *Cam. Bibl. English Lit.* (1940) I, 307–11; *DTC*, XV, 2, 3613–14; É. Gilson, *History of Christian Philosophy in the Middle Ages* (1955), pp. 771–2.

[2] For Wyclif's early career we generally follow Workman (cf. esp. I, 52–102, 151–206), but disagree over Wyclif's residence in Merton, for which see below, pp. 11–13. [3] Workman, I, 22 ff.; McFarlane, *John Wycliffe*, pp. 14–15.

we know for certain neither when nor where he was born. The venerable patriarch who meets the visitor to the Senior Common Room at Merton conveys nothing except the artist's delusion that old men are always wise men. Beyond the fact that he reached full middle life, we cannot fix with any precision the year of Wyclif's birth; and the recent and intriguing suggestion that the stroke which killed him in 1384 was the result of high blood pressure also argues against a long life.[1] Like most medieval academics he is met for the first time when already graduate—as a probationary fellow of Merton in 1356.[2] The evidence for his presence in the college is of some interest, and will bear setting out in full.

It was the custom of the college for each fellow to take his turn as steward of the week, when it was his duty to pay the bills for fellows' commons. His expenses were refunded by the bursar, who entered the sum in his account roll. It is in the roll for 1356, when Richard Billingham[3] the logician was Third Bursar, that Wyclif's name is found. The Merton year ran, as indeed it still runs, from August to August,[4] and for financial purposes was divided into three quarters. The final quarter for 1355/6 lasted from March to mid August 1356, and Wyclif's turn of office from Rogation Sunday, 28 May, to 4 June, the Saturday after Ascension Day. He was therefore responsible for the entertainment of the eighteen guests of the college—for which an outlay of £4. 7s. 5½d. does not seem excessive.[5]

[1] McFarlane, *John Wycliffe*, p. 85.

[2] Workman, I, 77, assumes that Wyclif first entered Balliol, because of the Yorkshire connections of the college, because he later became Master, and because of the presence of a William Wyclif among the fellows. This is very possible, but cannot be proved. Cf. also Lechler, p. 87.

[3] For Billingham (fellow 1344, Warden 1357–61) see A. B. Emden, *Biographical Register of the University of Oxford to A.D. 1500* (1957–9), I, 188–9.

[4] A college meeting is held to this day in August, as the founder's instructions direct; it is followed by a feast.

[5] G. C. Brodrick, *Memorials of Merton College*, OHS, IV (1885), 216; Lechler, p. 98; *FZ*, p. 511. This entry has not been printed before, and I must thank Dr J. R. L. Highfield for help in transcription.

Merton Record 3690

Compotus Ricardi Billingham tercii bursarii de administratione sua a die Sabbati proximi post festum Annunciationis Sancte Marie usque ad diem

The authority for stating that the Wyclif of the bursarial roll is the subject of this study is the *Catalogus Vetus*, a list of fellows of Merton, arranged alphabetically by reigns and compiled by Thomas Robert who, as the *Catalogus* itself tells us, became a fellow *tempore* Richard II, and was Third Bursar in 1411.[1] He ceased to be a fellow in 1422, which gives the *terminus ad quem* for his inventory, which shows 'the earliest instance of a fellow of an Oxford College being at pains to compose a list of his predecessors'. Wyclif's name appears[2] under the reign of Edward III and against it, as with many others, a note has been added. The hand of the annotation was studied by the distinguished palaeographer and historian, Falconer Madan, who divided the entry into three parts, as follows:

(A) Wyklyf (B) doctor in theologia qui tamen nimium in proprio ingenio confidebat ut dicitur

(C) nec erat socius istius domus nec annum probacionis habuit plenarie in eadem

veneris proximum post festum quod dicitur Ad Vincula per XIX septimanas, anno regis Edwardi tercii tricesimo....

In primis compoti liberati pro communis sociorum et famulorum per talleam: Bukingham xxxixs id / Toneworth xxixs iiid / Wanham xxxis iiiid obol / Billingham xxxiis viiid obol / Tecron iiii lib. ixs viiid in septimana Pascatis / Cotesford xxiiis iiid obol / Sutton xxvis xd obol / item Berton xxviis xd obol / Benger xxviiis vid obol / Wyklif iiii lib. viis vd obolus pro festo sancto in die Ascensionis pro xviii extraneis / Rok xxxis xd obol / Redyng lvis vid obol / Westebruk in festo Trinitatis et Nativitatis Sancti Iohannis iiii lib. xis iid / Reynham xlis / Ffarnilaw xxxiis iiiid / item Reed xxxs vid obol / item R. Lamborn xxviiis viiid / item Buryng xxvs iid / item Simon Lamborne xxviis iiid obol item   Summa xxxviii lib. vis ixd. obol.

H. S. Cronin's comment that Wyclif 'spent a good deal of college money on entertaining strangers' wrongly supposes that he did so on his own account. Cf. *TRHS*, 3rd ser. VIII (1914), 73.

[1] On Thomas Robert and his catalogue see Emden, *Biographical Register*, I, xiii.

[2] The faulty transcription in Brodrick, *Memorials of Merton College*, p. 215, is reprinted by Workman (1, 67), who also states incorrectly that it is in the *Catalogus Vetus* itself that the annotation 'aᵒ xxx Edw. Ter.' appears against Wyclif's name (that is, a reference to the bursarial roll of 1356). This in fact exists in a copy of the list of fellows under Edward III, enrolled by Robert on a bursarial indenture. A facsimile of the *Catalogus Vetus*, fo. 64v, containing Wyclif's name and comments thereon, is printed by P. S. Allen and H. W. Garrod, eds., *Merton Muniments*, OHS, LXXXVI (1928), 37, and is reproduced below with one emendation.

Madan considered that (B) was apparently contemporary with (A); that (C) seemed to be in the same hand as (B); and that 'in my opinion (B) and (C) are, and (A) very probably is, in Thomas Robert's hand'.[1] We have surely the strongest reasons for assuming that the annotation is contemporary with the compiling of the *Catalogus Vetus* and was made by someone in authority. It remains to consider its value.

The note is in two parts, the first of which is a comment on character incapable of proof or disproof, the second factual but self-contradictory. As Garrod and Allen say, 'the note appended to Wyclif's name, though designed to assert that he was not a Fellow, shows conclusively that he was admitted as a Bachelor-Fellow for the customary year of probation'.[2] It is true that Thomas Robert depended for his information on the bursar's rolls, which in general record surnames only; so that there is a possibility of confusion. But college memories are long and retentive, whilst there was nothing to be gained from falsely claiming a condemned man. On the contrary the accusation of overweening self-confidence was an admission of his presence in Merton, even if it was also an attempt to blacken his character. And even of that failing, at least at that time, we cannot be sure; it was, after all, a retrospective judgement and only hearsay—'ut dicitur'. But in matter of fact we have no good reason to question Thomas Robert, and the Wyclif whom he included in his catalogue is certainly he who appears in the accounts for 1356. For a number of rough drafts of the *Catalogus Vetus* survive on the backs of bursars' rolls, and in one of these against Wyclif's name stands the note 'a° XXX Edw. Ter.'[3]

That he was in Merton and a Bachelor of Arts by this time is all that we know for certain, and speculation on his conduct and the

---

[1] Madan's opinion (referred to by Allen and Garrod, *op. cit.* p. 37) is contained in a private letter in the Merton Archives, which I was able to see through the kindness of Dr Highfield. It will be seen that it rejects the suggestion (Workman, I, 67; Brodrick, *Memorials of Merton College*, p. 215) that annotation against Wyclif's name has subsequently been touched up. The emendation of 'tum' to 'tamen' in the transcription from the *Catalogus Vetus* I owe to Professor C. R. Cheney.

[2] Allen and Garrod, *op. cit.* p. 37.   [3] Brodrick, *op. cit.* p. 215.

cause of his leaving is profitless. Unfortunately the rolls which precede and follow that in which Wyclif is named are missing; so his residence of under a year may have fallen at any time between August 1355 and Lady Day 1357. It is true that at this time one of those disputes which too frequently disturbed the college led to an official visitation by Archbishop Islip in November 1357. But to suppose[1] Wyclif a *borealis militans* from Balliol (to which he may or may not have belonged), and the source of the trouble, is greatly to exaggerate the importance of his position, and to forget how accustomed was Merton, as the only well endowed college, to absorbing outsiders. Since when have colleges been at the mercy of junior fellows?

Not later than 1356 Wyclif had graduated Bachelor in the Faculty of Arts; four years later he had become *magister* and Master of Balliol. Three documents attest his presence there. The first, from 1360, reports a dispute between the Master and fellows of the college and one Nicholas Marchaunt over some property in St Lawrence Jewry, and appears to be an extract from an official record—perhaps that of the Court of Hustings, where the plea was heard. On 18 May 'Johannes de Wyclyf, Magister domus scolarium aule vocate La Baillohalle de Oxon' was summoned to give reasons why, two months previously, he had extracted pledges to the value of forty-eight shillings from Nicholas Marchaunt, though the said Nicholas held his tenement in Old Jewry by freehold.[2] Balliol ultimately won the case by establishing its ownership of the property. Just under a year later Wyclif was party to a deed by which the church of Abbotsley was appropriated to the college. Dated 7 April 1361, it was witnessed by the Master and ten fellows; and a companion notarial document of the same date expressly describes 'John de Wykclyff' as 'magister sive custos collegii predicti'.[3] One would dearly like to know the relationship of the William de Wycklyffe, fellow,

---

[1] As H. S. Cronin, 'John Wycliffe, the Reformer, and Canterbury Hall, Oxford', *TRHS*, 3rd ser. VIII (1914), 73 n. 2.

[2] *Historical Manuscripts Commission*, app. to 4th report, p. 448.

[3] Balliol Deeds, Abbotsley 9 and 10, summarised in *Hist. MSS. Comm.*, app. to 4th report, p. 447.

who also witnessed the deed of transfer, to the Master. But in an age when identity of surname may indicate only a common place of origin and not a family connection, it is unwise to assume a relationship between the two men. The Abbotsley transaction must have been one of the last with which Wyclif was concerned as Master, for in the following month he was inducted into the college living of Fillingham in Lincolnshire.[1]

Such is the slender evidence for his career as student and Artist. For the degree of Bachelor of Arts the Faculty required a course of study of four or five years, a period of not less than three years as *scholaris* and *sophista* being followed by a year in which the student, first as questionist and then as responsionist, took part in the academic exercises. On satisfying these tests, he would be allowed to make his first determination as a graduate; but at least a further three years had to elapse between determination and inception (*creatio magistri*).[2] We must suppose, therefore, that Wyclif came up to Oxford about 1350 or a little before. Of his masters and mentors we know nothing.

It seems clear that he resided at Fillingham for the first two years after leaving Balliol, though his name appears on the roll of masters deserving provisions which the University submitted to Avignon in 1362.[3] The petition requested a canonry at York. Instead Urban V granted the prebend of Aust in the collegiate church of Westbury-on-Trym,[4] which Wyclif held thereafter as a non-resident pluralist. In the next year his short separation from university life was ended; on 29 August 1363 the bishop of Lincoln, John Buckingham, granted him a licence of non-residence for study.[5] In the autumn Wyclif returned to Oxford to begin the long course in theology.

---

[1] Workman, I, 80 and n. 1.

[2] Strickland Gibson, ed., *Statuta antiqua universitatis Oxoniensis* (1931), pp. lxxxix–xcviii.

[3] J. A. Twemlow, 'Wycliffe's Preferments and University Degrees', *EHR*, xv (1900), 529. In the roll, submitted on 24 November 1362, the scribe mistakenly wrote 'Wychif'.

[4] Workman, I, 153; M.-H. Laurent, ed., *Urbain V (1362–1370). Lettres Communes*, fasc. IV (1957), no. 3662.

[5] Workman, I, 153.

To graduate Bachelor in theology (*admissio ad lecturam libri Sententiarum*) a Master of Arts had to attend lectures on the set books for four years (which included hearing the Bible read *biblice* for three); to oppose—not before the fifth year; and to respond—not before the seventh. In this or the following year he was admitted to read the *Sentences*. Two further years were required for the doctorate (*magister theologiae*), during which the Bachelor, besides 'reading' the Lombard, must oppose and respond in all the theological schools, preach publicly and lecture on some book of the Bible.[1] In all, therefore, the regulations required six or seven years' study before graduating Bachelor, and eight or nine to reach the doctorate. Wyclif is first described as *in sacra theologia bacallarius* in a document of May 1370, promulgating the judgement given against him in the Curia on 23 July 1369 over the Canterbury Hall dispute.[2] He is again described as Bachelor in January 1371 by Gregory XI, who provided him to a canonry, with reservation of prebend, at Lincoln; but by December 1373, when the provision was renewed on more favourable terms, Wyclif had become Master.[3] If the 'two year rule' for promotion to the magistracy was followed in his case, Wyclif must have graduated doctor between the summer of 1371 and the autumn of 1372.

When Wyclif returned to Oxford in autumn 1363, he took lodgings in Queen's, a poor college which made a habit of letting rooms to scholars. His set was repaired at a cost of 5s. 7d., and he remained there for two years at a rent of £1 a year.[4] Possibly he would have continued to reside at Queen's had not the unexpected appointment to the Wardenship of Canterbury College seemed to provide him with a permanent home in Oxford.

Canterbury College[5] was the fruit of the zeal of Archbishop

---

[1] Gibson, ed., *Statuta antiqua universitatis Oxoniensis*, pp. cix–cxii, 51, 195.

[2] W. A. Pantin, *Canterbury College Oxford, OHS*, new ser. VIII (1950), III, 184.

[3] J. A. Twemlow, *loc. cit.*, *EHR*, XV (1900), 530; M. E. H. Lloyd, 'John Wyclif and the Prebend of Lincoln', *EHR*, LXI (1946), 388–94; Workman, I, 203.

[4] J. R. Magrath, *The Queen's College* (1921), I, 112–13.

[5] The authoritative account of Wyclif's wardenship is by H. S. Cronin, 'John Wycliffe, the Reformer, and Canterbury Hall, Oxford', *TRHS*, 3rd ser. VIII (1914), 55–76; the latest edition of the relevant documents in Pantin, *Canterbury College*, III, 158–206; see also Workman, I, 172–94.

Simon Islip (inspired perhaps by the memory of the founder of his own college, Walter de Merton) for promoting the further education of both secular and regular clergy. The college, designed as a mixed community of monks (from Christ Church, Canterbury) and secular clerks, received its foundation charter in 1361; and the next year Islip appointed as first Warden Henry Wodehull, monk of Christ Church. The arrangement was a failure. The parties quarrelled; the seculars drove out Wodehull; and in 1365 Islip himself drew up fresh statutes, heavily weighted in favour of the seculars.[1] It was in these circumstances that Islip appointed Wyclif as Warden in December 1365. We may happily pass over the course of the prolonged and finally successful appeal of the monks to Rome, the recovery of the college for the religious and the expulsion of Wyclif and his allies. It is but one example of the baleful struggle of secular against regular which was so marked a feature of ecclesiastical and scholastic life in the fourteenth century. It is enough for our purpose that the documents attest Wyclif's residence in Oxford over a period of five years—for he was certainly not ejected before the summer of 1370. No doubt the Franciscan, William Wodeford, a contemporary whose judgement merits confidence, was right in stating that Wyclif's antagonism towards the religious was first aroused by his disappointment over the Canterbury College case.[2] But Islip himself must bear a good deal of the blame for an appointment which seems clearly to have run counter to his own statutes.

Throughout this institutional fracas Wyclif must have continued to lecture in the Oxford Schools, where by 1372 he was acknowledged as the leading master. But the years 1371–3 were a turning point in his life. For the first time his philosophy (particularly his rigid metaphysical principles) began to attract hostile attention, and he was compelled to wage a vigorous pamphlet war with John Kenningham, the Carmelite controversialist.[3] In brief, the explanation is that Wyclif's long held metaphysical axioms (innocuous enough when taken by themselves), were now

[1] Printed Pantin, *Canterbury College*, III, 159–72.
[2] Workman, I, 186; *FZ*, p. 517.   [3] See below, pp. 161 ff.

being applied, with radical results, to problems of the nature of the eucharist and the authority of Scripture. The arguments of the Master of Arts suddenly seemed much more questionable when invoked by the Master of Theology. At the same time, at some stage between taking his doctorate and the diplomatic mission to Bruges in 1374 his previous whole-hearted and wholly to be expected concern with questions of pure scholastic philosophy came to be replaced, rapidly and completely, by an equally total absorption in the problems of the nature and structure of the church —a subject hitherto not touched upon in his writings. This change of interest is, of course, closely related to his entry into the service of John of Gaunt (which probably took place in 1371 or 1372). With the exception of the *Commentary on the Bible*, to which a firm date has yet to be assigned,[1] Wyclif's academic, non-controversial scholastic work was completed by 1373/4. Though he remained the schoolman in technique and temperament, he had in reality abandoned the study of philosophy for that of political theory; and, if he employed scholastic forms of argument, he had by the mid 1370's ceased to think creatively in the field of scholastic studies.

We shall, therefore, do no violence to the truth in considering the achievement of Wyclif's earlier years as complete in itself and as a chapter in the history of medieval philosophy: the achievement of a man who was in 1370, by general consent, the outstanding philosopher of his generation at Oxford, and whose tragic future none could have foreseen. The principal materials for assessing his position at this date are to be found in the collection of treatises, metaphysical and theological, which has subsequently been named the *Summa de ente*. The metaphysical works were certainly written during Wyclif's years in the Arts faculty, that is, between the late 1350's and the late 1360's; and the theological treatises, it will be suggested, are in content, though not strictly in form, the product of his reading the *Sentences*, and so composed during his two years as Bachelor of Theology, c. 1369–1371. Here is the mature expression, undistorted by the needs or dis-

---

[1] Beryl Smalley, 'John Wyclif's Postilla super totam bibliam', *Bodleian Library Record*, IV (1953), 186–205.

tractions of controversy, of Wyclif's teaching on the fundamental problems of philosophy and theology.

But his ideas can only be properly understood in relation to the
world of thought in which he was educated.

II

Wyclif stands not at the beginning but at the end of an age in
medieval thought, an age of radicalism and innovation, which
dawned in the last decade of the thirteenth century and reached
its climax in the second quarter of the fourteenth. Even after the
first flood tide had begun to ebb, its impetus continued to a
marked degree to control the subject of debate and the manner in
which it should be tackled. In surprising measure, and whether
they supported or opposed this movement, Wyclif and his contemporaries were prisoners not only of their own generation but
of the previous one also.

The origins and nature of the New Way are still matters of dispute. But two cardinal features can be recognised. First, a radical
dissociation between theology and metaphysics, between divine
and human knowledge; and secondly a questioning of the possibility (even, on occasion, the desirability) of attaining a perfect
and co-ordinated explanation of things within those sciences. In
some way the urge towards a balanced, explicable synthesis was
replaced by more exciting goals. It is very much still open to
debate whether this movement was solely critical and destructive,
or rather was the necessary and inevitable attack on the received
synthesis that must precede the formulation of a new one. Recent
expositors have been anxious to restore a positive content to the
logical and cognitive systems put forward by Ockham and his
followers.[1] However, creative or destructive, the New Way

---

[1] See, in particular, P. Boehner, *Medieval Logic* (1952); 'The Realistic Conceptualism of William Ockham', *Traditio*, IV (1946), 307–35; 'Ockham's
Theory of Signification', *Franciscan Studies*, new ser. VI (1946), 143–70;
'Ockham's Theory of Supposition and the Notion of Truth', *ibid.* VI (1946),
261–92; *William Ockham, Summa Logicae pars prima*, Franc. Inst. Publ., text ser. 2
(1951); E. A. Moody, *The Logic of William of Ockham* (1935).

I have to thank Professor H. S. Offler for criticisms of statements on Ock-
hamism in an earlier draft.

shaped the course of thought in the schools of the fourteenth century; and Wyclif stands as the last important spokesman at Oxford of the conservative reaction, whose tenets were moulded in opposition to scholastic radicalism.[1]

The Augustinian tradition—*the* great tradition in medieval thought—sought to unite ratiocination and illumination in the pattern of a Christian neoplatonism. And ironically it was Aquinas, the greatest of the synthesists, who, by founding reason in a Christian Aristotelianism based upon sense perception, first decisively separated reason from faith. For Thomas, of course, reason and revelation were complementary. But already by the last quarter of the thirteenth century there had arisen a powerful sentiment, for many irresistible, absolutely to distinguish the two. This corresponded to no mere appetite for linguistic innovation, but represented an important change in theologians' approach to God. In brief, Augustinian neoplatonism was criticised for confounding God and man in a single metaphysical system, for excessive determinism, and for depreciating unduly the play of divine and human will. Against this the new philosophers placed the transcendence of God (and the impossibility of knowing him except in so far as his nature was expressed in the world of being), the primacy of his will, and the radical contingency of all divine and human acts. Such general preoccupations are quite compatible with dispute over particular theological issues and with profound disagreement in the whole field of metaphysics; and the fact that such preoccupations are patent in philosophers so metaphysically opposed as Scotus and Ockham illustrates their overriding and universal quality. It is misleading to read the history of fourteenth-century thought solely in terms of the battle of realist against nominalist, for disputes on the reality of universals were in large part prompted by wider struggles. The agreement upon the issues of debate, which united philosophers of the day, is at least as important as the opposing solutions, which divided them. As pure philosophers, Ockham and Wyclif have more in common than is often allowed.

[1] The following paragraphs, which make no claim to originality, owe much to Robert Guelluy, *Philosophie et théologie chez Guillaume d'Ockham* (Louvain, 1947).

The supposition that what was germane to theology might not be accessible to rational enquiry, that theology in short was not a science as other sciences, goes back to Alexander of Hales (d. 1245) who posited the question, with which the fourteenth-century Commentaries so often begin, 'Utrum theologia sit scientia'. The question at issue was that of the character of the act of faith, at once meritorious and rational, and the intelligibility of revelation. Has in fact plain intellectual endeavour a religious and theological value?[1]

The answers of three masters, whose metaphysical teaching ranged from strongly realist to openly nominalist, and who were frequently cited by Wyclif, reveal the changing current of opinion.

As master in theology at Paris from 1276 to 1292 Henry of Ghent[2] had full opportunity for appreciating the reasons which led Bishop Stephen Tempier to condemn the Averroist theses of 1277.[3] Though himself a realist he had no cause to welcome opinions which, by their emphasis on the First Cause, on which all secondary causes depended, led to an inevitable determinism. He stressed the Thomist doctrine of analogy, whereby the universal in man represented but was not directly moved by the divine idea, and in which ideal existence in God corresponded to the actual essence in the world. Distinguishing clearly God's knowledge of possible being from divine ideas, Henry was free to preserve the primacy of his will. As a theologian Henry of Ghent recognised the transcendence of the world of faith, whilst claiming to leave dogma open to intellectual enquiry. What belongs to faith can be assured both by faith and by reason; and he explicitly associates that which is known by faith with what can also be deduced by philosophy.[4] Showing himself a platonist of the traditional school, Henry states that for certain knowledge we depend on the illumination of divine ideas. But just as he emphasises the freedom of God's will, so he stresses the need of a willing disposition

---

[1] Guelluy, *op. cit.* pp. 25–6.

[2] J. Paulus, *Henri de Gand: essai sur les tendances de sa métaphysique*, Études de philosophie médiévale, xxv (1938). His *Summae questionum ordinariarum* are conveniently reprinted (from the 1520 edn) in Franciscan Inst. Publ., text ser. 5 (2 vols., 1953).

[3] É. Gilson, *La Philosophie au moyen âge*, 2nd edn (1944), pp. 386 ff.

[4] Guelluy, *op. cit.* p. 54.

in man to be illumined. Thus Henry remains within the Augustinian and realist tradition, whilst showing the influence of the voluntarism which was to be such a marked feature of the *via moderna*.

Scotus also makes the distinction between metaphysics (the study of being) and theology (the study of God). The first is known by reason; the second, strictly speaking, is only intelligible by revelation—though the manifestations of God's work can be the subject of deductive knowledge. Scotus thus followed Thomas in stating that a scientific knowledge of God cannot be reconciled with the attitude of faith in those without the gift of revelation; but, stricter than Thomas as to what human reason can deduce, he underlined the unfailing liberty of divine action. We cannot know without faith, and our knowledge, as analysed by reason, must be contingent. He also repudiated the doctrine of direct illumination, on the ground that this would cause human knowledge to depend on ideas present in God and not on his will.[1]

Scotus therefore is justly regarded as the first great figure of the *via moderna*, because he stressed the distinction between theological and 'scientific' knowledge, because he denied certainty to human reason, and limited the sphere of its application, and because of his emphasis on God's freedom to will and to act. Yet far from decrying metaphysical systems, it was Scotus who made the last great effort to adapt the realist tradition to the new theological concepts which he had done so much to promote. For his doctrine of the univocity of being (which posited a universal order of fundamental being, common to God and creatures, and preceding actual being) in fact passes beyond Henry of Ghent by propounding a system of being which is univocal rather than analogous in God and creation.[2]

William of Ockham[3] shared the preoccupations of Henry of

[1] *Ibid.* pp. 67–72; G. Leff, *Medieval Thought* (1958), p. 268.

[2] Leff, *Medieval Thought*, pp. 264–8.

[3] See L. Baudry, *Guillaume d'Occam: sa vie, ses œuvres, ses idées sociales et politiques* (1949); Guelluy, *op. cit.*; *DTC*, XI, 864–904; P. Vignaux, article 'Nominalisme', *DTC*, XI, 717–84; *idem*, *Nominalisme au XIVe siècle* (1948); Gilson, *La Philosophie au moyen âge*, pp. 638–86; Boehner, *The Tractatus de successivis, attributed to William Ockham* (1944), pp. 1–15; H. Rashdall, *Universities of Europe in the Middle Ages*, ed. Powicke and Emden (1936), I, 562 ff.

Ghent and Scotus; and to them he added a genius in logic which was to help carry the New Way to its extreme. It is the combination of theological radicalism with logical innovation which made Ockham's work so potent.[1] None of his *sequelae* shared to the full both the theological and logical capacities of their master.

Ockham's fundamental metaphysical concept is that of the singularity of the real. Nothing can remove the self-identity of the real, which is distinct in its own nature—*seipsis differunt*; and to know an object one need know nothing outside that thing. Human knowledge is therefore conceptual, though Ockham would argue that it was none the less real. How then does the mind synthesise what it perceives? Our concepts signify subjects by relating them to a reality distinct from that subject. But unity in the concept implies no corresponding unity in reality, for neither universals nor properties are real; and the universality of concepts does not derive from any reality inherent in the objects defined.

We can agree that Ockham accepted the reality of singulars. But his system utterly repudiates any hierarchy of universal reality. To admit that the universal could be really distinct from its singular would be to question God's transcendence in respect of his work, and to admit an element of determinism into nature. Whether Ockham devised such a logical system in the service of his theology, or found his theology determined by his logic, is a question impossible to answer, and perhaps foolish to ask. Does his theology depend on his theory of cognition, or is it independent of it? Does it rather follow from some more immediate religious imperative—the determination, for example, to preserve the sphere of divine revelation? Certainly these questions are interlocking; for Ockham's teaching as to what can be known answers at once the scholastic dispute 'utrum theologia sit scientia'.[2]

The distinction between philosophical and theological knowledge is fundamental to our understanding of Ockham. Though reason can be applied to the divine, the answer can only be partial.

[1] Cf. M. H. Carré, *Phases of Thought in England* (1949), p. 164.
[2] Guelluy, *op. cit.* pp. 315, 322, 342–4.

Ockham expresses this by distinguishing intuitive from abstract knowledge. It is impossible, he states, for the ordinary Christian in this world, the *viator*, to attain, unaided by revelation, the intuitive knowledge which gives a full apprehension of God; and abstract knowledge, that which is deduced by reason, is both contingent and uncertain. For to know God (the object of theology) is to pass beyond the arrangement of concepts into the realm of faith. Here Ockham followed Scotus and his successors, who declared that theology allowed one to put certain propositions, but that only faith could judge which were acceptable. So we know the divine by revelation, but revelation is never the source of the rationally deduced. Ockham, therefore, rejects the doctrine of illumination. The mortal accepted by God sees and believes, but does not, in the metaphysical sense, know.[1]

The second feature of Ockham's theology is the impossibility of distinguishing between God's attributes and capacities, for the self-contained realm of theology is impenetrable to graceless man. This distinction was one of the propositions most strongly censured by the masters at Avignon in 1326.[2] We know God, declared the Venerable Inceptor, as manifested in this world— that is, in the sphere in which he is accessible to rational enquiry. We know that he is supremely good, for goodness is within the mind's grasp. But we cannot know (though we believe) that he is three Persons; we cannot know him in his divinity.[3] What validity then have the statements which all theologians must make concerning God's attributes? The truth, replies Ockham, is that in these moments we perceive not God himself, but concepts only. He is simple, and to know him is to know all of him. If our knowledge, therefore, is diverse, it is because it terminates not in God, but in 'rational beings' representing him. Using the notion of *suppositio*, he argued that it was possible to describe divine properties because they were not really distinct from, were not

[1] *Ibid.* pp. 125, 248–9, 254.

[2] A. Pelzer, 'Les 51 articles de Guillaume Occam censurés, en Avignon, en 1326', *Revue d'histoire ecclésiastique*, XVIII (1922), 240–70; J. Koch, 'Neue Aktenstücke zu dem gegen Wilhelm Ockham in Avignon geführten Prozess', *RTAM*, VII (1935), 353–80; VIII (1936), 79–93, 168–97.

[3] Pelzer, *loc. cit.* p. 257 (art. 12).

individuated realities inhering in God, but concepts distinguished for purposes of comparison.[1]

Correspondingly Ockham's logic and theology demand the disappearance of all intermediaries between God and subject; for no universal or attribute can determine his acts, which are utterly free. Following the course first charted by Scotus, and abandoning all efforts to propound a method of knowing, Ockham 'places the faithful before the absolute and incomprehensible liberty of God'. In the 1330's an unknown disciple summed up in his *Tractatus de principiis theologiae* the two cardinal principles of his master. The first was that of God's omnipotence; the second that of 'Ockham's razor'—*quod entia non sunt praedicanda praeter necessitatem*. Here was an Augustinianism shorn of determinist overtones, emphasising God's supreme liberty of will, and denying the possibility of fathoming his purpose.[2] Ockham is often accused of a radical scepticism; but the principle of economy is in fact thoroughly fideist.[3]

III

Wyclif was but one of those who reacted against the *via moderna*, while being also greatly influenced by it. The radical theology was met by the counter-attack of Thomas Bradwardine; the new logic, physics and metaphysics by the replies of Walter Burley and others, and by the concerted activity of the whole Arts faculty at Paris. Ockham was delated to Avignon, and a long list of opinions culled from his works condemned by a papal commission. The nature of this reaction at Oxford is discussed in the following chapters.

Conservative philosophers drew their material from the inexhaustible reservoir of the Augustinian tradition. The genius

---

[1] Guelluy, *op. cit.* pp. 74, 331.

[2] *Ibid.* p. 19; L. Baudry, *Le Tractatus de principiis theologiae attribué à Guillaume d'Occam*, Études de philosophie médiévale, XXIII (1936).

[3] Professor E. F. Jacob notes that it is a common fideism that explains the alliance of Ockhamists and the 'conventionally devout' in the fifteenth century against Pecocke and the attempt to provide a rational basis for faith; cf. E. F. Jacob, *Some Recent Contributions to the Study of the Later Middle Ages*, Inaugural Lecture, Oxford (1951), p. 19.

of Plato and Paul, transmitted from antiquity in the monumental work of Augustine of Hippo, cast upon the medieval mind a spell which none could avoid. Thomas Netter of Walden noted of Wyclif's followers that 'his disciples called him John son of Augustine'.[1] But later commentators were surely incorrect in assuming that this distinguished Wyclif from his contemporaries. Indeed it is hard to think of any century (except perhaps the seventeenth) more soaked in Augustine than the fourteenth. Raised upon the great synthesis of Pauline theology and neo-platonist philosophy, it is easy to understand why, in one form or another, realism remained the dominant strand in medieval metaphysics. Wyclif made his own distinctive contribution to this school of thought. We cannot tell how he came to cleave to this party or whether any teacher influenced him directly in this direction. Probably none did. For it is a notable fact that, when his metaphysics were seen to lead to radical and dangerous conclusions, no one other than Wyclif was accused of propagating them, nor any master suspected of foisting them upon him. We are therefore entitled to suppose that he found them for himself. Nor is this at all incredible. Walter Burley, a moderate realist of the old school, had still been active at Oxford in the 1330's; and it has recently been established[2] that, in later life, he revised much of his work in order to refute the terminist attacks of Ockham. The library catalogues of the later fourteenth century (of the Benedictines at Durham, of the Austin Canons at Leicester, of John Erghome, O.S.A., at York)[3] show that Burley was respected and read. Moreover recent research has served to point out the realist elements in writers usually classed as nominalists, Ockham himself included.

[1] *Thomae Waldensis Doctrinale antiquitatum fidei catholicae ecclesiae*, ed. B. Blanciotti (Venice, 1757), I, 186 (Book I, ch. 34); Workman, I, 119.

[2] See below, pp. 99–100.

[3] Pantin, 'Catalogue of the Books of Durham College, Oxford, c. 1390–1400', in H. E. Salter, W. A. Pantin, H. G. Richardson, eds., *Formularies which bear on the History of Oxford, c. 1240–1420*, OHS, new ser. IV (1942), I, 244; M. R. James and A. H. Thompson, 'Catalogue of the Library of Leicester Abbey', *Trans. Leicest. Arch. Soc.* XXI (1939–41), 17; M. R. James, 'Catalogue of the Library of the Augustinian Friars at York', *Fasciculus J. W. Clark dicatus* (1909), p. 51.

But no such qualifications can explain the ultrarealist nature of Wyclif's metaphysics; nor did he claim to follow any current school. On the contrary, he repeatedly states that he bases himself on the teaching of Robert Grosseteste, the first Chancellor of his university.

Wyclif's devotion to the memory of Grosseteste and indebtedness to his works has long been appreciated.[1] But recent scholarship has brought out the extraordinary revival of interest in the work of Lincolniensis, which preceded Wyclif's entry into the schools and persisted into the fifteenth century. Miss Smalley[2] has noted the degree to which we depend on fourteenth- and fifteenth-century MSS. for our knowledge, for example, of Grosseteste's biblical scholarship. His *Moralitates* survive only in two thirteenth-century and two fifteenth-century copies, and these last, Miss Smalley comments, 'witness to a post-Wyclif cult of Grosseteste which led to a revival of interest in his lesser known commentaries'. At the beginning of our period Richard Fitz-Ralph was incorporating his teaching on divine illumination;[3] and, after its close, the passionately orthodox Thomas Gascoigne was citing Lincolniensis, and actually using a copy of St Paul carrying Grosseteste's own glosses.[4] This active concern in the later Middle Ages was the counterpart to a positive neglect in the

[1] For Grosseteste and Oxford philosophy see: D. A. Callus, ed., *Robert Grosseteste, Scholar and Bishop* (1955); Callus, 'The Oxford career of Robert Grosseteste', *Oxoniensia*, x (1945), 42 ff.; A. C. Crombie, *Robert Grosseteste and the Origins of Experimental Science, 1100–1700* (1953); L. Baur, *Die philosophischen Werke des Robert Grosseteste, Bischofs von Lincoln*, Beiträge zur Gesch. der Phil. des Mittelalters, IX (Münster, 1912); L. Baur, *Die Philosophie des Robert Grosseteste, Bischofs von Lincoln, ibid.* XVIII, 4–6 (Münster, 1917); D. E. Sharp, *Franciscan Philosophy at Oxford in the Thirteenth Century* (1930), pp. 9–46; Workman, I, 115–16.

For Wyclif and Grosseteste see: Lechler, pp. 20–40; J. Loserth, 'Johann von Wiclif und Robert Grosseteste, Bischof von Lincoln', *Sitz. Akad. der Wissenschaften in Wien* (phil.-hist. Kl.), 186 (1918), fasc. 2, 1–83; B. Smalley, 'The Biblical Scholar', *Robert Grosseteste, Scholar and Bishop*, ed. Callus, esp. pp. 70, 83, 95–7; S. H. Thomson, 'The Philosophical Basis of Wyclif's Theology', *Journal of Religion*, XI (1931), 105 ff.

[2] Smalley, 'The Biblical Scholar', pp. 70, 74.

[3] See below, p. 76.

[4] Smalley, 'The Biblical Scholar', pp. 74–5. Gascoigne's notebook (MS. Bodleian, lat. theol. e. 33) is full of references to Grosseteste.

fifty years after his death, a contrast which Miss Smalley finds important—and explicable. Grosseteste, she suggests, was 'old fashioned' even in his own day, and out of sympathy with the new movement to divide the teaching of theology from biblical study, still believing that theology should be tied to exegesis. To this he added a preference for scholarship to dialectic which was individual and not merely old fashioned, and which served only to alienate the rising generation of dialecticians.[1]

Several strands, besides the appeal of his metaphysics (with which we are immediately concerned) bound Wyclif to the memory of Grosseteste: the emphasis on Scripture, opposition to papal abuses, pastoral excellence.

Many external reasons must have led Wyclif to cultivate Grosseteste. Here was an Englishman who taught at Oxford, a doctor who reduced theology to Bible study, a reformer who criticised papal provisions, a bishop who devoted himself to pastoral care. Admiration does not always induce study; it can remain purely Platonic. Wyclif's did not. He quoted and knew very well a great variety of Grosseteste's works. ...He used them with scrupulous fairness...so Grosseteste was no mere legend to him nor a mouthpiece for his own views, but a source of genuine mental satisfaction....

The wheel had come full circle. The archaic, unscholastic strain in Grosseteste had repelled his contemporaries. It brought him a late but warm recognition in his own university.[2]

Drawing principally on Augustine, Denis, Avicenna and the *Liber de causis*, Grosseteste's realism was the product of various strands of neoplatonism. Its kernel was his theory of light.[3] If this was a blend of diverse materials,

his genius gave order, cohesion and unity to these scattered members. It pervades the whole of his philosophy as well as his theology, and is applied by him to every being, from God to inanimate things. God is *the* Light, the source of all light; all other beings simply participate in that Light. In the scale of created beings, a thing is more or less perfect according to its greater or less participation in light. Thus at the summit are the *intelligentiae*, the angels, wholly luminous. Next comes the

[1] Smalley, 'The Biblical Scholar', pp. 84–5, 94.
[2] *Ibid.* pp. 95–6.   [3] Crombie, *op. cit.* pp. 128–34.

human soul, whose apex, *acies intellectus*, is akin to the *intelligentiae*. Light is the bond which unites and keeps together the soul, pure spirit, with the human body. Through light the soul acquires knowledge from the senses, and through an irradiation of divine light the truth of things is perceived.[1]

These ideas are elaborated in the *Commentary on the Posterior Analytics*,[2] so often cited by Wyclif. For Grosseteste the formal cause is always more important than the material. Matter is by nature inferior to and only perfected by form; indeed matter exists simply as something caused and employed by form, the material substance of effected cause. This argument controls absolutely his theory of cognition. Assisted by common sense, imagination and memory, our sense faculties become the medium but never the cause of knowledge. Not only is the inferior unable to modify the superior, but sense alone cannot apprehend universals, which are the material cause of our knowing. The senses, in fact, perceive things as they actually are, that is imperfectly. Grosseteste does not deny that the senses contribute to knowledge but he 'never completely tears himself away from the notion that they restrict' it. If our intelligence, he believed, which is the highest element in the human soul, was not weighed down by the body, it would through divine illumination have a perfect knowledge that owed nothing to and was uncorrupted by the senses.[3] It is interesting to note that this very passage, epitomising so much of the realist tradition, was cited by Richard FitzRalph,[4] one of the two Oxford masters of the mid-fourteenth century whose inspiration Wyclif acknowledged.

Nevertheless, Grosseteste argued, it is from sense data, whether distorted or not, that the intellect elicits the universal. This act has three necessary characteristics. The complete universal must be free from the phantasms of material things; it must involve the experience of many singulars; and, in eliciting the universal we actualise our potentiality for comprehending first principles. In

---

[1] Callus, 'Robert Grosseteste as Scholar', *Robert Grosseteste, Scholar and Bishop*, pp. 23–4.
[2] Printed Venice, 149.   [3] Sharp, *op. cit.* pp. 16, 30.
[4] See below, p. 76.

universals we find absolute truth, or as near as we can approach to it; they are the material for demonstrable scientific knowledge, because they conform to the unchangeable prototypes or ideas existing in the divine mind. And through ideas, he teaches, we may even in this life know God fully; for, in a state of grace, the mind 'transcends the contents of consciousness', because 'subject to a kind of radiation from the First Cause that illuminates intelligible things and imparts to the mind a clearer under-standing and an infallibility proportionate to its penetration'.[1]

The Franciscans, whose first Oxford master he had been, were in the forefront of those in England who cherished Grosseteste's teaching and the neoplatonist tradition in general. Their loyalty to his memory, even when this meant running counter to current opinion, is shown, to take one example, in their support for his tendency, against Aristotle, to identify the *intellectus agens* with God.[2] In this view Lincolniensis had been followed by Roger Bacon and John Pecham. Rejecting the argument that the *intellectus agens* could inhere in the human intellect, Pecham denied that its identification with the Prime Mover deprived the human soul of rationality or choice, or that to posit this was to fall into the Averroist heresy. As archbishop Pecham was ruthless in his suppression of anything even remotely connected with the 'Latin Averroist' movement. Yet in his philosophical works he had shown the influence of the Oxford Franciscans. Another dis-ciple of Grosseteste amongst the Oxford Minorites was Thomas of York; following Lincolniensis, he taught that divine illumina-tion and sense perception are the two ways in which we know universals.[3]

The metaphysical tradition of the English Franciscans was con-tinued, though modified, by Scotus. Duns was a moderate realist (for Wyclif he was *constans universalium explanator*);[4] and some recent research[5] has sought to qualify his voluntarism, and

---

[1] Sharp, *op. cit.* pp. 31-3.   [2] Callus, 'Robert Grosseteste', p. 24.
[3] Sharp, *op. cit.* pp. 100, 196, 198, 394.
[4] MS. Trinity College, Cambridge, B. 16. 2, fo. 21v, and see below, p. 151.
[5] É. Gilson, *Jean Duns Scot: introduction à ses positions fondamentales*, 2 vols. (1952); on this point cf. Sharp, *op. cit.* pp. 362-3.

to insist on the priority in his system of the divine intellect to the divine volition. Certainly the doctrine of ideas (prominent in the work of those who, like Wyclif, emphasise God's intellect against his will) is of great importance in the Scotist system. In his *Opus Oxoniense* (Book I, d. xxxv) Duns poses the nature of the eternal relations between God's knowledge and what he knows. He considers three solutions. First, that God has, as an eternal relation which in some way corresponds to actuality, a simple and essential knowledge of things. Secondly, that he knows things first as relations in himself, and afterwards (because relations are the image of the actual) as they exist. Thirdly, that in the act of intellection God knows ideas. In accepting the last, Scotus proclaims the reality of ideas as relations eternally known to God, though not *naturally* prior to the actual. Correspondingly he dismisses the first two solutions as positing a mutual dependence of the relation and the known, and so (because the relation is in God's essence) of God himself and the known. All divine intellections, Scotus states, are essentially eternal and as such are ideas, according to Augustine's interpretation of Plato.[1]

The Franciscan tradition was a lasting one in medieval Oxford. And, in a quite literal sense, Wyclif would not have to go far to find Grosseteste's works and Grosseteste's ways of thought; several of his books were available in the library of the Friars Minor.[2] In one other way also, it may be, Grosseteste may have bequeathed to his successors an abiding interest. For the same platonism to be found in his writing fructified the work of mystical writers of the fifteenth century, like Cusanus. This group has usually been classed as anti-scholastic; and so, in a sense, they were. But they too had attended the schools, and it may well be that, despite their attitude to academic learning, they found there the platonism they later expounded as a rival to dialectic. We shall

---

[1] *Oxoniense scriptum in librum primum sententiarum P. Lombardi* (Coimbra, 1609), pp. 615–16, 619, 621.

[2] R. W. Hunt, 'The Library of Robert Grosseteste', *Robert Grosseteste* (1955), pp. 130, 135–8. For Wyclif's accurate, and often lengthy, citations from Grosseteste (especially the *Dicta*), see Loserth, 'Johann von Wiclif und Robert Grosseteste', *Sitz. Akad. Wissen. Wien* (phil.-hist. Kl.), 186 (1918), fasc. 2, pp. 15–40.

not forget that Grosseteste himself had set on foot the revised translation of Denis, the inspiration of the 'learned mystics' of the late medieval world.

In the old fashioned realism of Lincolniensis Wyclif found the strongest support for his metaphysical views.

Confusion and discord in metaphysics and theology: this was the climate in which Wyclif's opinions were moulded. And the eddying cross-currents of philosophical dispute in the Oxford of his day is matched by the uncertainties of modern interpretation. Indeed the course of speculation at Oxford between 1340 and 1370 is almost *terra incognita*: a landscape fitfully illumined by the rigorous predestinarianism of Bradwardine or the radical doctrine of grace propounded by Uthred Boldon. Yet it is precisely in these years that we must seek the themes which connect Wyclif with contemporary opinion. We know that teachers arose to refute Ockhamist propositions, and that by 1370 Wyclif was himself the leader of the conservative school. But little is known of the course of this reaction or of how successful it was. The evidence is sparse. There survive many fewer major treatises from the Oxford schools for these decades than for the previous generation, 1310–40. Probably there were simply fewer masters in Oxford. This, surely, is itself significant, and may do much to explain Wyclif's sudden rise to prominence.

Amongst the upholders of tradition at Oxford in these years two masters are outstanding: Thomas Bradwardine and Richard FitzRalph. It is they almost alone of the generation preceding his own whom Wyclif cites, and who clearly represented in his eyes the best answer to the radical theologians. We are entitled to take them as seriously as he did. Yet, though the nature of Bradwardine's refutation of the *moderni* is sufficiently well known, the reaction of Oxford to the *De causa Dei* awaits investigation; whilst FitzRalph's theology remains quite unexplored. A study of these questions will combine an enquiry into Wyclif's sources with an attempt to illumine some features of Oxford speculation in the middle decades of the fourteenth century.

CHAPTER II

THOMAS BUCKINGHAM AND THE REACTION TO THE 'DE CAUSA DEI'

I

IN analysing the ideas of philosophers and theologians of the past, the historian naturally emphasises distinctions and individualities. But the clash of Ockhamist and anti-Ockhamist can only fully be understood by recognising the common ground between them. For, if they disputed the answers, conservative and radical thinkers were generally agreed as to what were the important questions. An Ockhamist like the young Thomas Buckingham, an Augustinian like Thomas Bradwardine, and a moderate eclectic like Richard FitzRalph, could concur in assuming that the major questions which confronted their generation concerned neither the nature of the Godhead nor the problem of human psychology (both matters which greatly exercised the minds of the thirteenth century), but the nature of God's activity to man, our knowledge of him and his of us, the relation of his will to ours, and the capacity of men to act freely and completely both in their own power and in respect of God's will towards them. The divine will was to be seen in every human act, and man's strongest desire was to be justified to God.[1] But in the answering of these questions there was no agreement: on the contrary, deep and passionate conflict. And it is a feature of philosophy in the age of Ockham that, in the solution of these controversies, there was propounded every extreme, from absolute scepticism to absolute

[1] The most perceptive of recent studies on these themes is by Paul Vignaux, *Justification et prédestination au XIVe siècle*, Bibl. de l'école des hautes études, sc. relig. 48 (1934). For Augustinianism at Oxford at this time see K. Werner, *Der Augustinismus in der Scholastik des späteren Mittelalters* (1883), pp. 234–306; J. Milner, *History of the Church of Christ* (new edn, 1847), III, 218–42; also D. Trapp, 'Augustinian Theology of the 14th Century', *Augustiniana*, VI (1956), 146–274.

fideism, from absolute free will to rigid predestinarianism, and from the natural and inalienable goodness of human nature to the total depravity of all men unsanctified by the gratuitous gift of grace.

In this theologians were not pursuing their own private obsessions, remote from the world of reality; for interest in such matters ranged far beyond the Schools, which only reflected a wider concern. Ockham once protested that laymen and old women used to badger university lecturers with their heretical views on necessity and contingency and the limits of God's power.[1] An outstanding example of the interest, even expertise, assumed in the laity is to be found in the text of *Pearl*. In this moving vernacular poem, which can be dated to 1360–95—Wyclif's years—the author tells his vision of the Pearl, in whom he gradually recognises the transfigured form of his little daughter, dead when but a tiny child of two. Pearl undertakes to assuage her father's grief by justifying the righteousness of God, and does so in explicitly theological terms. The doctrinal theme is the nature of salvation, and the core of the poem, some 300 lines, is 'nothing more than a sustained theological argument'. 'Without the elegiac basis and the sense of great personal loss which pervades it', wrote E. V. Gordon, '*Pearl* would indeed be the mere theological treatise on a special point which some critics have called it. But without the theological debate the grief would never have risen above the ground.'[2] Throughout it is the reality and mercy of divine grace with which Pearl comforts her father, with her repeated refrain of 'the grace of God is great enough'.

Whilst in logic, physics and metaphysics (the disciplines pursued in the Arts faculties) it can be argued with much conviction that the innovations of Ockham and his followers were constructive and beneficial, we can well understand why their theological deductions were profoundly unacceptable to conservative masters. For if the final effect of the new ideas was to free men from a dogmatic rigidity which could not comprehend the over-

[1] *Guillelmi de Ockham Opera politica*, ed. H. S. Offler, III (1956), 231 (noticed by B. Smalley in *Journal of Ecclesiastical History*, IX (1958), 94).
[2] *Pearl*, ed. E. V. Gordon (Oxford, 1953), pp. xviii–xix, 127.

whelming majesty and power of God, the immediate effect was to
undermine the accepted balance in dogma.

The Ockhamist attack was as various as pertinacious, 'now
appearing as Terminism, now as extreme voluntarism and semi-
Pelagianism, now as fideism'.[1] The more 'ultra' theologians,
questioning the possibility of a reasonable faith, drifted imper-
ceptibly towards the extremes of scepticism or blind faith, and
often to combining strands of both. The tendency to divorce
reason from faith led some to dubious conclusions. An exaggerated voluntarism allowed some to suppose God to be irrational
or contradictory, whilst from another angle a strong Pelagianism
undermined his omnipotence by denying an absolute relation
between human merit and sanctifying grace. Extreme Ockhamism was attacked by contemporaries on the grounds that it broke
the unity of philosophical and theological experience and, in
particular (to take the burning problem of the day), because it
denied the accepted relation between man's will and God's,
between grace and merit, and between his foreknowledge and
man's free choice. This is the substance of the first nine articles
extracted from Ockham's *Sentences* and condemned by the masters
at Avignon in 1326.[2] Nominalism could lead to speculative
doubts of the same kind in logic and metaphysics. John Buridan,
who as Rector of the Arts faculty at Paris forbade in 1339 the use
of Ockhamist techniques, admitted in his own *Commentary on the
Nicomachean Ethics* that the existence of free will cannot be
proved, but only believed. To admit determinism would be to
reduce men to the level of beasts; but the reality of free will was
purely a matter of faith.[3]

The course of heterodox theology in these years, except in so
far as it shaped the reaction of the new orthodoxy, is outside the

---

[1] M. D. Knowles, 'The Censured Opinions of Uthred of Boldon', *Proceedings of the British Academy*, XXXVII (1951), 308–9. On the significance of
Ockhamist criticisms see Gilson, *La Philosophie au moyen âge*, pp. 638–86.

[2] Pelzer, 'Les 51 Articles de Guillaume Occam censurés, en Avignon, en
1326', *Rev. d'hist. ecclés.* XVIII (1922), 250–5; Gilson, *La Philosophie au moyen âge*,
p. 639.

[3] C. Michalski, 'Le Problème de la volonté à Oxford et à Paris au XIVe
siècle', *Studia Philosophica* (Lemberg, 1936), II, 324.

scope of this study; and we shall give but two well-known examples to portray the radical speculation of the 1340's, the years which witnessed its first effective refutation at Oxford. Both are Parisian but, we believe, illustrative also of trends at Oxford.

In 1346 Nicholas Autrecourt,[1] a licentiate in theology, was deprived of his *magisterium* in the Faculty of Arts and forbidden to proceed to the senior degree. He was condemned for meta-physical and logical errors, of which the chief was that of pro-pounding the uncertainty of human knowledge and reason. This doctrine underlies nearly all the individual propositions which the university censured. Nicholas, for example, does not say out-right that something other than God may cause an effect, but only that we cannot prove that it is not so—'non potest evidenter ostendi quin...'. There is no certainty in logic or causation; cause may produce its effect, and yet it is possible that the effect is not the product of the cause. Nor does the natural illumination of men's minds prove *evidenter* the existence of anything, not even that of the First Cause.

In the following year, Jean de Mirecourt[2] was censured for opinions contained in his *Sentences* (read in 1344–5). Here is the Ockhamism of the theologian, and all the more remarkable for the pertinacity with which it is defended. For in hardly an article of the retraction, which he was required to make, does he make a complete withdrawal, but defends at least one interpretation of his original proposition. First, by distinguishing between analysis *de virtute sermonis* and *de usu loquentium*, he is able to maintain as logically consistent propositions which, as habitually understood, he admits to be untenable. Secondly Jean de Mirecourt dis-tinguishes between God's activity *de potentia ordinata* and *de potentia absoluta* (an accepted scholastic distinction), in a way which would permit God to act quite contrary to his own nature.

[1] Cf. Gilson, *La Philosophie au moyen âge*, pp. 665–73; the text of the con-demnation in H. Denifle and A. Chatelain, eds., *Chartularium universitatis Parisiensis* (1889–97), II, 576–86, esp. 577, 583.

[2] Cf. Gilson, *La Philosophie au moyen âge*, pp. 662–5. The condemnation of 1347 is printed by Denifle and Chatelain, *Chartularium universitatis Parisiensis*, II, 610–13; Mirecourt's retraction by F. Stegmüller, 'Die zwei Apologien des Jean de Mirecourt', *RTAM*, V (1933), 40–78, 192–204.

He could, for example, *absolutely* cause men to sin; he could in the same way have caused Christ to err; and he can even cause men to hate himself.[1] By the use of such techniques Jean de Mirecourt was able to extend the range of deductive possibility to its limits, and beyond. Apart from this vigorous use of the uncertainty principle, we should also note in his theology a strong element of voluntarism, particularly in his admission that *privative* or *pro causa permissiva* God is the cause of sin. On the other hand, by allowing that good works can effect the gift of grace and that human merit can elicit divine acceptance, he detracts from God's omnipotence.[2]

II

Of the reaction at Oxford by traditional theologians to these arguments the most distinguished monument is the *De causa Dei*[3] of Thomas Bradwardine, a major work in its own right and long known to be an important source for the thought of Wyclif (who cites it countless times).

Like many of the great Mertonians, Bradwardine was a recruit from outside.[4] As a Bachelor of Arts he had been a fellow of Balliol in 1321;[5] but within two years had migrated to Merton,

[1] Stegmüller, *loc. cit.* p. 193 (2nd Apol. a. 2), 54–5 (1st Apol. aa. 19–21).

[2] *Ibid.* p. 75 (1st Apol. a. 60).

[3] The primary source for the study of Bradwardine's thought is *De causa Dei contra Pelagium*, ed. H. Savile (1618). For his theology see G. Lechler, *De Thoma Bradwardino Commentatio* (Leipzig, 1862); S. Hahn, *Thomas Bradwardinus und seine Lehre von der menschlichen Willensfreiheit*, Beiträge zur Gesch. der Philos. des Mittelalters, v (Münster, 1905); G. Leff, *Bradwardine and the Pelagians* (Cambridge, 1957); H. A. Oberman, *Archbishop Thomas Bradwardine, a Fourteenth Century Augustinian* (Utrecht, 1957).

Bradwardine and his relation to Wyclif are treated by Lechler, pp. 64–70; F. Ueberweg and B. Geyer, *Grundriss der Gesch. der Phil.* (1928), II, 623; Gilson, *La Philosophie au moyen âge*, pp. 618–20; J. F. Laun, 'Thomas von Bradwardin, der Schüler Augustins und Lehrer Wiclifs', *Zeitschrift für Kirchengeschichte*, new ser. 10, XLVII (1928), 333–56, esp. 353–6; idem, 'Recherches sur Thomas de Bradwardin, précurseur de Wyclif', *Revue d'histoire et de philosophie religieuses*, IX (1929), 217–33, esp. 226–31; idem, 'Die Prädestination bei Wyclif und Bradwardin', *Imago Dei*, ed. H. Bornkamm (1932), pp. 63–84; *DTC*, XV-2, 3586.

[4] For his career see *DNB*; Emden, *Biographical Register*, I, 244–6; Oberman, *op. cit.* pp. 10–22; Leff, *Bradwardine and the Pelagians*, pp. 2–3.

[5] E. B. Fryde and J. R. L. Highfield, 'An Oxfordshire Deed of Balliol College', *Oxoniensia*, XX (1955), 40–5.

whose wealth enabled it to draw members from the whole university, and whose pre-eminence was not seriously challenged until William of Wykeham erected a college even more lavishly endowed. Bradwardine's deep respect for fellows of Merton is reflected in the celebrated preface and postscript to the *De causa Dei*, which is the most eloquent expression of this camaraderie. His words confirm that the college was not merely an agreeable companionship but a true intellectual society. Only 'at the repeated requests of his beloved brethren, the Warden and fellows of Merton Hall' had he consented to put into writing the opinions that they knew him to hold; and he was conscious of the standards they would expect.

I have sometimes found it to have happened that, in treating difficult subjects, either the stupidity of the lecturer corrupted his listener or the rashness of the listener maligned the lecturer. Wherefore these seem equally to be avoided, and especially in that place where any other course cannot be entertained without danger, and where we would not lightly assert nor rashly judge the opinions of others.[1]

It was with the same warmth (though in a less solemn vein) that John Ashenden dedicated a treatise to his sodality a few years later in these words:

This work... I have written for the general use of students of astronomy, and especially for the occupation and amusement of the fellows of Merton Hall in Oxford. May God on high preserve them and the college for ever.[2]

Bradwardine remained a fellow of Merton from 1323 to 1335. He had a notable career in the Arts faculty as a mathematician and physicist, and must have lectured on the *Sentences* during 1333-6 (when he is named Bachelor of Theology). At this time he had the good luck to gain the patronage of Richard Bury, who secured for him the Chancellorship of St Paul's and a position in the royal household (1337). In 1349, only three months before being carried off by the Black Death, he received the supreme accolade of the clerical civil servant, promotion to Canterbury.[3]

---

[1] *De causa Dei*, ed. Savile, 'Ad suos Mertonenses epistola prior' (unpaginated).
[2] MS. Bodleian, Digby 176, fo. 40r, for which see below, pp. 101 ff.
[3] Emden, *Biographical Register*, I, 245.

Recent study has established that the *De causa Dei* was composed in 1344.[1] When therefore Bradwardine yielded to the entreaties of the fellows of Merton, he had been away from Oxford for about eight years. His rod had been long in pickle, and his work is a criticism of twenty years of battle in the schools of Oxford and Paris. The radical theologians whom he attacks are called by Bradwardine the Modern Pelagians; they are not named, but their opinions, which he refutes, correspond significantly with many of those of Ockham and his *sequelae*. But if he attacked the Modern Pelagians, he was himself a product of his times, exhibiting a voluntarism as extreme as any Ockhamist's and erecting a 'system of determinist theology which departs from orthodoxy in one direction almost as clearly as do the "Pelagians" whom he was attacking on the other'.[2]

The insistence on the primacy of the will, human and divine, is a characteristic of fourteenth-century theology. But it is the overriding importance which Bradwardine places upon grace which gives the *De causa Dei* its unique quality. His conversion to a knowledge that without God's ineffable and gratuitous gift of grace all human activity is worthless and even impossible (the key to his critique of Ockhamism) is described in a famous autobiographical passage in the *De Causa Dei*.[3] But his words must be read with care. He writes that when reading Arts ('quando philosophicis literis intendebam') he was 'far from the true knowledge of God and held captive in opposing error', and that in the Arts faculty ('in scholis philosophorum') he rarely heard anything of grace. But this is hardly a criticism of his teachers, since the doctrine of grace was essentially a theological problem which the Artists were forbidden to discuss. At the time of the Averroist controversy of 1270-7, Masters of Arts at Paris had been rebuked for impinging on theological issues; and in the 1350's, as will be seen,[4] a fellow of Merton could attack another member of his own

---

[1] Oberman, *op. cit.* pp. 18-19; Leff, *Bradwardine and the Pelagians*, pp. 265-6.

[2] Knowles, *loc. cit.*, *Proceedings of the British Academy*, XXXVII (1951), 308.

[3] *De causa Dei*, Book I, chap. 35, p. 308, printed in translation in Workman, I, 120-1; cf. Oberman, *op. cit.* pp. 14-15.

[4] Below, p. 102.

college for the same offence. Topics like free will did indeed overlap the two disciplines, but an Artist could only treat them 'philosophically'. Bradwardine therefore 'rarely heard anything of grace' because at that stage in his studies it was not in his syllabus. But he makes it plain that his conversion took place when still a member of the junior faculty—'before I became a student of theology'—and so, we may assume, was not the result of attraction to any particular theologian then lecturing at Oxford. He was converted by the direct words of Scripture: 'Therefore it is not in him that willeth nor in him that runneth, but in God that sheweth mercy.' The contrast with Wyclif's intellectual progress is marked. Bradwardine's words reveal that his vision of God's grace, and the determinist theology he deduced from it, came to him during, but did not arise out of, his philosophical studies—whereas Wyclif's plainly did.

Fundamental to Bradwardine's restatement of orthodoxy is his conception of the divine omnipotence effected through 'the grace of God as it is prevenient both in time and nature to all good works'. God is all: without him men's puny efforts are nothing. But besides remarking on the strong predestinarianism of the 'Doctor Profundus', the student of Wyclif will note a further marked feature of the *De causa Dei*. Bradwardine believed that there lay in the Ockhamist denial of certainty in dogma not the genuine humility of one who knows that God's purpose is always a mystery, but a taste for irresponsible speculation, the instrument of which was an extension of the doctrine of possibility to its limit. This technique, whether leading to scepticism or fideism, was repugnant to him; and the *De causa Dei*, therefore, was concerned not merely to restore, albeit with a determinist gloss,[1] the old relation between will, power and grace in God, but also to assert that of these and all other divine truths we have a sure and certain knowledge. And in this, at least, he was at one with Wyclif, though the two reached the same conclusion from different premises.

[1] For a contrary view of Bradwardine's determinism see J. A. Weisheipl and H. A. Oberman, 'The *Sermo Epinicius* ascribed to Thomas Bradwardine (1346)', *AHDL*, xxv (1958), 295-329.

III

It has long been appreciated that the *De causa Dei* struck a power-ful and effective blow for traditional Augustinianism, and its influence is marked by the numerous citations in the *Commentaries* read at Oxford and Paris in the following twenty years.[1] This influence was indeed somewhat equivocal. The 'ultra' volun-tarism, for example, which Bradwardine shared with many of the radical theologians whom he attacked (and which, in its extrem-ism, renders the *De causa Dei* as typical of its times as many an Ockhamist work), could be put to use by the radicals themselves. The Cistercian Pierre de Ceffons, who argued in his highly Ockhamist *Sentences* (Paris, *c.* 1360) that God was the cause of sin, was able to quote the 'Doctor Profundus' in support.[2]

If the *Chartularium* is to be trusted, heterodox speculation con-tinued to be a feature of Parisian philosophy between 1340 and 1360.[3] Was this true of Oxford also? And, if not, how thoroughly did Bradwardine succeed in silencing his opponents? In any attempt to assess Wyclif's theological position and the move-ments in Oxford theology during his formative years this question must be faced.

A quantitative answer we cannot expect: the extant texts are too few. But in the intellectual journey of one man at least, an Oxford theologian and a Mertonian to boot, we have the most striking evidence of a change of heart directly caused by the argu-ment of the *De causa Dei* (and, very possibly, by immediate inter-course with the author himself). Thomas Buckingham, fellow of Merton and Chancellor of Exeter, began his career as a Modern Pelagian; he ended as a moderate and conservative Augustinian. His change of heart has been suspected, but not adequately investigated; and in the dearth of material for Oxford theology *c.* 1345–65 his *Sentences* and *Questions* cannot be neglected. 'One

[1] Oberman, *op. cit.* pp. 186–223.
[2] Michalski, 'Le Problème de la volonté à Oxford et à Paris au XIVe siècle', pp. 359–61. For Ceffons see D. Trapp, 'Peter Ceffons of Clairvaux', *RTAM*, XXIV (1957), 101–54.
[3] Cf. censures of 'advanced' propositions in Denifle and Chatelain, eds., *Chartularium*, III, 11–12, 21–3, 95–7, 108.

gets the impression', writes Professor E. F. Jacob,[1] 'that Bucking-ham is a philosopher of considerable importance in the Oxford schools and that a study of him is a necessary precursor to any analysis of Wyclif's philosophy.'

Buckingham[2] was born c. 1300 and died shortly after 1356. He was fellow of Merton 1324–40 and, though he was certainly absent from Oxford during the years 1346–9 (and possibly at other times), it was to Merton that he returned in later life—per-haps to die there. Like many of his colleagues he was interested in science and mathematics and at least one of his tracts composed as an Artist has survived.[3] He lectured in college, and was a bene-factor to the library, to which he left copies of the *Confessions* and *De civitate Dei* and Higden's *Polychronicon*.[4]

But his importance lies in his theology. The date of his reading the *Sentences* is unknown, but since his *Commentary*[5] displays some typical features of the *via moderna*, and quotes such theologians of the 1320's as Chatton and Holcot, this is unlikely to have occurred before 1330. And there is evidence that Buckingham's *Com-mentary* may have been delivered as late as c. 1335, and that his master may have been none other than Richard FitzRalph. This may seem surprising, for FitzRalph, though too subtle not to be influenced by the currents of the age, remained fundamentally

---

[1] *Journal of Ecclesiastical History*, IX (1958), 96.

[2] Emden, *Biographical Register*, I, 298–9; C. Michalski, 'Le Problème de la volonté', pp. 233 ff.; *idem*, 'Les Courants philosophiques à Oxford et à Paris pendant le XIVe siècle', *Bulletin international de l'académie polonaise des sciences et des lettres* (Cl. hist. et phil.) (Cracow, 1922–4), pp. 68–9; *idem*, 'Le Criticisme et le scepticisme dans la philosophie du XIVe siècle', *ibid.* (1927), p. 69; F. M. Powicke, *The Medieval Books of Merton College* (Oxford, 1931), p. 113; Leff, *Bradwardine and the Pelagians*, pp. 227–41; Oberman, *op. cit.* pp. 118–94; W. A. Pantin, *The English Church in the Fourteenth Century* (Cambridge, 1955), pp. 113 ff., 263 ff.; Brodrick, *Memorials of Merton College*, pp. 202–3.

[3] MS. Erfurt, Amplonius F. 135, fo. 48, noted in Powicke, *Medieval Books*, p. 113.

[4] Powicke, *op. cit.* pp. 34, 57–8. He also left a copy of Peter Lombard to Exeter Cathedral Library; cf. Emden, *loc. cit.*

[5] *Questiones Solertissimi viri Johannis* (sic) *Bokinkam genere anglici in quattuor libros sententiarum* (Paris, 1505). This erroneous title has led to the *Commentary*'s being attributed to John Buckingham, bishop of Lincoln (for whom see *DNB*, s.v. Bokyngham, where the confusion is suspected).

orthodox in a way quite contrary to the young Ockhamist. But the suggestion is plausible,[1] and it would not be the first time that a conservative teacher had hatched a radical pupil.

The supposed relation between the two depends on a single text. In Qu. 6 of his *lectura* Buckingham advances his characteristic argument that God could produce a creature deprived of justifying grace, and yet without demerit or mortal guilt.[2] Amongst the objectors to this proposition had been one man of distinction, whose argument Buckingham states.

And if in the aforesaid case the loss of grace would not then be a sin, now also in fact and by common usage there would be no sin in children, as my lord and master has said; and this was the opinion of the reverend doctor, who not long ago was Chancellor.[3]

It is true that the opinion here expressed, that infants too young to act meritoriously and without the grace conferred by baptism are still unjustified, was a contemporary orthodoxy. But it is also true that of the Chancellors of the university at this time none has left any theology except FitzRalph, who held office from May 1332 to May 1334 and in whose *Commentary* this opinion can be found.[4] In so far as we can wring a meaning from one oblique reference, the probability is that Buckingham was indeed FitzRalph's pupil, and incepted *c.* 1335.

It is also possible that he visited Paris (where two copies of his *Sentences* survive).[5] A collection of Parisian incepting exercises, belonging to Thomas of Cracow, who was a student at the

---

[1] Michalski, 'Le Problème de la volonté', p. 250.

[2] *Ed. cit.*, qu. 6, fo. L 4r[a].

[3] Qu. 6, fo. M 2r[b]. Ad idem, si in casu predicto privatio gratie non foret peccatum tunc, et nunc de facto et lege currenti (*sic*), non esset peccatum in parvulis, sicut dixit Dominus meus et Magister; et fuit hec opinio reverendi doctoris, et non diu est Cancelarii.

[4] MS. Oriel College, Oxford, 15, qu. 28 a. 2, fo. 105r[b].

[5] MSS. Paris, Bibliothèque Nationale, lat. 15888, fos. 2r–109v; 16400, fos. 6r–64v. Cf. Michalski, 'Les Courants philosophiques', pp. 68–9; M. D. Chenu, 'Les *Quaestiones* de Thomas de Buckingham', *Studia medievalia...in honorem R. J. Martin* (Bruges, 1948), p. 231; F. Stegmüller, *Repertorium commentariorum in sententias Petri Lombardi* (Würzburg, 1947), I, 415. Another copy (MS. Madrid, Biblioteca Nacional 133, fos. 1–92) has been identified by V. Doucet, 'Commentaires sur les Sentences', *AFH*, XLVII (1954), 170.

university about 1350, cites him as an opponent of Bradwardine on the question of created will. Buckingham incorporated this proposition into his *Questions*.[1] His visit, if it did occur, is likely to have taken place between 1344 and 1346, when he became Chancellor of Exeter. But Thomas of Cracow may simply have been recording an Oxford dispute; the reference does not in itself imply Buckingham's presence at Paris.

Buckingham's *Sentences*, which we suppose to have been read *c.* 1335, are notable for the refusal to regard the states of grace and sin as absolute contraries. Quite the reverse: in Qu. 6 he seeks to establish a neutral state between grace and sin in which the absence of the one does not compel the existence of the other.[2] Since our first parents and the angels were both without sin and grace, and yet were guiltless, there must be a *medius status* between sin and grace in which both are reconciled.[3] And if grace and sin can coexist, then the loss of grace is equally immaterial involving, if one continues to act meritoriously, neither sin nor guilt.[4] The basis for such propositions was the belief that there is a natural justice in men which does not require the divine habit of charity and by which men can naturally be justified;[5] and the consequence was to render superfluous the infused grace by virtue of which, as orthodox theologians understood, we receive justification.

[1] B. Hauréau, 'Notice sur le numéro 16409 des manuscrits latins de la bibliothèque nationale', *Notices et extraits des manuscrits de la Bibliothèque Nationale*, xxxiv, pt. ii (1895), 319, 324–5; Michalski, 'Le Problème de la volonté', pp. 250–1, 'Les Courants philosophiques', pp. 68–9. On fo. 23 v of this MS. it is stated: 'Ponit Bokinham talem conclusionem contra auctorem De causa Dei: voluntas creata potest libere libertate contradictionis producere actum suum.' This is the ninth conclusion of Buckingham's *Questions* (MS. New College, Oxford, 134, fo. 324r).

[2] Leff, *Bradwardine and the Pelagians*, p. 232.

[3] *Ed. cit.*, fo. L 6vᵇ. Ad idem arguitur sic: primi angeli et primi parentes in statu innocentie erant sine gratia gratum faciente et sine peccato et culpa mortali et veniali, et per consequens inter peccatum et gratiam est medius status possibilis....

[4] Fo. M 3r. Ad istum articulum respondeo et dico quod si deus aufferret a creatura gratiam seu iusticiam sine tamen demerito suo vel alieno, vel si deus crearet creaturam rationalem sine tali iniusticia, non requiritur quod privatio illius iusticie sit peccatum nec culpa....

[5] Fo. M 3rᵇ. Concedo: preter tamen charitatem est una naturalis iusticia quo creatura rationalis potest esse iusta et recta sine charitate.

Created grace is not a divine habit necessarily existing in the righteous, for God accepts men through their natural virtues as well as through his grace. So men may be graceless and yet without sin, and justified without receiving the infusion of divine charity.[1]

The God of this system has a will which is untrammelled but not determining. Freed from the obligation to relate reward to merit or penalty to guilt, he can by his absolute power produce creatures who are naturally without sin but deprived of grace.[2] From him we receive the power to will but, just as God's will is not necessitated but is changeable, so also are ours. Buckingham indeed turns the traditional determinist thesis inside out; the argument from analogy is reversed. It is God's knowledge which is the reflection of human knowledge, and like us he knows the future only contingently. Thus we reach a conclusion arrived at by many of Bradwardine's opponents, that it is the freedom of the divine will and its inherent contingency which prevents it from being determining.[3]

But Buckingham is prepared to take this argument to the extreme. God's promises, he declares, are merely contingent, as is the revelation granted to the blessed and even the truth revealed to Christ; for he willed future events contingently, and he and we know them also in the same way. Within this conception of a radical contingency in the universe Buckingham can admit that God wills the existence of sin, for in such indeterminacy he cannot be thought to be the cause of the particular sins of men.[4]

[1] Fo. L 5r^b, printed Leff, *Bradwardine and the Pelagians*, p. 230 n. 3.

[2] Fo. L 5r^b. Ad idem arguo per rationes sic: si carere gratia in creatura rationali semper foret peccatum et culpa mortalis, sequeretur quod deus de potentia sua absoluta non posset creaturam facere esse in puris naturalibus sine peccato et sine gratia gratum faciente, quod esset quidam habitus additus suis naturalibus. Consequens est falsum.

[3] Fos. F7v^b, G1r^b, G3v^b, printed Leff, *op. cit.* pp. 235 n. 3, 237 n. 2, 238 n. 4.

[4] Fo. F4r^b. Et eodem modo, si deus promittat aliqua contingenter, promittit et contingenter iurat; et eodem modo dico de beatis qui vident futura contingentia in Verbo, et maxime de Christo, qui fuit deus et homo, quod scivit in Verbo contingentia et contingenter sciunt illa; et [quod] scivit, contingenter sciunt. Sic contingenter voluit ita et ea esse futura asseruit.

Fo. O2v^a. Ad articulum principalem, nichil asserendo, sed tantum gratia exercitii disputando, dico quod deus vult peccatum fieri et esse et hominem peccare mortaliter et venialiter.

In his *Commentary*, therefore, Buckingham put forward two of the major theses which Bradwardine tried to combat in the *De causa Dei*. He implicitly denied the accepted doctrine of grace by making it a neutral term reconcilable with unpurged sinfulness, and he stated that the acts of God and man were utterly contingent. We can only speculate on his attitude to Bradwardine at this time. They had become fellows of Merton within a year of each other (both were in residence from 1324 to 1335), and Buckingham once referred to his colleague as 'doctor noster Bardvardinus'.[1] And in an important reference in his *Questions* (c. 1350) to a 'certain reverend doctor', who is identified below as Bradwardine, Buckingham actually speaks of himself as a disciple and pupil in the schools of the 'Doctor Profundus'. He admits, however, that then, and when reading the *Sentences*, he put forward a solution hostile to his master's.

Pro hiis et similibus argumentis doctori et domino reverendo, in scolis doctoris suus scolaris et discipulus, respondebam, et in legendo Sententias idem dixi, quod nullum infinitum est alio infinito eiusdem speciei maius....[2]

But it is difficult to believe that Buckingham can have been one of those Mertonians who 'implored' the Chancellor of St Paul's to publish his great refutation. Whatever their personal relations, doctrinally they were poles apart. The well-known predestinarianism of the latter was anathema to Buckingham.

He vacated his fellowship in 1340; and is next discovered in 1346, already installed as Chancellor of Exeter Cathedral.[3] John Grandisson,[4] bishop of Exeter 1327-69, was a notable patron of art and learning, justly proud of his cathedral school. We shall

---

[1] A. Maier, *Die Vorläufer Galileis im 14. Jahrhundert*, Storia e Letteratura, XXII (1949), p. 96 n. 27. Cf. Buckingham's *Sentences*, ed. cit., fo. C 31r-v, where the surname is omitted.

[2] MS. New College 134, fo. 364r^b.

[3] F. C. Hingeston-Randolph, ed., *Register of John de Grandisson, Bishop of Exeter (A.D. 1327-1369)*, Episcopal Registers, diocese of Exeter (1894-9), II, 1005.

[4] For Grandisson and his relations with Buckingham and FitzRalph see Pantin, *The English Church in the Fourteenth Century*, pp. 113 ff., 151 ff., and below, Appendix.

meet him again as the benefactor of Richard FitzRalph. No doubt he selected Buckingham as an accomplished scholastic who would bring distinction and perhaps a spark of controversy to a provincial town; and he was not to be disappointed. But Buckingham must have left by 1349, for in that year Grandisson, again looking for a theologian to preach and teach, complained that he was once more without any master of divinity.[1] He later returned to Merton; and his last appearance in the college records is notable, for it is in that list of stewards for 1356 which also contains Wyclif's name.[2] Of all those who took part in the 'Pelagian' controversy Buckingham is the only one whom we know for certain that Wyclif met. Nearly all the protagonists were dead by 1350. Thomas Buckingham, critic of the 'Doctor Profundus', is the sole physical link between Wyclif and Bradwardine.

IV

Shortly after leaving Exeter, Buckingham composed a second major work, valuable for three reasons. First it reveals a significant modification of his previous opinions; secondly it provides a critique of the *De causa Dei* and helps us to measure the reaction to it; and finally it throws light on just that period when it is most difficult to plot the course of speculation at Oxford.

Buckingham's *Questions*[3] survive in two manuscripts, MSS. New College 134, fos. 322r–441v and Merton M. I. 11, fos. 1–83. The New College MS.,[4] the more legible and, we believe, the earlier of the two, is a magnificent codex containing the *De causa Dei* followed by the *Questions*. The copy of Bradwardine's work

---

[1] Pantin, *The English Church*, pp. 115–16. [2] See above, p. 11 n. 5.

[3] Powicke, *Medieval Books of Merton College*, pp. 30, 113, 243; Pantin, *The English Church*, pp. 114–15, 263–6; Oberman, *Thomas Bradwardine*, pp. 192–4. The MSS. are described and the incipits printed (from the New College MS.) by Chenu, 'Les *Quaestiones* de Thomas de Buckingham', *Studia medievalia in honorem...R. J. Martin*, pp. 229–42.

[4] H. O. Coxe, *Catalogus codicum MSS....in collegiis aulisque Oxoniensibus* (1852), I, 49 of separate pagination. For the history of MS. New College 134 see Powicke, *op. cit.* pp. 30, 91, 243.

was a legacy to New College from William Rede, sometime fellow of Merton and bishop of Chichester. Rede's will of 1382 makes no mention of the *Questions*,[1] and the hand of these is not that of the scribe of the *De causa Dei*. The two treatises have a common subject (indeed the one is in part a commentary on the other), but it must therefore have been after 1382 that the link between them was recognised and the opportunity taken to bind them together.

Buckingham apparently gave none of his own works to the the Merton library, whose copy of the *Questions*[2] was acquired in the fifteenth century. Although there are some textual variants, there can (because of the identical displacement of a part of a question in both MSS.) be little doubt that one is a copy of the other; and it seems clear that it is the Merton text which is a copy of the New College MS.[3] Moreover the Merton scribe carelessly and erroneously associates Buckingham with Oxford instead of Exeter—twice out of three times reading 'Oxonie' or 'Oxoni-

---

[1] Powicke, *op. cit.* p. 91.   [2] *Ibid.* pp. 243–4.

[3] MS. New College 134 breaks off in the middle of fo. 437r[a], leaving 35 blank lines, and resumes at the head of fo. 437r[b] with the words, 'Ad primam instanciam respondetur quod per meditacionem intelligit propositum et vult quod virginitas sit virtus...'. It can be shown by reference to the Merton MS. that this is the concluding section accidentally omitted at the end of the series of questions 'de augmento gracie et de merito creature'. The New College MS. ends this section thus (fo. 390v[b]): '...usque in finem. Quod hic deficit quere in fine libri.'

MS. Merton M. I. II repeats this misplaced order without any break, merely noting in the margin of fo. 50v, 'Quod hec defficit quere in fine libri in penultimo folio ad tale signum $\lambda_{\lambda\lambda}$', and repeating the key ($\lambda_{\lambda\lambda}$) against 'ad primam instanciam' on fo. 82v[a], which is written continuously. The exact repetition of the misplacement indicates that one MS. is a copy of the other, and the broken nature of the New College MS., compared with the continuous and unbroken script of the Merton MS., shows that it is the Merton MS. which is a copy of the New College MS.

This comparison explains an error of M. D. Chenu, 'Les Quaestiones de Thomas de Buckingham', p. 231 (repeated in Oberman, *op. cit.* p. 190 n. 1), who states that the Merton MS. contains only the first three sections of the *Questions*. Chenu saw that the end of section three had been misplaced in the New Coll. MS. to the end of the whole work, but did not note that exactly the same misplacement had occurred in the Merton MS., and therefore assumed that the final sections were missing. The Merton MS. is complete.

ensis' for 'Exonie' and 'Exoniensis'. Indeed in the incipit he manages with the aid of an erasure to turn the Chancellor of Exeter Cathedral into the Chancellor of the university, an office Buckingham never held.[1] But the value of the Merton MS. lies, not in its text, but in the marginalia of its unknown owner, where the 'quidam doctor' whom Buckingham attacks is identified as Bradwardine, and, on occasion, the relevant chapter of the *De causa Dei* is cited.

Buckingham's *Questions*[2] are in reality a collection of five groups of questions, the first three of which (on future contingents, divine causation and grace and merit) contain explicit references to the 'Doctor Profundus' and can be treated as a unity. The fourth group is concerned with original sin and includes a long account of a dispute with an unknown doctor at Exeter[3] (who is certainly not Bradwardine and seems, on the contrary, to have put forward 'Pelagian' propositions). The work ends with a set of questions posed by Buckingham on the problem of merit and demerit, though whether argued at Oxford or Exeter is not made plain. In any case all the *quaestiones* were written within a few years of each other, those criticising Bradwardine's 'ultra' doctrine sometime after 1344 and those on the Exeter dispute shortly after 1349, since the author is described in the incipit as 'nuper ecclesie Exoniensis cancellarium'. The *terminus ad quem* is Buckingham's death *c.* 1356, and we have taken *c.* 1350 as a mean date for the *Questions*.

Buckingham's *Sentences* are most striking in their treatment of contingency and free will, and it is with this problem, argued

[1] Cf. incipit of New Coll. MS., 'Questiones tractate per Thomam de Bukyngham nuper ecclesie Exoniensis Cancellarium' with Merton MS., 'Questiones tractate per Thomam de Buckingham [erasure] Oxoniensis Cancellarium'. The Merton scribe correctly copies (fo. 54 v^a) 'Exonie' for New Coll. MS. fo. 395 v^a, but again misreads (fo. 65 r^b) 'Oxonie' for the 'Exonie' of New Coll. MS. fo. 409 v^a. This clears up the doubts expressed by Pantin, *The English Church in the Fourteenth Century*, p. 114 n. 2.

[2] In MS. New Coll. 134 the groups are foliated as follows: future contingents, fos. 324 r^a–352 r^a; divine causation, fos. 352 r^a–369 r^a; grace and merit, fos. 369 r^a–390 v^b; original sin, fos. 390 v^b–409 v^a; merit and demerit, fos. 409 v^a–438 v^a.

[3] See below, Appendix.

under fifteen conclusions, that his *Questions* begin. But if the topics remained the same, his understanding of them had profoundly changed, as the opening paragraphs showed:

The questions treated by Thomas Buckingham, lately Chancellor of the church at Exeter, showing that between the errors of Pelagius, Cicero and Scotus there exists a middle catholic way, and that an eternal predestination, preordaining and forewilling, and God's concurrence with them, are compatible with free will and merit in creatures. And the following *opusculum* takes its name from the demonstrable effect of the merit of freedom of action; and after the custom formerly observed at Oxford, at the time of inception or inauguration, the author has proposed a question, covering matters which he has decided to treat in this form: whether it is meritorious for a creature to believe a prophecy of some contingent future.

First I have treated on the contingency of future events and the freedom of the will, countering with various evidence those who attempt to destroy the freedom of choice and freedom to reject both alternatives which rational creatures possess (by supposing that everything that will happen necessarily happens); and also attacking those who with too facile a judgement strive to take away from God the free exercise of power, under the impression that the divine ordering restricts and binds his infinite power. And so that my listeners can more easily grasp my words, I have proposed some conclusions for discussion and, when they are declared, what I intend to assert and maintain on this subject will, I think, become clear.[1]

---

[1] MS. New College 134, fo. 324r[a] (all references, unless otherwise stated, are to this manuscript). The text is printed in part by Pantin, *The English Church*, p. 263.

Questiones tractate per Thomam de Bukyngham, nuper ecclesie Exoniensis cancellarium, ostendentes inter errores Pelagii, Cicheronis et Scoti catholicum medium invenire ac predestinacionem, preordinacionem, prevolucionem eternam concursumque Dei stare cum libera voluntate et merito creature; et ideo ab effectu ostensivo meriti libere accionis sequens opusculum nominatur, et iuxta modum Oxonie actenus observatum in sua incepcione seu principio, Questionem, materias quas tractare disposuit continentem, proposuit sub hac forma: utrum credere prophecie de aliquo contingenter futuro sit meritorium creature.

Primo tractavi de contingencia futurorum et arbitrii libertate, obiciendo diversis evidenciis contra illos qui contradiccionis et indifferencie libertatem a creatura racionali nituntur destruere, opinantes de necessitate autem cuncta que evenient evenire, ac contra illos qui nimis faciliter iudicantes a deo nituntur

In these words we find, if not a complete reversal, at least a drastic shift in Buckingham's standpoint. He is still, as the second paragraph shows, an enemy of extreme determinism, still the advocate of the freedom of men's wills. But whereas in his *Sentences* an all-pervading contingency of things human and divine was seen to affect even God's faculties and powers, here Buckingham undertakes to justify a moderate predestinarianism. God's preordinance and forewilling, he says, complement rather than contradict human liberty and a true understanding of his relation to men's acts must avoid both the humanistic error of Pelagius (that we can merit salvation without the gift of grace), the Stoic indeterminism of Cicero, who believed, as Buckingham had done, that even God does not know the future, and the unlimited voluntarism which Scotus attributes to God. Buckingham in fact had moved from the left to the centre and had secured an impregnable position from which to criticise the extreme Augustinianism of Bradwardine. So he is able in his first conclusion to state briefly, 'and so that I should not seem to be agreeing with the Pelagians', that nothing happens without God's co-operation, and then without more delay to plunge into the central question of relating his necessitating power to man's freedom of action.[1]

Medieval theologians recognised that God's omnipotence and compulsive power cannot be adequately described in terms of simple coercion and, in refining their definitions, had come to distinguish between the necessity, deriving from a divine imperative *tout court*, and the necessity which results from given circumstances, or, to use the scholastic jargon, between antecedent and consequent necessity. Circumstances can never be absolutely compelling, and however pressing they may be, our ultimate freedom of choice is not impaired. Yet can we deny God's direct

---

auferre liberam potestatem, credentes divinam ordinacionem eius infinitissimam potestatem restringere et ligare; et ut audientes facilius caperent mea dicta, conclusiones quasdam proposui pertractandas quibus, ut reputo, declaratis patebit in hac materia quid intendo asserere et tenere.

[1] Fo. 324r[a]. Prima conclusio fuit ista: nulla res secundum suam essenciam seu substanciam potest fieri nisi deo ipsam per se et proprie faciente et eternaliter prevolente; [fo. 324v[a].] Primam conclusionem ad presens solummodo introduco ne Pelagiis videar consentire.

forewilling of our acts? Buckingham discusses necessitation explicitly in five of the fifteen conclusions on future contingents with which the *Questions* begin, and at once clashes with Thomas Bradwardine.

He begins with a series of negative premisses. First he insists on a strict definition of antecedent necessity; not every act which we judge inevitable is 'antecedently' necessitated. He declares secondly that it is erroneous simply to equate the divine will with antecedent necessity; and thirdly that man, even if he has the power absolutely to cause some act, is still not its antecedent cause in the sense of having an irresistible will.[1] Behind this we may assume another fundamental premiss, that absolute necessity is as derogatory to God's liberty as it is to man's. This is, of course, the precise opposite of Bradwardine's belief than any admission of contingency, human or divine, is derogatory to the divine will and power. But Buckingham roundly declares that if God's acts were bound by antecedent necessity, his liberty of action would be curtailed (and it is an axiom of his system that God's freedom of choice must be absolute).[2] With an echo of his radical views on contingency, he adds that not even the consequences of predestination, which is 'the gift of present grace and future glory', are irrevocable, should God will otherwise.[3]

As medieval theologians did not cease to point out, determinism resulted in reward and punishment ceasing to be related to merit or demerit, since men's acts were divinely necessitated and so without moral content. But it was unnecessary to go to the other extreme and say that moral worth requires that our acts be entirely unassisted even by God's support. This indeed (the belief

[1] Fo. 324r^a. Conclusio secunda; non omnis causa activa, qua positiva, cum omnibus suis disposicionibus previis quibus causat suum causatum, necessario et indefectibiliter sequitur illud causari, est necessitas antecedens. Conclusio tercia; voluntas divina non est respectu cuiuslibet effectus futuri necessitas antecedens. Conclusio quarta; non in cuiuscunque libera potestate est aliquod consequens in eius libera potestate est omne ad idem consequens necessario antecedens.

[2] Fo. 324v^a. Secundam conclusionem multipliciter confirmabo et simul cum illa probatur conclusio tertia; primo sic, sequitur, si omnis accio dei ad extra esset a necessitate antecedente, sic non posset deus aliquid ad extra agere libere libertate contradictionis, quod videtur erroneum.

[3] Fo. 324v^a.

that we can merit justification without the infusion of grace) was an aspect of the Pelagianism so fashionable in Buckingham's youth. We can, he writes in his *Questions*, accept the fact that God rewards many meritorious acts which nevertheless appear to men to be necessitated, without having also to accept the repugnant notion that he can punish us for sins which we cannot avoid:

For there is nothing unfitting in the fact that his mercy and goodness are declared by rewarding a necessary act... but it would not accord with reason, and would argue cruelty in him, that he should punish us for an act that is either necessitated or without demerit.[1]

Buckingham followed contemporary practice in the emphasis laid on that *potentia absoluta* by which God may transcend his own laws,[2] but in truth he does so only to remark that St Thomas and the Lombard are hostile to a misconception which divorces merit from the free act.[3]

It is in fact his principal thesis that God's omnipotence and human freedom of choice (the 'freedom of contradiction', to use the theologian's technical term) are not incompatible. Who dares to say, he asks, that omnipotent God cannot create a person who has freedom of contradiction? The answer is, of course, that he not only can but does, and that his prevenient will effects and preserves rather than denies our freedom. Buckingham assumes, therefore, that there is a clear distinction between the two kinds of necessity, and (implicitly) that we are rarely if ever subjected to the extreme form.

But another view could be taken and had indeed been taken by a distinguished contemporary named, after the manner of the schools, merely as a 'certain doctor'. The argument and objection can best be given in Buckingham's own tortuous but precise language.

---

[1] Fo. 342r[b].

[2] This argument was noted by Wyclif, who refers in his *De volucione Dei* to the modern Pelagians, characterised as 'those who assert that we can merit grace by God's absolute, even if not by his ordinate, power'. Cf. M. H. Dziewicki, ed., *De ente librorum duorum excerpta* (*WS*, 1909), p. 195, and see below, p. 211.

[3] Fo. 342r[b].

In a necessary consequence [he writes], if the antecedent is not in the free control of the person concerned, then neither is the consequence; and if the consequence is under his control so is the antecedent; and the rules brought with authorities and arguments against my second, third, ninth and tenth conclusions have (I hope) been fully refuted to the understanding of those who uttered them. But to what has been said here a certain doctor objects, by proving that whoever has free control over a consequence is also in control of whatever follows from it and whatever is necessarily antecedent. And he says that he understands this only of any antecedent which is not absolutely impossible: and it is his 13th conclusion.[1]

The opponent can be identified without difficulty. He is Bradwardine (as the marginal annotation in the Merton MS. tells us), and the reference is to the *De causa Dei*, Book III, ch. 5, cor. 13.[2]

On the question of free will Bradwardine and Buckingham are utterly opposed. The 'Doctor Profundus' is a determinist theologian, whose conception of the supremacy of God's will leaves no room for uncontrolled free will in men; or rather, he argues that to act freely is to fulfil those acts to which we have been

---

[1] Fo. 327r[a]. In consequentia necessaria, si antecedens non est in cuiusquam libera potestate secundum contradiccionem, nec consequens, et si consequens est in cuiusquam libera potestate est similiter et antecedens; et hee regule per auctoritates et raciones, que diversis locis contra conclusionem secundam et terciam, nonam et decimam adducuntur, ut spero, plenarie reprobantur et hoc ad dicencium intellectum. Sed contra nunc dicta obicit quidam doctor et probat quod in cuiuscunque potestate simpliciter libera est aliquod consequens, in eius simpliciter libera potestate est quodlibet ad idem consequens, in consequentia formali et necessaria [sic] antecedens. Et dicit quod intelligit solum de quocunque antecedente simpliciter possibili, quod scilicet non est impossibile absolute; et est conclusio sua 13[a].

[2] MS. Merton M. I. 11, fo. 31r[b] in margin, 'Doc[tor] Pro[fundus]'; cf. Savile, ed., *De causa Dei*, p. 654. I must thank Dr G. Leff for help in identifying the relevant passages from the *De causa Dei*. Shortly before the present writer, Dr H. A. Oberman, who had not seen the evidence of the Merton MS., also examined the New College MS. and deduced from internal evidence that the 'quidam doctor' must be Bradwardine. The writer made his identification independently, before hearing of Dr Oberman's conclusions; but Dr Oberman deserves credit as the first to identify in print Buckingham's opponent as Bradwardine (see *Archbishop Thomas Bradwardine*, pp. 192–4). He does not identify this reference.

necessitated by God—a most Hegelian concept. So he equates determinism with orthodoxy and its denial with an outright rejection of the accepted doctrine of grace.

But the pernicious Pelagians, ungrateful of the manifold grace of God, strive to take from him his due grace and the acts of grace. For they deny his predestination and divine providence in good and evil, and they deny his co-operation and especially his pre-efficacy, in the exercise of the free will in its free acts.[1]

How then is our understanding of contingency affected? Brad-wardine replies, in the 'r3th conclusion' to which Buckingham refers, that supreme 'freedom of contradiction' and supreme contingency lie in the divine will and are the cause of freedom in all other wills.[2] But, as interpreted by the 'Doctor Profundus', this represents the very opposite of the liberty it purports to guarantee. For what, as he understands it, is God's freedom? It is a boundless liberty to determine men's acts, whilst ours is the freedom to do that which his will has predestined us to do. To read the *De causa Dei* is, again and again, to be reminded of the mechanistic errors condemned in 1277, to which Bradwardine so often refers. God's will, he believed, must act directly, for to posit a hierarchy of will was to derogate from his supremacy. So Bradwardine wields his own razor: that wills are not be predicated beyond necessity.[3]

As Buckingham notes,[4] the 'Doctor Profundus', in his definition of necessity, denies the distinction between 'antecedent' and 'consequent' necessity, subsumes the latter in the former and

---

[1] *De causa Dei*, III, 1, p. 637.

[2] *De causa Dei*, III, 5, cor. 13, p. 654. Decima tertia, quod prima et summa libertas contradictionis similis quoque contingentia ad utrumlibet est in volun-tate divina; et quod hae sunt causae similis libertatis et contingentiae in aliis universis.

[3] *De causa Dei*, III, 6, p. 667. Veruntamen mihi videtur, quod deus primo vult seipsum, et secundo caetera ad et propter seipsum; nec videtur mihi neces-sarium ponere voluntatem aliquam mediam inter istas....Si quis tamen sit consiliarius dei in tantum, ut securus audeat ponere voluntatem mediam inter istas, qua videlicet deus velit se velle extrinseca, vitet processum infinitum in voluntatibus talibus essentialiter ordinatis, et superfluitatem ponendi plura, ubi sufficiunt pauciora.

[4] Fo. 327r^a–r^b.

equates the whole with the divine will.[1] It is, he says, logically and theologically impossible to suppose that one kind of necessity binds us but that another does not; it must be all or nothing. And it is just because Buckingham does insist on this distinction that he can assert that God's will, even if it should necessitate the future 'antecedently', still would not destroy merit in human beings.[2]

It is now possible to see how Buckingham relates will to necessity. He affirms what in his *Sentences* he had denied, that God's prevenient will is the necessary first cause of any effect. But this he understands in a non-determinist sense, declaring that no effect is so willed or known by God that he cannot will or know (and cannot eternally have willed or known) the opposite, notwithstanding his immutable and irresistible power to cause.[3] It is indeed God's co-operation and his forewilling that are the guarantee of contingency and of our freedom of choice.[4] For we either do or do not necessitate some future event. But God, who by his forewilling causes all things to be, necessitates events without losing his inalienable power to will and foreknow that they have never been. In him there lies always the possibility of reversing the apparently inevitable; it is only we who, within the limits of human action, cause that which is irrevocably necessary.

So Buckingham reconciles liberty and necessity and avoids 'the

---

[1] Cf. *De causa Dei*, III, 2 cor., p. 649. Unde consequitur evidenter, quod aliqualis necessitas antecedens et libertas ac meritum non repugnant, et quod nulla causa inferior, sed tantum superior, scilicet dei voluntas, est necessitas antecedens.

[2] Fo. 340v[b]. Conclusio 10[a] est, si dei voluntas esset et semper fuisset omnium futurorum necessitas antecedens, nullum esset demeritum creature.

[3] Fo. 327v[b]. Hec est, cuiuslibet effectus futuri, quem deus vult et scit esse futurum, potest deus eternaliter voluisse et scivisse oppositum et non ipsum, non obstante quod ipse deus sit non mutabilis, non frustrabilis, nec impedibilis sed universaliter efficax in causando.

[4] Fo. 331v[a]. Conclusio octava est illa: nisi esset dei prevencio et concursus in accione creature nulla esset contingencia vel libertas contradiccionis in voluntate creata. Patet hec conclusio per dominum Lincolniensem, De libero arbitrio, dicit, quod que est vera potuit fine immo non fuisse vera, ex qua potencia sequitur rerum contingencia. Videtur quod illa libera potencia et potestas que est in deo ad volendum antichristum fore, et antichristum nunquam fore, et ad producendum et non producendum antichristum, sit causa libertatis contradiccionis in creatura.

errors of the Stoics who, to posit foreknowledge in God, took away man's free will and put him under necessity in every act'. In doing this he again came into conflict with Bradwardine. In Conclusion 6 Buckingham declares that any future event willed or to be willed by God can be voided or reversed; any other assumption, he says, leads to determinism. Nevertheless his argument had been challenged. An opponent, 'quidam doctor', had argued as follows: any effect in an object is inseparable from it and necessarily present; but the effect of being future (*futuricio*) necessarily exists in a future event, which therefore must take place.[1] This thesis is expounded in the *De causa Dei*, Book III, ch. 25. We might well suppose, argues Bradwardine, that all past, present and future events are contingent in God's knowledge and will; indeed he admits that he himself was once tempted to allow this. And it is true that in him all is contingent; but this contingency cannot be transferred to the human will which has never known the antecedent power that ultimately controls events.[2] From this Bradwardine concluded that one cannot speak of God's activity as past, present or future since he is eternal and outside time. There is in him no distinction of past, present and future; all is eternally present.

This assumption, intimately associated with a determinist theology, radically affects the interpretation of statements which

[1] Fo. 329 v^b. Et ideo oportet necessario quod dicens hanc opinionem teneat quod omnia que evenient de necessitate evenient...; hanc opinionem reputo heresim manifestam et ex defectu scientie cogitatam. Contra hanc opinionem sextam quidam multipliciter contradicit, primo sic: quam inpossibile est aliquid ab alio recedere cui inest, tam necesse est illud ei inesse; sed futuricio sic inest omni futuro quod non potest ab eo recedere, nisi per exhibicionem futuri inesse, igitur omni futuro necesse est quod ei insit futuricio, igitur omne futurum quod erit, necesse est quod erit.

[2] *De causa Dei*, III, 25, p. 701. Amplius autem et 32^a opinio, nondum quod sciverim ab aliquo opinata, sed forsitan opinanda, quae et me, ut verum fatear, aliquando tentavit, ex dicendis fortassis probabiliter oritura, praesumet astruere, quod in omnibus rebus futuris, praesentibus atque praeteritis, respectu scientiae et voluntatis divinae, est semper contingentia ad utrumlibet....Licet enim actus liber humanus futurus posset contingenter et libere non esse futurus, et econtra per potentiam voluntatis divine, hoc tamen non est simpliciter, sufficienter et antecedenter in potestate humana; cum voluntas humana in suis actionibus universis divinam (voluntatem) praecedentem necessario subsequatur.

literaliter the determinist may share with others. So, in the question at issue here, Buckingham agrees that effects once predicated of an object cannot 'recede' from it; everything simply by existing has futurity, which like all things comes from God's will. But it does not follow that the future of anything is incontrovertibly determined. If God knows anything, as he must know all, he must know it in all its forms, past, present and future. Yet for Buckingham it is axiomatic that his will is free and contingent; therefore in respect to God the future is mutable, and in respect to man it can only be necessitated 'consequently' (so remaining subject to contingency).[1]

The argument is renewed in the ninth Conclusion which, as has been noted,[2] is that which Buckingham sustained against Bradwardine. 'It is extraordinary', he says, 'to have to accuse such profound philosophers of incapacity to conceive how God's prescience is compatible with freedom from coercion.' But their arguments are singularly perverse in posing the false antithesis that, either man must have the power to determine God's ordinance or he the power to determine ours. The first, they argue, is untenable because his prescient will ordains, and has eternally ordained, how man shall act; therefore we are without option.[3]

And so to Bradwardine: 'iterum arguit Dominus Reverendus'.[4] In the *De causa Dei*, Book III, ch. 2, he had declared it demonstrable 'that God in some way necessitates all created will in any free act, and in its ceasing from that act, by a necessity that is naturally precedent'.[5] Once again, as Buckingham saw, he had returned to the doctrine of 'antecedent necessity'.

Likewise the Reverend Doctor, arguing in opposition to this conclusion, says that unless we admit antecedent necessity, we must admit it possible for the whole of God's church to fall, collapse and perish, for the whole vessel of Peter to suffer shipwreck and drowning, for all

---

[1] Fo. 330v[a]. Ad confirmandam aliam dico quod me velle que volo, et voluisse que volui, est necessarium necessitate consequenti, non tamen deum velle ea que vult, vel voluisse ea que voluit, de futuris est necessarium necessitate consimili.

[2] Fo. 324r[b]. Conclusio 9[a]: voluntas creata potest libere libertate contradictionis producere et non producere suum actum, dei ordinacione et prescientia non obstante.

See above, p. 43.

[3] Fo. 333r[b].   [4] Fo. 335r[a].   [5] *De causa Dei*, III, 2, p. 646.

Christ's faith before the Day of Judgement to be defective and shattered (and even that all the articles of faith concerning the future should be, and should always have been, false and erroneous); that Christ should have lied and all the Saints, Apostles, Martyrs and Confessors who formerly lived in this faith should have been deceived.[1]

This caricature of the alternative to a rigid predestinarianism Buckingham flatly rejected in a moving passage, which we may fairly call central and orthodox.

To the other argument alleged by the Master and Reverend Doctor, that unless we admit antecedent necessity in all acts of the will, we must admit the possibility of the whole church being destroyed, and so forth: in reply, I wish to know whether God is free to change his ordinances; and, if he is, whether he cannot by his free will effect and fulfil all those things here named. And my opponent must first reply for me and others and avoid these difficulties.

For I think that the created will has liberty of contradiction, and that no man has the power to destroy Holy Church.... And I know that, as logic demands, [I must affirm] the co-operation, grace, predestination, and prescience of God, which I shall not deny. Nor like the Fool shall I deny his existence, nor like Pelagius do I wish to exalt my will as master and God's as mere handmaid. But I wish to attribute to God, as first agent, every good we have and to declare that we are in many things his free instruments, not coerced, and also fit to be rewarded out of his abundant mercy for which, as I am bound, I return all the thanks I can.[2]

---

[1] Fo. 335r[a].

[2] Fo. 338r[b]–v[a]. Ad aliud quod inponit Dominus et Doctor Reverendus, quod nisi necessitas antecedens in omnibus actibus voluntatis et aliis admittatur, oportet concedere possibile esse totam sanctam ecclesiam etc.; pro responsione, quero sic dicente utrum deus habeat libertatem contradiccionis; si habeat, numquid potest tunc deus per suam arbitrii libertatem facere et implere omnia que superius numerantur; et habet sic arguens sibi pro me et aliis respondere et illa inconveniencia evitare.

Ego enim reputo voluntatem creatam habere libertatem contradiccionis, et tamen in nullius hominis esse positum potestate sanctam ecclesiam ruere....Et scio quod, logica conpellente, dei preaccionem, coaccionem, auxilium, graciam, predestinacionem, prescientiam, efficienciam, conservanciam, etc. huius non negabo, nec tandem cum incipiente insipientissime, deum esse. Nec volo cum Pelagio meam preponere voluntatem ut dominam et divinam / preponere ut ancillam; sed deo ut principali agenti attribuere omne bonum nostrum, et nos esse in multis ipsius instrumenta voluntaria, non coacta; et ideo ex immensa misericordia premianda pro quibus, ut teneor, gratias quas valeo sibi reddo.

The two theologians were in conflict once more on the issue of mutability in time. The predestinarian believes that in God's eternal being it is meaningless to speak of distinctions in time, and that we cannot therefore attribute to the future a degree of contingency which we do not allow the present or the past. Both Bradwardine and Wyclif argued in this spirit. Buckingham, however, like the majority of medieval theologians, whilst aware of the pitfalls of attributing distinctions of time to God, still believed that one could distinguish degrees of necessity and contingency in the events of this world. Not being an extreme voluntarist, he was free to accept the truth of God's prevenience, whilst asserting that *naturaliter* (eternally) objects necessarily existed before God actively willed their necessary existence; similarly the change from 'present' to 'past' existence in eternal being was also prior to his willing such change.[1] Buckingham here made two assumptions: that past and present are distinct tenses, not merely contingent in time; and that it is not the divine will which makes the past or present necessarily so. Nor did he agree that this was to admit God's will to be caused by its object; 'the necessary existence of the object is not the cause of his necessary willing'.[2]

But if we can distinguish tenses in eternity and, whilst accepting God's prevenience, remove their dependence on his volitions, we can also distinguish degrees of contingence and necessity in this world. Buckingham agrees that the present and past, by existing or having existed, are or were necessarily so; but the future he saves for contingency. 'The 13th conclusion', he says, 'is that the divine will in respect of future contingents, so long as they are future, is free with "freedom of contradiction"; but

---

[1] Fo. 343 v[b]. Conclusio II[a] fuit ista: de re posita in esse ac etiam quam est pro tunc necesse deum velle esse, prius naturaliter est necesse illam rem esse, quam est necesse deum velle illam rem esse; et modo consimili, de re lapsa in preteritum est dicendum quod prius naturaliter est necesse illam rem fuisse, quam est necesse deum velle illam fuisse.

The clause inserted by Chenu, *loc. cit.* p. 233, after 'in esse' ('quam rem pro tunc est necesse esse') is found in neither MS., and does not seem to be required.

[2] Fo. 345 r[b]. ...quoniam necessitas in re extra non est causa quare deus necessario vult.

when they have been present and become past, it ceases to be free and begins to become necessary in respect of them, without any change being posited or to be posited in God.'[1] This is precisely the opposite of Bradwardine's position. In his cosmos the past, the present and the future comprise an indivisible unity, which is God himself; if one tense is necessary, so are all. According to the 'Doctor Profundus', God's will is necessary in respect of past and present, *therefore* it is necessary in respect of the future also.

And if it should be said [he had declared] that the divine will towards the past and present is an antecedent necessity, but not towards the future, this is to make his will variable (and is against Book I, chapters 5 and 23).

For it makes God's will towards the future contradictorily free, so that at the same moment in which a volition exists it has the possibility of not existing in the future; and when that future becomes the present, or lapses into the past, it causes that volition to be necessary. But why cannot omnipotent God be as great a necessity towards a future effect as towards one that is present or past?[2]

V

For the theologians of our period the solution of the problem of determinism and predestination began with a correct understanding of how God wills and knows our acts. They conceived of him as the divine cause in a way which, intelligible enough to the sixteenth and seventeenth centuries, might seem today somewhat mechanical. And, granted this conception, they had further to consider the extent or limitations of his power. Is God the direct and immediate cause of our every act? Is he, above all, the efficient cause of our positive sinning? The question of divine participation in evil exercised the medieval mind in much the same way as, for example, the problem of pain has occupied

[1] Fo. 324r[b]. Voluntas divina respectu futurorum contingencium, quamdiu sunt futura, est libera libertate contradiccionis, sed cum fuerint presencia (et) in preteritum velabuntur, desinit esse libera huiusmodi libertate, et incipit esse necessaria necessitate opposita respectu eorum, sine mutacione in deo posita vel ponenda; et consimiliter est dicendum de dei prescientia futurorum.
Cf. also fo. 345r[b].
[2] *De causa Dei*, III, 2, p. 647.

Christian philosophers in more recent times. It was natural, therefore, that Buckingham should discuss the topic of sin and evil in
the context of divine causation.[1]

To determine whether God is the Universal Cause, he says, one
must first ask if everything past, present or to come is the product
of his will as the principal efficient cause. Obviously this is true of
the good; but of evil also? Very different as is Buckingham's
answer, the owner of the Merton copy of his *Questions* kept in
mind that of an earlier and more celebrated Mertonian; for he
here made the marginal annotation: 'Nota Doctorem Profundum
li. I c. 34, quomodo deus vult et non vult peccatum.'[2]

Most scholastic theologians of the fourteenth century supported
a moderate predestinarianism; we may say that it was a contemporary orthodoxy. Buckingham in his *Sentences*, it is true, had
denied this, like some but not all the Ockhamists; but in his
maturity he came to conform. Though making a far less rigid
interpretation than Bradwardine, he admits in his *Questions* that
'all things that have been, are and will be are so from the divine
will'. But, whilst God wills all things in that eternity which precedes and is outside time, we need not conclude that anything
effected in this world, and much less the world itself, is eternal.
God has ordained the future and in the fulness of time it will
become a present reality. But, for Buckingham, the actual pro-
duction of this effect requires an act of his will;[3] and it is, as will be
seen, by insisting on this act of volition that he guards himself

[1] Thus Buckingham explains the relation of Section 2 to Section 1 of his
Questions; fo. 352r^a. Quia ad materiam de necessitate essendi rerum et contingencia futurorum est pertinens et anexum de causalitate divina tractare, pro
noticia planiori habenda et precipue pro declaracione conclusionis prime, talem
in scolis proposui questionem: utrum omne bonum et malum effective et
formaliter sit a deo, in qua questione quosdam articulos disputavi. Et est
primus: utrum omnia que fuerunt, sunt et erunt, fuerunt, sunt et erunt ex
voluntate et ordinacione divina, causa efficiente principali et prima.
[2] MS. Merton M. I. II, fo. 251r^b.
[3] Fo. 368v^b. Videtur quod similia argumenta sunt contra futuricionem
eternam sicut contra mundum eternum. Numquid ante futuricionem non fuit
futuricio? Nonne in instanti eternitatis preordinavit omnia que temporaliter
post produxit; et quare non potuit tunc illa in re et realiter produxisse? Nonne
omnia futura habuerunt ab eterno esse in mente divina et non a se, sed a deo sic
volente, ordinante, et quodammodo efficiente?

against determinism. In his *Sentences*, of course, there had been
no danger in this quarter; and Buckingham's emphasis on the
absolute contingency of things had amounted to a doctrine of
radical indeterminacy. It is all the more interesting, therefore, to
discover in his *Questions* a much more cautious and conservative
approach.

He examines the problem of direct causation under three heads.
Are things rational and just because God has willed them so? Are
they necessary or impossible for the same reason? And, does anything become possible simply and directly because he wills it?[1]
To these questions, which are the touchstone of the degree of
voluntarism in his theology, Buckingham replies that things are
not just or unjust, rational or irrational merely because he has
willed them as such, and that his will cannot be arbitrary or irresponsible. Certainly he does not deny the primacy of will
(Wyclif was one of the few in fourteenth-century Oxford to do
that); but his is not an untrammelled will and it obeys an internal
discipline. There are many things outside God, says Buckingham,
which are irrational but which nevertheless he might will to happen. But within himself he is by no means absolutely free. He
must always love good and hate evil, and will all things subject to
him. Moreover these things are true and just, not merely because
he has so willed them, but because his goodness has ensured that
they must be. It is his will which causes truths to exist; it is his
goodness which makes them rational. God's will is moral.[2]

Nor is Buckingham prepared to make divine will the sole

[1] Fo. 353 vᵇ. Secundus articulus: utrum omne racionabile sive iustum sit
racionabile sive iustum eo quod est a deo volutum esse tale. [Fo. 355rᵃ.]
Articulus tercius: utrum cuiuslibet necessitatis seu inpossibilitatis sit per se
divina volucio prima causa. [Fo. 355vᵃ.] Articulus quartus: utrum cuiuslibet
possibilitatis est dei omnipotencia, non volucio ut volucio, prima causa.

[2] Fo. 354vᵃ–vᵇ. Ad istud dubium respondetur quod, de racionabilibus sive
iustis in esse creature, aliqua sunt sic racionabilia sive iusta, quod possunt esse et
esse irracionabilia . . . et in hiis velle divinum est causa quare hec sunt racionabilia
sive iusta; et prius sunt voluta quam racionabilia sint sive iusta. Alia sunt sic
racionabilia sive iusta quod non sint, non possunt esse, nisi racionabilia atque
iusta; et tale est omnia esse deo subiecta, deum bonum diligere ac peccata odire,
et horum velle dei est causa ut sint. Sed bonitas, dignitas et similia, que essencialiter insunt deo, sunt causa ut racionabilia sint et iusta, si sint.

cause of necessity, possibility and impossibility. He rehearses the classic text of Henry of Ghent (Quodlibet 6, qu. 3) that the ultimate cause of the impossibility of anything lies in God. But the burden of his case is simply that the possibility of change is inherent in the universe he has created; and, against Anselm, he restricts God's absolute and irresistible acts to those which he has antecedently necessitated or forbidden.[1] So the tenor of his *Questions* is hostile to extreme voluntarism. His position is summed up in his reply to the query, Can we defy God's will? With his freshly acquired moderation, he answers that it is 'always expedient to conform' to his will, to which also our will to good always conforms.[2]

But what of our will to sin, to do evil? Buckingham's reply is quite traditional. Two arguments had been proposed to justify the belief that God actively wills men to sin. The first is that all our acts are predestined by God, in whose preordinance there is no distinct 'future' (so neither sin nor merit is in our free power). The second is that his will cannot be less than total, so that to say that God permits but cannot cause men to sin is an unreal distinction. Both propositions he firmly rejects. He had, in any case, already dismissed the argument that one cannot speak of future in respect of God. No doubt the eternal future differs from the created future, but that is not to equate it with past or present. We can, he says, accept predestination and still allow that a future sin requires an agent (the sinner) to make it a reality.[3] In insisting on the distinction between permission and volition, and that it is in this sense that God allows man to sin, he was only repeating accepted teaching.

[1] Fos. 355r^b–v^a, 355v^b.   [2] Fo. 357v^a.

[3] Fo. 358r^a Sextus articulus: utrum velle divinum causa efficiens sit peccati, et quod sic arguitur multis modis; primo sic, peccatum antichristi futurum vel antichristum esse peccaturum non est nec fuit de se futurum, sed ab eterno a deo factum est esse futurum.... [Fo. 359r^b.] Respondeo, futuricio rei vel rem esse futuram non est res aliqua creata, nam si foret ab eterno fuisset aliqua creatura; immo esse futurum inportat quod erit et nondum est. Quoad hoc quod nondum est, cum sit totaliter privativum, non proprie habet causam; modo tamen quo causam habet, deus est causa quare nondum est. Quoad hoc quod dicitur 'erit', non requiritur nec causam esse [sic: habet?], sed sufficit quod causam habebit in futurum, quoniam peccator sic erit causa.

In these highly orthodox sentiments Buckingham does not refer to a contemporary opponent. But the owner of the Merton MS. clearly assumed him to be countering Bradwardine. For at the head of the page where the problem of sin is treated he has written: 'Nota in ista materia Doctorem Profundum li. 1 cc. 33 & 34; facit ibi illa argumenta et tenet contrarium huius doctoris: et libro 2° cc. 30 & 31.'[1] And twice on the opposite page he has noted—'contra Doctorem Profundum 1 c. 34'.[2] It is indeed difficult to imagine that Buckingham was thinking of anyone but the Mertonian. Bradwardine starts from the conviction that every human act is the consequence of a divine volition naturally preceding it. The created will always depends on the uncreated. From this he drew three conclusions: that God's willing as the Primary Cause invariably precedes human volitions; that he can never will conditionally; and that only the divine will is primary. Such thoroughly voluntarist beliefs necessarily determined his treatment of sin. Bradwardine abolished the distinction, on which Buckingham had naturally insisted, between God's permission and volition. Everything which he permits, he says, he also actively wills; and since experience shows that God permits men to sin, he must positively will them to do so.[3]

Buckingham's analysis of the problem of sin, and its relation to merit and justification, is remarkable not for any eccentricity of doctrine but for the contrast with the radical opinions put forward in his *Sentences*. One of the most striking features of his *Commentary* had been the refusal to relate sin and grace in any coherent theology, by positing between them a *medius status* in which we might gain acceptance without absolution and without showing merit. This proposition was itself illustrative of the indeterminacy so widespread amongst theologians of the 1330's.

By the time of the composition of his *Questions*, c. 1350, Buckingham had completely abandoned these youthful indiscretions. We are surely justified in attributing this in part to the

---

[1] MS. Merton M. I, II, fo. 30v.   [2] *Ibid.* fos. 31r[a], 31r[b] in margin.
[3] *De causa Dei*, I, 32, p. 282; 33, p. 289; 34, p. 294; II, 30 and cor., pp. 578, 596.

influence of Bradwardine, and his change of heart is one of the most valuable pieces of evidence we have for assessing the reaction of Oxford to the *De causa Dei*.

But of this abandonment of old opinions Buckingham gives no hint in the later work. Without a note of apology and as though answering a simple request—'pro mea doctrina scolariumque instanter iam petencium'—he relates grace to merit[1] in a strictly orthodox fashion. Between them there is a clear relation. But is it directly causal? Is our merit given in simple proportion to his gift of grace? And if grace naturally precedes the meritorious act, does the loss of grace also precede our rejection of his love? Buckingham replies that grace does naturally precede merit, and always in greater power than our ability to deserve; but he also allows that the gift of grace is related to (but not, of course, caused by) the disposition of men to receive it. To the second he answers that the loss of justification follows the act by which we have rejected God, but that *iniusticia* as such precedes the individual sinful act.[2] The primacy of God's love is thus assured. But is it the absolute primacy of an acceptance or rejection which we can in no way merit? The annotation of the Merton MS. at this point, 'Nota Doctorem Profundum li. I c. 39 post',[3] is a reminder of the bitter divisions of the period on this issue. Moreover the text contains an attack on 'a doctor who holds the opposite view', who can be no other than the Mertonian.

There is no suggestion in the *Questions* that grace is a *medius status*. The grace of God, which is the act of love through which creatures are made acceptable to himself, must be absolutely gratuitous. Yet human merit is not shown in vain; it is not ignored by God. But how can it be made graceful, without seeming to

---

[1] Fo. 369r[a]. Post materiam de contingencia futurorum et arbitrii libertate, ac de causalitate et quibusdam effectibus voluntatis divine, pro mea doctrina scolariumque instanter iam petencium, de augmento gracie et de merito creature tractabam articulos qui sequntur: utrum augmentum in merito prioritate nature precedat augmentum in gracia vel econtra.... [Fo. 369v[b].] Utrum prius naturaliter sit iniusticia quam iniuste agere.

For fo. 369r[a] Chenu, *loc. cit.* p. 236, incorrectly reads 'necesse precedit' for 'nature precedat'.

[2] Fos. 369v[a], 370r[a].　　　　　[3] MS. cit., fo. 37v[a].

elicit grace? The answer is that merit is also a gracious gift, by which God implants in us the spur to good acts that we may fittingly achieve acceptance through his love. Those who will enjoy salvation, says Buckingham, are first predestined to their heavenly rest; for God's predestinating love is the final and principal cause of salvation. So merit becomes a mediating cause of election, dependent on the original divine will that we should be saved;[1] and Buckingham escapes the Scylla and Charybdis of, on the one hand, destroying the efficacy of merit, and, on the other, admitting that it can directly cause the gift of grace.

Yet he remained anxious to allow a genuine place to merit in the mystery of election and reprobation; and recalling his former opinions, we can hardly be surprised. But where he had once exalted merit by weakening the doctrine of grace, Buckingham now gave it its due place by traditional arguments.

Scholastic theology distinguishes the absolute merit, which cannot exist in men naturally, but is a supernatural quality deriving from grace (*meritum de condigno*), from the disposition to good which has a certain claim to grace, though not possessing it (*meritum de congruo*). God's grace is his free gift which renders our works condign, a double reward of merit and acceptance following from his promise that what is done with his love should merit eternal life. In the light of this promise, says Buckingham, we cannot doubt that men do in some way merit acceptance; and he even admits that merit sometimes precedes the gift of grace.[2] Conversely he declares that the grace whereby the penitent sinner is reconciled to God naturally precedes the remission of sin and the meritorious act of repentance which justifies it. But this does not make men ciphers for God to accept or reject at his whim. For by true repentance we exhibit merit which, though not condign (since we can never recompense him for our deeds), God

---

[1] Fo. 374r^b–v^a.

[2] Fo. 376r^a. Unde iuxta modum loquendi doctorum et sanctorum teneo, semper salvo iudicio meliori, quod homo per opera in caritate facta meretur aliquo modo vitam eternam, et hoc ut premium debitum et condignum....Ad primum dico quod deus dat gratissime sua dona et est infinite liberalis, et tamen dat multa bona, quamvis non omnia alico merito precedente.

may still fittingly (*de congruo*) reward. Even if *naturaliter* his grace precedes our merit, *temporaliter* our good works are prior to the remission of sin.[1]

The place of merit is therefore assured. And on this matter Buckingham affords one of the few reminders in his *Questions* of his more radical days. Cannot we go further, he suggests, and admit that man can possess merit which derives from purely natural causes and is in the strictest sense graceless? He imagines a man of uncorrupted natural goodness who would show merit and even, to the extent of his natural powers, do so on account of God's love;[2] and this, he adds, would be the reverse of the error of Pelagius who had said that we could elicit by our natural power the *supernatural* reward of grace. Buckingham was also at pains to deny that all acts of a mortal sinner are necessarily sinful. It had been argued, he wrote, either that all acts of a mortal sinner are without merit or that, by his failure to repent, he deprives his actions of any merit. But it is in fact plain that sinful men often do good works precisely to regain that grace of which their sin has deprived them. Buckingham's answer is that such men do merit and that even mortal sinners can earn merit

---

[1] Fo. 380r[b]. Unde dico quod prius natura est a solo deo gracie infusio, secundo peccati remissio quo ad culpam et penam eternam, et tercio est virtuosa operacio, et sic actum iustum et peccati satisfaccionem iustificacionem sequi natura posterius, in omni adulto est necessarium de communi lege. Ad primam formam in dubio principali, quando deducitur, arguendo de remissione pene, numquid aliquis posset mereri remissionem pene debite pro peccato, dico, ut potest faciliter elici ex predictis, quod remissionem pene temporalis meretur penitens, non remissionem pene eterne loquendo de merito condigno; de congruo tamen potest, ut de prima gracia superius erat dictum.

[2] Fo. 382v[a]. Omnia inanimata deum super omnia diligunt suo modo; quoniam sicut deus est finis omnium et terminus naturalis, sic omnia naturaliter referuntur in deum. Sed alio modo est deus finis creature racionalis, et per quemdam modum essendi supernaturalem.... Est alia dileccio accualis informis, qua quis aliquid facit principaliter propter deum, ponens deum finem et terminum ultimatum in suo facto (ut si daret principaliter propter deum elemosinam); et sic puto quod aliquis maxime existens in naturalibus non coruptis potest aliquod bonum opus facere principaliter propter deum, et sic deum super omnia diligere.

Even this modest assessment of man's ability to love God by his natural powers was regarded as 'Pelagian' by Bradwardine (*De causa Dei*, I, 35–40).

de congruo, at least as far as the temporal reward of this world is concerned.[1]

Cautious though Buckingham's opinions now were, compared with the more exhilarating novelties in his *Sentences*, they remained incompatible with those of Bradwardine. We have already noted the marginal reference in the Merton MS. to his view of the cause of sin. The comment was apt, and is reinforced by an aside which again surely refers to the 'Doctor Profundus'. The saints and Scripture, says Buckingham, all agree that we can merit grace and glory and that God rewards each one of us according to his deserts.

Almost all the doctors take that side, and so it ought to be sufficient that I take it for the truth and reply to the reasons put forward by the Doctor from the opposite side. And I have been anxious to treat this matter so that I might reply to his arguments for this opinion.[2]

But for Bradwardine this was a position so erroneous as to be almost heretical. In his theology, where the majesty of divine grace and will is so exalted as to become the sole efficient cause of every human act, there can be no place for merit uncaused by God. Not only can the meritorious act never precede the reward

[1] Fo. 383r[b]. Secundum dubium fuit tale: utrum omnis actus liberi arbitrii sine caritate et gracia sit peccatum seu culpa.... [Fo. 385r[a].] Ad istud dubium, semper salvo iudicio meliori...credo quod habens fidem, licet maneat in peccato mortali, potest elemosinam facere, orare et alia bona similia ut vitam eternam habeat. [Fo. 385v[a].] Tercium dubium fuit tale: utrum existens in peccato mortali existens [*sic*] posset pro tunc mereri saltem aliquod premium temporale, quod sic videtur. [Fo. 386r[a]–r[b].] Ad istud dubium respondeo: dico quod cum peccato mortali stat meritum de congruo premii temporalis, et hoc secundum liberalitatem illius qui nullum bonum dimittit inremuneratum; non tamen hoc reputo esse verum de merito de condigno.

These statements are directly opposed to Bradwardine, who regarded all free acts by one in mortal sin as sinful, and denied that one in mortal sin could merit *de congruo* (*De causa Dei*, I, 39).

[2] Fo. 375v[a]. Ad oppositum istius dubii, quod graciam et gloriam aliquis mereatur, clamant omnes doctores et sancti, 'Si graciam vel gloriam nemo posset mereri, cur vita eterna tam frequenter in scriptura merces et premium nominatur, et cur deus iuxta valorem operum dicitur reddere unicuique premium et mercedem?' Illam partem quasi omnes doctores affirmant, et hinc sufficere mihi debet pro vero eam supponere et racionibus respondere, que per doctorem pro parte opposita sunt adducte, quia ut suis evidenciis responderem hanc materiam pertractare curavi.

of grace; merit itself becomes all but valueless in the light of his omnipotent grace. Merit *de congruo* disappears, subsumed in merit *de condigno*; and condign merit becomes in reality nothing but God's gratuitous gift. For to accept meritorious works as causal, in however limited a manner, would be to necessitate grace—a monstrous proposition.[1] One can hardly doubt that here as before it is against Bradwardine that Buckingham is tilting.

Buckingham had his other opponents,[2] but the controversy here analysed more clearly reveals the structure of the principal dispute in dogmatic theology in the Oxford schools *c.* 1350. We see the *De causa Dei* closely discussed; and one can recognise yet again how central were the questions raised by Bradwardine to the disputes of his time. Wyclif therefore was in no way eccentric in returning to the problems which absorbed, indeed obsessed, the 'Doctor Profundus'. He and his generation were the natural heirs to the contentions which filled the schools in their youth.

But in Buckingham's progress we have evidence also for the efficacy of Bradwardine's counter-attack. In later life Buckingham remained as he had been when young an advocate of free will and contingency; but he now believed these to be compatible with a moderate predestinarianism. Abandoning the extremism of his *Sentences*, he agreed that contingency could be combined with divine prevenience, and that the state of grace was not an indeterminate *medius status* but bore a defined relationship to sin and redemption. In part this may be due to the eclecticism of middle age succeeding the immoderation of youth. But in significant measure his *Questions* are testimony to a genuine change of opinion and to the effectiveness of a remarkable treatise and suggest that, after two decades of upheaval, Oxford theology was returning to more conservative ways.

---

[1] Cf. *De causa Dei*, I, 35, p. 307; 39, p. 325; 40, p. 364.
[2] For the dispute with the 'Exeter master' see below, Appendix.

CHAPTER III

RICHARD FITZRALPH AND THE CONSERVATIVE TRADITION

I

APART from Thomas Bradwardine, Wyclif cites only one other Oxford theologian of the previous generation: Richard Fitz-Ralph of Armagh (d. 1360). FitzRalph[1] has long been recognised as one of the great personalities of the English church in the fourteenth century. He was a notable primate, a powerful controversialist and a determined litigant: a familiar figure in Oxford, Ireland and Avignon. He was also embroiled in the quarrel between the friars and the secular clergy, which raged so bitterly during his lifetime; and from his pen came the attack upon the mendicants, the *De pauperie Salvatoris*,[2] which so deeply influenced Wyclif, when he came to dispute the question of 'lordship'. But we are here concerned with his importance as a philosopher and theologian.

FitzRalph was born at Dundalk *c.* 1300. Like Bradwardine he held a Balliol fellowship (which he had resigned by 1325), and like the 'Doctor Profundus' he had to leave when he began to read theology. He graduated Bachelor of Theology by 1329 and incepted Master in the summer of 1331.[3] He was lucky in his

[1] FitzRalph's biographer is Professor Aubrey Gwynn, S.J. For his academic career see Gwynn, 'Richard FitzRalph at Avignon', *Studies*, XXII (1933), 591–607; 'Archbishop FitzRalph and the Friars', *Studies*, XXVI (1937), 50–67; 'The Sermon-Diary of Richard FitzRalph', *Proceedings of the Royal Irish Academy*, XLIV (1937), 1–57; and, for other aspects, see Gwynn, *Studies*, XXII (1933), 389 ff.; XXIII (1934), 395 ff.; XXIV (1935), 25 ff., 558 ff.; XXV (1936), 81 ff. See also Gwynn, *The English Austin Friars in the Time of Wyclif* (1940), pp. 66–75, 79–95; 'Two Sermons of Primate Ric. FitzRalph', *Archivia Hibernica*, XIV (1949), 50–65; Pantin, *The English Church in the Fourteenth Century*, pp. 151–65.

[2] Ed. R. L. Poole (*WS*, 1890).

[3] Career summarised in Emden, *Biographical Register*, II, 692–4; see also *Hist. MSS. Comm.*, app. to 4th report, pp. 442–3.

patronage, and became the protégé of Bishop Grandisson of Exeter (later to be Buckingham's patron), whose nephew he accompanied to Paris as tutor in 1329.[1] Grandisson thought much of FitzRalph, and he might well have settled at Exeter to take charge of the cathedral school. But a greater honour came his way; he returned to Oxford as Chancellor from 1332 to 1334 (years made difficult by the secession of a group of scholars to Stamford).[2] About this time he was befriended by the redoubtable Richard Bury and so became acquainted (had he not done so earlier) with Bradwardine.[3] In fact the papal registers show evidence of a Grandisson–Bury connection. In September 1331 a benefice in the gift of the abbot of St Albans was reserved at the king's request for Thomas Buckingham (with a copy of the mandate to Richard Bury, canon of York). In December 1335 FitzRalph was provided to the deanery of Lichfield, with concurrent mandates to John de Northewode, archdeacon of Norwich, and Thomas Bradwardine, canon of Lincoln (to which benefice he had been provided at Bury's request two years previously).[4] Clearly the two patrons and their circles were close to each other. Twelve years later the dean of Lichfield was promoted archbishop of Armagh; he was consecrated in Exeter Cathedral by Grandisson on 8 July 1347.

FitzRalph composed two major theological treatises, his *Commentary on the Sentences* (read shortly before his journey to Paris with Grandisson's nephew) and the *De questionibus Armenorum*, written mainly at Avignon, 1334–7. The Armenian questions, from which alone Wyclif quotes, have received considerable attention.[5] The incessant appeal to scriptural rather than scholastic

---

[1] *Reg. Grandisson*, I, 233. Grandisson appointed as tutor for his nephew John de Northwode Richard FitzRalph 'Magister in Artibus et in Sacra Pagina egregius Bacularius, inter omnes studentes et legentes Universitatis Oxoniensis eminenter dinoscitur intelligens et subtilis'. He incepted Master in Theology between May and October 1331 (*Reg. Grandisson*, II, 616; *Calendar of Papal Letters*, ed. W. Bliss, II, 355).

[2] H. E. Salter, 'The Stamford Schism', *EHR*, xxxvii (1922), 249–53.

[3] Wharton, ed., *Anglia Sacra*, I, 766.

[4] *Calendar of Papal Letters*, II, 365, 524.

[5] Gwynn, 'Archbishop FitzRalph at Avignon', *Studies*, xxii (1933), 600–2; Pantin, *The English Church*, pp. 153–4.

proof and the dramatic autobiographical prayer, in which Fitz-Ralph voices his disgust with the schools and announces his repudiation of academic theology, have been cited as evidence of a growing revolt against scholasticism. If his words are unequivocally true, they are clearly of the first importance. Such a statement by a former Chancellor, delivered not long before Wyclif must have begun his studies, would be strong evidence for a deterioration in vigour and morale in the Oxford schools, or at least for a significant discontent with the accepted ethos.

But in fact his words cannot be accepted without strong qualification. Many of the propositions which he sustains in the *Armenian Questions* (particularly those on the nature of free will) are not only thoroughly scholastic, and argued in the appropriate language, but simply reformulate identical propositions main-tained in his *Commentary on the Sentences*. FitzRalph's *Commentary* has never been examined either in its own right, or in connection with the presumed anti-intellectualism of the *Armenian Questions*. But it is a revealing and important work: revealing, not indeed for any eccentricity of doctrine, but as a statement of moderate realism and moderate Augustinianism at Oxford, *c.* 1330. For the historian of scholasticism it is evidence of the moderation still pursued by some Oxford theologians in the high noon of Ock-hamism. And the student of Wyclif will note the continuity of a metaphysical teaching uninfluenced by nominalism, whilst con-trasting the reconciliation of free will and realism in the one philosopher with the realist predestinarianism of the other.

II

An exhaustive examination of his *Sentences* (not here attempted) would require the establishing of a full critical text, which Fitz-Ralph's *Commentary* has not yet received.[1] The problem seems to

---

[1] For MSS. of FitzRalph's *Commentary* see Stegmüller, *Repertorium Commentariorum*, I, 349; V. Doucet, 'Commentaires sur les Sentences', *AFH*, XLVI (1953), 94; XLVII (1954), 159–60. Four complete texts are listed: MS. Oriel College, Oxford, 15, fos. 4vᵃ–112vᵇ; Florence, bibl. naz., conv. soppr., A. 3. 508, fos. 1r–109v; Florence, bibl. naz., A. 6. 611; Paris, bibl. nat., lat. 15853. A nearly complete text is MS. Troyes 505. Despite a misleading explicit, 'Bradwardi lectura seu expositio in 1ᵐ et 2ᵐ librum Sententiarum', it

be rather one of ordering the individual questions than of proving their authenticity, and of relating groups of *quaestiones* to the complete *Commentary*. Nevertheless, while many judgements must remain provisional, we are entitled to make certain deductions on the broad outlines of the interests and opinions displayed in this work.

In structure FitzRalph's *Sentences* are typical of the time.[1] No comprehensive or systematic survey of the Lombard is even attempted; and correspondingly there is an overwhelming concentration on certain topics habitually discussed in Books 1 and 2 of the *Sentences*. In MS. Oriel College, Oxford, 15 (the text cited in this chapter) the *Commentary* consists of an undivided series of twenty-six questions. In MS. Florence, Bibl. Naz. (Conventi Soppresi), A. 3. 508, which is divided, Books 1 and 2 comprise fifteen and nine *quaestiones* respectively, while Books 3 and 4 have a single *quaestio* apiece. That for Book 3 was considered so minor by the redactor of the Oriel MS. that he attached it as a dependent article to a question in Book 1.[2] The foliation of the four books in the Florence MS. is equally arresting: 1r^a–76r^b; 76r^b–104v^b; 104v^b–107r^a; 107r^a–109v^b. This emphasis can be compared with the seven questions which comprise Buckingham's *lectura* on the *Sentences*.

FitzRalph has received scant attention or respect from historians of medieval philosophy. His *Sentences* are hardly original; and he has suffered for his eclecticism. He belongs, as Gilson bitingly puts

is in fact FitzRalph, Books 1–2, at the end of which some *questiones* of Bradwardine have been added (cf. Glorieux in *DTC*, xv-1, 766). Some *questiones* extracted from the *Commentary* follow the text in MS. Florence, A. 3. 508 ('Hic incipiunt determinationes Ybernici', fos. 109v–134v); others are in MS. Worcester Cathedral Chap. Lib. F 65, fos. 63–92, and Q 71 (cf. S. L. Forte, *Some Oxford Schoolmen of the Middle of the Fourteenth Century*, unpubl. B.Litt., Oxford, 1947). The following pages are based on MS. Oriel 15, compared with MS. Florence, bibl. naz., A. 3. 508 (I have to thank the staff of the library at Florence for supplying a microfilm of this text).

[1] For the changing nature of *Commentaries* in the fourteenth century, see Glorieux, 'Sentences', *DTC*, xiv, 1860–84.

[2] MS. Florence, bibl. naz., conv. soppr., A. 3. 508, fos. 104v^b–107r^a (Utrum in voluntate sit aliquis habitus allectivus vel inclinativus...nisi quod causat delectacionem et tristiciam: 1^m de tercio libro et non plus)=MS. Oriel 15, qu. 10. a. 3, fo. 37r^b.

it, to 'la race aimable de ceux qui pensent qu'on exagère les différences'.[1] Fundamentally he was, like Wyclif, a disciple of the old school of platonising Augustinianism, a tradition he found in Averroes, Grosseteste and Henry of Ghent. It is interesting that both depended so much on these authorities. The emphasis might vary. FitzRalph more frequently invokes Henry of Ghent, because of his interest in psychology, which Wyclif lacked; on the other hand, Wyclif's devotion to Grosseteste is notorious. But Lincolniensis is cited by almost all the Oxford masters of the age. This was partly, no doubt, local patriotism; Oxford looks after her own. But more important is Grosseteste's blend of Augustinian Aristotelianism, which had a marked appeal for the theologians of FitzRalph's generation and its successors at Oxford. A century later we find Thomas Gascoigne's theological notebook studded with references to Lincolniensis.[2]

FitzRalph's theories of cognition derive from Henry of Ghent. Henry propounds a qualified platonism. He rejects, for example, the doctrine of innate ideas; it is, he says, the mind which gives form to ideas by knowing them as intelligible species under its own categories of essence and quiddity.[3] The theory of illumination, therefore, had to be modified to allow the human mind to realise the original impulse from the divine mind. FitzRalph agrees that there is a basic distinction between reality and speculation, between the mental concept and the apprehension of the actual. What the mind deduces from itself is unspecific: what is external it knows through species in particular acts of knowledge.[4]

---

[1] Gilson, La Philosophie au moyen âge, p. 687.

[2] MS. Bodleian, lat. theol. e. 33 (for example, pp. 37, 38, 39, 41, 46, 47). Gascoigne not only cultivated Grosseteste, but also owned some of his books (for example, MS. Bodleian 198, De civitate Dei, containing Grosseteste's own marginalia); cf. R. W. Hunt in Robert Grosseteste, ed. Callus, p. 121; J. E. Thorold Rogers, ed., Loci e libro veritatum (1881), pp. vii, 12, 102–3, 126–7, 140–2, etc.

[3] Paulus, Henri de Gand, p. 9, citing the Summa Aurea, 1, 5, 5 and 1, 11, 16.

[4] MS. Oriel 15, qu. 9, fo. 29v[b]. Utrum mens ipsa et ceteri habitus sibi presentes sint principaliter in memoria respectu sui. [Fo. 30v[a]–v[b].] Ad articulum: opinio Gandavensis, Doctor Solempnis, 3° Quod. qu. 7, utrum intellectus intelligat se et alia que ipsa per essenciam sunt in personis per se vel

This is distinct from but not necessarily opposed to the doctrine of illumination. FitzRalph quotes Henry of Ghent to show that the mind knows qualities inherent in itself prior to any individual act of cognition, and that it does so by the *actus impressus* of Eternal Light. If man had retained his primal innocence, wrote Henry, there could be no reason why we should not always receive the gift of divine illumination. But alas, we are born of corrupted flesh and see but through a glass darkly, sometimes gaining the true light, but more often deceived by our own fantasies.[1] FitzRalph naturally denied the Averroist interpretation of this statement, that the light of the divine mind is immanent. On the contrary, illumination is not present in the mind, but 'irradiates our power to know'.[2] So, says FitzRalph, confirming the words of Henry of Ghent, 'what the doctor says concerning the union of the eternal light with the rational soul seems to be demonstrable', though he agreed that the *habitus* by which the mind knows God is unique.[3]

Granted this, he declares that little by little and by increasing effort we can truly apprehend God, at first mainly by the natural operation of the mind guided by the divine light, but finally by an

per suas species, tenet quidem nec respectu sui nec respectu alicuius secundum essenciam suam existentis in ipsa indigent specie alia a se...sed de intellectu nostro pro statu nature, tenet quod nullam actualem noticiam habet de se, nisi per speciem suorum effectuum.

All subsequent references are to the text of this MS. (which is described in E. Harris, ed., *Johannis Wyclif tractatus de benedicta incarnacione*, WS, 1886, p. xv). At the beginning of the Oriel MS. (fos. 1vᵃ-4vᵃ) two *questiones* have been inserted which do not belong to the *Commentary* (cf. Doucet in *AFH*, XLVII (1954), 159, correcting Stegmüller, *Repertorium Commentariorum*, I, 349), so that the true incipit ('Circa primam distinctionem quaeritur utrum sola trinitate incommutabili') is here numbered three. This numbering has been retained.

[1] Fo. 30vᵇ, citing Henry of Ghent, 9° Quodl. qu. 15.

[2] Fo. 30vᵇ. Addit tamen iste Doctor [*sc.* Solempnis], in hac questione 15, quod ista illustracio naturalis non est in luce eterna sicut in obiecto, sed sicut in ratione cognoscendi.

Cf. Michalski, 'Le Criticisme et le scepticisme', p. 53: 'Sous l'influence de Henri de Gand FitzRalph admet la théorie de l'irradiation de la lumière divine (*intellectus agens*) dans notre intelligence, de sorte qu'elle intensifie la faculté de connaître de celle-ci.'

[3] Fo. 30vᵇ-31rᵃ.

unalloyed perception of the light itself (a light seen so intensely that the mind can fully discern it without sensible acts).[1] From this it is plain that FitzRalph's theory of cognition is as much indebted to Averroes as to Augustine. Dismissing the heresy of the universal soul, he accepts the identification of God and the *intellectus agens*. The latter does not inhere in the mind, for it is the prime form which is God himself.[2] As Gilson has noted,[3] we find here, inspired by Henry of Ghent, an 'augustinisme averroisant'.

FitzRalph was clearly expounding a pronounced but not excessive realism; and within this framework he was concerned with the ways in which our minds act on the received intimations of truth. Here no absolute distinctions were possible, he believed, since all our acts of knowing are a mixture of sense perception, dependent on species ('per species impressas a sensibus'), and the direct but never unclouded knowledge by which we know the *intellectus agens*.[4] However in so far as it is possible, we can distinguish three kinds of knowledge of God: the first through species, which is always speculative; the second through his supernatural gifts of charity; and the third through the ideas of himself which he imparts to the imagination. For FitzRalph the divine idea can be enjoyed by all and is distinct from the clear vision of the blessed, of which he has much to say elsewhere. We may con-

---

[1] Fo. 31r^a. Sed dico paulatim de crescentibus tribulacionibus naturaliter causatis in anima a suo corpore, per exercitium speculacionis crescit illa illustracio et coniunctio cum hoc lumine, primo scilicet cum intellectu agente, et paulatim intelligit anima per illum, tamquam per representans quicquid intelligit per aliquid aliud in ipsa....Et tandem per excercitium et subtraccionem intellectus rebus sensibilibus, clarius et clarius oritur in ipso ista cognicio et splendor lucis agentis, ita ut tunc per maximam [*sic*] exercicium posset homo intelligere absque adminiculo sensuum, sicut dicit Lincolniensis, primo Posteriorum, c. 14.

[2] Fo. 46r^a–r^b. Propter argumenta predicta videtur mihi esse dicendum quod intellectus agens non est pars ymaginis mentis racionalis, quia est forma prima, scilicet deus ipse, quatenus sic coniungitur menti hominis, ut preparet ipsam ad recipiendam passionem ab intencionibus in virtutibus materialibus hominis, et etiam quatenus illuminat mentem hominis, ut possit inspicere intra se in natura divina....

[3] *La Philosophie au moyen âge*, p. 687.

[4] Fo. 31r^a.

fuse true perception with our own romancing, but no mortal can be deprived of the power to know God.[1]

But mental activity must be related more precisely to the perception of the real. Is there, asked FitzRalph, a necessary connection between apprehending the species and understanding it? Can the mind be informed by the species without reacting to it, and conversely can it make an act of intellection without being informed by the real? He replies that provided there is no impediment in our understanding, and the *habitus* of the idea is sufficiently intense, the mind must form an act of intellection upon receiving the species; *naturally* it can do no other.[2] Nevertheless our minds are not blind agents of divine form. First the mind can freely be moved by an internal volition, presenting an image to itself independent of any external force; and secondly, the external habit never deprives the will of its power to reject what is perceived. Every time we defy temptation we acknowledge both that we must know the idea and that we can will its opposite.[3]

FitzRalph clearly distinguishes cognition from volition. Many of the *moderni*, on the other hand, had questioned whether it was at all possible to separate the faculties of the mind. FitzRalph opposed this view; but it is typical of his state of mind that he was sufficiently influenced by the current of opinion to discuss the problem at some length,[4] and sufficiently out of sympathy with it

---

[1] Fo. 32v^b. 3º modo cognoscitur deus a nobis tanquam obiectum vel potest intelligi cognosci sic, non ut est essencia sed vera ydea in ymagine [*MS.* ymago] alicuius creature....Unde videtur mihi quod isto tertio modo adhuc deus cognoscitur a viatoribus et clarius cognoscitur isto tertio modo quam a secundo a viatoribus [et] a comprehendentibus econverso, vel saltem equaliter.

[2] Qu. 10 (Utrum ex presencia speciei sequatur necessario cogitacio actualis per illam), fo. 35r^b. Ad 8^m argumentum, concedo quod species est agens naturale, et quod causat actualem cogitacionem naturaliter et necessario, positis condicionibus numeratis in posicione, scilicet quod sit sufficienter dispositus per habitum intellectus agentis, et quod species sit satis intensa et non sit aliquid inpediens alico modo....

[3] Fos. 35r^b, 35v^a, 39r^b.

[4] Cf. qu. 6 a. 2, fo. 11r^b. Utrum delectacio sit ipsa volucio; qu. 7 a. 1, fo. 17r^b. Utrum memoria, intelligencia et voluntas distinguantur abinvicem realiter et ab ipsa mente; qu. 7 a. 3, fo. 19r^b. Utrum cognicio et volucio sint idem realiter.

to come down on the side of tradition. He denies the identity between cognition and volition and, if his words are not without qualification,[1] it is plain from his supporting arguments that he stands with the conservatives. He denies that if we refuse to identify the faculties they may be contradictory. Why cannot we love that for which we do not hope? In any case all is ultimately resolved by God's absolute power. It is noteworthy that this stand earned the disapproval of Adam Woodham, one of Ockham's most intimate disciples, who displays to the full in his *Commentary on the Sentences* the tendency to reduce the faculties to unity. It is true, wrote Adam, that Hibernicus distinguishes acts of knowing and willing; yet elsewhere he admits that in some sense all volitions are cognitions since we can only will what we know.[2] But only at the level of simple apprehensions would FitzRalph have agreed that these faculties merge; in positive acts they are quite distinct.

But if these mental processes are distinct, is one dependent on the other? Or, to be more precise, is our will controlled by our knowledge?[3] At root this is a question of free will, the theological problem on which FitzRalph felt most intensely. He set out three opinions on the matter, 'two extreme and one moderate'. The first (embodying the new urge to extend the range of possibility and to limit necessary relations, whether in human psychology or in divine power), was that of those who declared that the will is utterly free to reject any intellection, even the 'clear vision' of God. To this opinion FitzRalph was totally opposed. He replied first that, though particular volitions are free, the will is limited by its own nature (it cannot, for example, wish its own non-existence), and secondly and more importantly that those who have seen the 'clear vision' cannot but will what God has commanded. The second opinion was that of the moderate determinists who believed that the will is controlled by our intellection,

---

[1] Fo. 19 vᵇ. Ad ista argumenta teneo hanc partem, scilicet quod volucio respectu actus rei non est cognicio eiusdem, quamvis fortassis volucio alicuius rei sit cognicio sui ipsius, per hoc quod ipsa presens est intellectui.

[2] Michalski, 'Le Problème de la volonté', p. 266.

[3] Qu. 8 a. 2, fo. 24 rᵃ. Utrum ex actuali noticia actus obiecti sequatur necessario amor seu volucio eiusdem.

though allowing that we could freely know some alternative truth. This also failed to satisfy FitzRalph. What we apprehend, he says, is not a single apprehension but many, and it is ridiculous to suppose that we must destroy one before willing another. Intuitions are not exclusive imperatives. So though we may say that the blessed in Heaven, who have seen God clearly, may be absolutely necessitated to will what he reveals, this is not so with mortals who have not yet seen him in his perfection. What he clearly reveals to us we must will; but in all that lies outside the 'clear vision', we can freely accept or reject. Cognition cannot play the tyrant over volition.[1]

III

FitzRalph's philosophical conclusions, especially those touching the will and the intellect, necessarily affected his approach to theological questions. He wished to reconcile free will with the apprehension of the 'clear vision', which cannot be denied; for we can only enjoy the love of God when we have a sure hope or a true vision of his majesty—'vel cum gaudio spei vel cum gaudio rei clare vise'.

But can they be reconciled? In his long discussion of *voluntas* FitzRalph went to the heart of contemporary controversy. If, having seen God, he states, we must inhere in his love, then our wills are not free but necessitated, and the merit of good works nullified. Indeed will is a meaningless term unless under our own control. On the other hand to admit that we can lose the sure acceptance of eternal life is to emasculate *securitas*. It seemed that theologians were quite opposed to one another: Scotus, at one extreme, saying that the will can deny the clear vision and Aquinas, at the other, declaring that, once seen, we must enjoy God's love. FitzRalph accepted neither argument, though he

---

[1] Fo. 25r^b. Responsio propria. In isto articulo... intelligendo questionem de necessitate naturali, dico sic quod patet in beatis in quibus necessitate naturali ad cognicionem claram dei sequitur amor ipsius. Set si articulus intelligitur de noticia illorum qui habent libertatem contradictionis, sicut habuerunt angeli ante confirmacionem et habent omnes homines in via, sic dico quod in angelis et in hominibus ad noticias actuales alicorum sequitur amor necessario....non tamen ad noticiam actualem cuiuscunque obiecti sequitur amor necessario...

remained as always a strong protagonist of free will. What, he asks, is the *libertas contradictionis*, the freedom of choice, that we believe all men to have? The answer is that our decisions are either the deliberate acts of the mind and will, or a choice based on partial knowledge. If we have seen with complete clarity the end to which God has directed us, we are not free to will any other; but if our vision is only partial, we retain the freedom *per accidens* which belongs to imperfection.[1]

FitzRalph restricts to the minimum the class of vision which permits no choice. Even the elect, he says, who of all creatures should see God with unclouded eyes, retain their free will because they enjoy His love by a natural and not an absolute necessity. For their assurance lies not in God himself, but in the knowledge received from him that to deny him is to gain eternal punishment.[2] God, though united to men's wills, can still permit the blessed to commit particular sins.[3] If this is not absolutely compatible with some of his other statements on the 'clear vision', it shows the lengths to which FitzRalph would go to safeguard freedom of the will.

His sensitivity to current controversy is again apparent in his discussion of the relative importance of will and intellect in attaining beatitude. He was here on bitterly contested ground. The *moderni*, influenced by Scotus, tended to assert the supremacy of the will, and some went further and confounded intellections and volitions (that is, as has been noted, to deny real distinctions between the mental faculties). FitzRalph's reply to this question is revealing because his indeterminacy, and indeed undignified hedging, on the first point contrasts so strongly with his crisp repudiation of the Ockhamist position on the second. Once again we recognise a mind susceptible to contemporary opinion but fundamentally orthodox. We may argue with Thomas, he says, that the 'clear vision', the highest form in which we can apprehend God, is essentially an act of intellection, or we may say that the supreme good of loving God depends on the will. In the event

---

[1] Fo. 9r^a. Si vero loquamur de libertate per accidens, sic concedo quod, ostenso ultimo fine clare, non confirmata ipsa voluntate, potest ipsa voluntas illud [*sc.* amare deum] non velle.
[2] Fo. 9v^b.   [3] Fo. 10r^a.

FitzRalph never fully resolves the problem; for, reproducing an argument of Aquinas that the intellect is superior *secundum ordinem* but the will *secundum perfectionem*, he comments:

In this article other doctors hold that the will is superior as such; but I hold to this opinion [of Thomas] for the present, although I think that the opposite opinion can perfectly well be argued.[1]

It is true that the tenor of FitzRalph's argument is to support the supremacy of the will (only the beatitude which comes from the 'clear vision', he decides, is an act of intellection), and that his *Sentences* become at times virtually a treatise on will. But his indecision is patent, and his only firm conclusion the denial of the *innate* superiority of will over intellect. At any rate, on both counts he earned the contemptuous scorn of Adam Woodham, who noted in his *Commentary*:

Hibernicus first admits the supremacy of the will over the intellect, but immediately declares that the mind contains both intellect and will, of which the first is superior *secundum ordinem* and the second *secundum perfeccionem*. But I support the conclusion that is a matter of reduction, that is, that neither the will nor the intellect is the higher faculty since both are aspects of the same mental substance, which exists both to will and to intuit.[2]

The rebuke may have been partially deserved, but the further conclusion drawn by Adam had been firmly rejected by Fitz-Ralph. Adam Woodham had resolved the question by denying

[1] Fo. 11rᵃ. In responsione ad primum articulum dicit [*sc.* Thomas] quod mens habet intellectum et voluntatem, quorum duorum intellectus est altior secundum ordinem [*MS.* originem] et voluntas secundum perfeccionem, et similis ordo est in habitibus et actibus. Hec ille, ubi expresse dicit quod voluntas est altior secundum perfeccionem....In isto articulo tenent alii doctores concorditer quod voluntas est potencia nobilior ut voluntas; unde teneo hanc partem ad presens, quamvis opposita pars sit valde probabilis.

[2] Michalski, 'Le Problème de la volonté', p. 265, citing Adam Woodham, I Sent. qu. 4. Hibernicus tenet cum Scoto contra Thomam in scripto, quod voluntas est potentia nobilior quam intellectus....Sed...statim dicit quod mens habet intellectum et voluntatem, quorum duorum intellectus est altior secundum ordinem et voluntas secundum perfeccionem....Teneo conclusionem ad viam reduccionis, cum dico scilicet quod non intellectus est potentia nobilior voluntate nec econverso, quia idem numero est intellectus et econtra in eadem substancia intellectuali...ipsa nata est intelligere et ipsa nata est velle.

that it existed, by treating will and intellect as facets of a single faculty. Nor was he alone in his opinion; it was a Modernist commonplace that had already drawn FitzRalph's fire. Almost all the *moderni*, he comments, declare that a volition towards anything is indistinguishable from the desire for that thing. For if this were not so, they say, men could desire what they have not willed and *vice versa*, and the different faculties could be predicated of each other in preposterous ways. FitzRalph was unimpressed. Men often act, he replies, in ways that show that they can enjoy what they do not will, or will what they do not like.[1] FitzRalph's psychology in fact discouraged the idea that our faculties are incapable of distinct and deliberate acts. Our will, he declared, is not merely the mind making a volition, but a separate faculty that can excite another (our desire, for example). In his rejection of the tendency to blur distinctions he showed himself strongly opposed to the Modernists.

IV

The God revealed to us in FitzRalph's *Sentences* acts towards men in a manner befitting his majesty and dignity. He is, above all, not an irresponsible God. FitzRalph is even anxious to establish that he is not absolutely omnipotent, in the sense of being able to do any conceivable thing.[2] His object was to limit not the range but the quality of God's acts. In him anything is possible, but his freedom to act is a *potestas supernaturalis absoluta* which, when manifested in particular events, does not permit the absurd or the unbecoming. This does not mean that God's power is imperfect. FitzRalph agrees that he cannot cause men to sin, but denies that is to limit his essential authority; for what is improper when present in secondary causes is natural and proper to God. The impulse which becomes an evil act in men is, as first cause, no evil but God himself; and though he may deprive creatures of his created love, he will never take away from those who truly serve him his uncreated and supernatural love and acceptance.[3]

[1] Fo. 11v^a–v^b.
[2] Qu. 21, fo. 80v^a. Utrum deus sit omnipotens.
[3] Fos. 85r^b, 85v^a, 86r^b.

His concept of the responsible God also turned FitzRalph from voluntarism. We have noted his preoccupation with the problem of will, but he held no brief for the extreme doctrine preached by Bradwardine. Discussing God's will as first cause,[1] he elaborates the disastrous consequence of assuming that all human acts are directly caused by his will. Men's sins, their salvation and reprobation, predestination and acceptance—all would follow ineluctably from God's will. Moreover the determinist thesis implies not only that human action cannot affect God's purpose, but that he himself cannot alter what has been eternally predestined. So crude an explanation of the working of the divine will, FitzRalph believed, broke down under its own contradictions; it required that, to allow freedom to the human will, one must admit that man could frustrate the divine will.[2] In reality, he says, God's will is not equally causal in all circumstances, and we must distinguish his first and supreme act of Creation from the lapses from perfection which are the immediate consequences of men's volitions. If God is the cause of the fact and possibility of our sinning, he bears no responsibility for the sinful acts that we deliberately commit.[3]

FitzRalph did not deny the reality of predestination, but sought to modify the rigour of its interpretation. He was, of course, convinced of the contingency of future events; but Buckingham (to mention only one name) had shown that a moderate could find contingency and predestination quite compatible. FitzRalph refuses to conceive predestination as a determining force outside the will of God or man. In his eyes it is that sure fulfilling of his purpose which comprehends divine and human will, which is, in fine, the actual exercise of such will. God wills, therefore, not that we be predestined, but the fact of our predestination. In this way our free volitions do not derogate from his authority, since he has

---

[1] Qu. 20, fo. 76r[a]. Utrum voluntas dei sit prima causa rerum.

[2] Fo. 76v[a]. Propterea si voluntas dei sit causa cuiuslibet creature, sequitur quod voluntas sit causa et predestinacionis...consequens inpossibile; et probo consequentiam quia, si predestinatus potest dampnari et voluntas dei beneplacita est ut salvetur, igitur creatura potest inpedire voluntatem ne inpleatur.

[3] Fo. 78r[a].

previously willed that we should exercise our freedom of choice.[1]
As for those deeds which will in the future bring down upon us the
wrath of God, we ought not to say that he has determined them, but
rather that he will mete out condign punishment to those who,
by his foreknowledge, he knows will sin at some later time.[2]

How then does God foreknow those elected to salvation or
foreseen to reprobation? FitzRalph refuses to deprive men of the
hope of attaining acceptance. Although, he says, the number of
the elect is certain, it is still possible for them to lose salvation by
sin; whilst the number of the reprobate is purely contingent,
depending upon the sinful acts which we freely commit. No
doubt the ultimate cause of acceptance lies in God himself, but the
immediate cause of justification is sincere repentance, and the
cause of losing his love the refusal to repent.[3]

But to speak of his foreknowledge is to beg the question of
what is 'future'. The problem was of universal concern to the
theologians of the fourteenth century. We have already referred
in this study to the opinions of Bradwardine and Buckingham;
and we shall later discuss in some detail Wyclif's views. The conclusion of the 'Doctor Profundus' had been as simple as it was
extreme. God, he had said, who is present in eternity, knows
everything past, present and future as a single fact in which there
can be no distinction of kind between his knowledge of the future
and of the past or present. Buckingham, on the other hand,
declared that his knowledge, though eternal, unitary and certain,
remained contingent towards future events until they had actually
occurred (this contingency being an inherent quality and not
imposed from without).

---

[1] Fo. 78v[b]. Respondeo et dico quod voluntas dei non est causa predestinacionis, quia ipsa voluntas dei est predestinacio, sicut dicit Magister li. I d.
35 in principio. Dico tamen quod voluntas dei est causa predestinandi
quemcunque predestinatum, et nego consequentiam, igitur predestinatus non
potest peccare mortaliter nec dampnari....Respondeo et concedo quod hoc
maxime est verum in hiis que fiunt a voluntate libera, scilicet quod, si voluntas
vult illa facere, [deus vult illa facere], et si voluntas non vult illa facere, deus non
vult illa facere, nec vult illa fore...licet voluntas creature sit causa quare deus
vult illa fore vel facere, tamen deus est causa quare voluntas creature illa
producere potest, scilicet quia dedit voluntati libertatem talia producendi.

[2] Fo. 79r[a].   [3] Fos. 79r[b], 80rb.

FitzRalph's reply to this question[1] is worth considering with some care. After all, to Oxonians at the end of the century he and Bradwardine stood out as the two great conservative philosophers of the previous generation, and in both his *Sentences* and the *Armenian Questions* he laid the greatest stress on the problem of free will and contingency. Like Wyclif, though unlike Bradwardine, FitzRalph was a metaphysician as well as a theologian; and we may note with interest that his defence of contingency not only conforms to but actually depends on his realism—the very factor which was to confirm Wyclif in his determinism. Ardmachanus demonstrated that one could be both realist and champion of free will.

Divine knowledge, he states, pertains first to the idea and the essence, outside time and place; and though God may know singulars also, his knowledge of them is mutable and contingent, because particular. It follows that what he knows in essence he knows perfectly, but not that he necessitates future events, which must be temporal and therefore contingent.[2] But, for FitzRalph, contingency does not depend solely on the temporality of events, since God's direct knowledge can itself be contingent. If he chooses to know not the simple idea (*racio simpliciter*) of an event but its particular form (*racio congregata*), he knows its past, present and future as distinct phenomena, having the contingency which belongs to all temporal things. Arguing that, though ideas can never be temporal, their singulars must be, FitzRalph admitted, as neither Buckingham nor Bradwardine had done, that God in his

---

[1] Qu. 15, fo. 54r[b]. Circa distinctionem 35 primi libri, queritur utrum deus sit prescius omnium futurorum.

[2] Fo. 54v[a]. Responsio: potest dici quod essencia divina representat contingenter et accidentaliter 'antichristum fore', non necessario nec naturaliter, propter hoc, quia essencia divina representat actu distincto omnia creanda et creabilia, sed tantum [*MS.* tamen] per simplicem representacionem, non per modum composicionis; et ideo per modum simplicis representacionis representat esse, tempus et omnem locum et omnem ordinem causarum...et ideo accidentaliter et non necessario cognoscitur 'antichristus esse futurus'.

Fo. 54v[b]. Responsio: pro ista dubitacione est notandum, quando divina essencia representat res. Pro quo dico quod essencia divina est ars seu racio vel species vel ydea cuiuslibet rei create vel creande.

own person can know future events as future and past events as past.[1] The whole of his argument is designed to support his belief in the contingency of things (*evitabilitas*, as he so often calls it), that is the leitmotiv of his *Sentences*.

It is again by using the realist concept of the *ydea* that FitzRalph explains how God reveals the future to us.[2] Because revelation is a true and certain knowledge of his purpose, we would seem to be necessitated to any future he reveals, and the future itself would seem to be determined. Can we possibly admit that revelation can be defied, however terrible? Clearly any solution of this problem must account both for the truth of revelation and the liberty of the human will. One explanation, FitzRalph noted, had been to say that, whilst creatures necessarily enjoy God's love in that their wills inhere essentially in his, their actual and temporal enjoyment remains contingent. In this way the freedom and frailty of human nature would be protected. This did not satisfy FitzRalph, who argued that it led to the error of supposing divine forms to inhere immediately in our wills.[3] He resolves the question by admitting that there is an ideal and perfect knowledge of things, the *nuda essencia*, which is timeless and which God may reveal to us. But this gift is as rare as it is precious. All other experiences, including those which we commonly call 'revelations', depend on apprehending God's purpose, and it is through our apprehension, which is imperfect, that this knowledge becomes contingent. He therefore does indeed reveal the future

---

[1] Fo. 54v[b]. ...et simili modo respectu cuiuscunque rei future potest esse aliqua talis racio conggregata, que representat illam particulariter dum futura est, et illa eadem racio conggregata non representabit illam rem distincte et particulariter quando erit presens, sicut illa racio conggregata 'sacerdos supremus' primus futurus representat papam antequam fuit papa...et per hunc modum [divina essencia] representat rem futuram ut futura est, et preterita ut preterita est, et hoc particulariter et distincte....

Fo. 55r[a]. Applicacio: sic dico quod pari modo essencia divina representat res futuras distincte ut future sunt...et tamen istam rem quam representat esse futuram non semper representabit esse futuram, quia contingenter representat...unde in uno tempore representat aliter unam rem quam in alio tempore.

[2] Qu. 16, fo. 55r[b]. Utrum deus possit revelare creature racionali futura contingencia.

[3] Fo. 56v[a].

to us, but seldom in a manner which renders it inevitable.[1] That we should believe is the necessary consequence of God's willing; but what we believe remains contingent through the possibility of error.

So FitzRalph's idealism avoids the pitfalls of determinism, and the stress laid upon free will allows him to emphasise our ability to earn the reward of God's love. As we should expect, there is no trace of Pelagianism in his *Commentary*; divine charity is a supernatural virtue that is his free gift to those whom he justifies to eternal life. Following Henry of Ghent, he confirms that we cannot in ourselves attain or lose the love of God, and that it is his love which induces the will to good. Merit, therefore, is the product of uncreated charity; but by showing merit we can certainly increase the *caritas creata* through which we experience divine love. Good works alone are impotent, yet the disposition to love which they reveal will surely bring its reward. Such convictions are the precise opposite of those of Bradwardine who, to preserve the absolute supremacy of God's will, denied all efficacy to merit. For FitzRalph it is only just and fitting that God should reward those who fulfil his word. Meritorious acts do not cause God's intentions but ensure that those who love him will indeed be rewarded by acceptance. For our merit would be in vain if we were not certain that it would elicit a condign reward.[2]

FitzRalph developed in his *Sentences* a moderate realism, in which his theory of illumination showed debts to Grosseteste and Averroes. His deep interest in the way in which we apprehend divine truth, and our reaction to these intimations, led to a con-

---

[1] Fo. 62rᵃ. Nichil asserendo igitur, dico quod mihi videtur inpossibile, quod in verbo deus revelet alicui aliquid esse futurum, id est scilicet, quod solum verbum divinum representet illi rem esse futuram, ymmo nec verbum potest precise presentare aliquam rem alicui creature racionali absque actu cognicionis in cognoscente....Sed aliter loquendo de revelacione per quam cognoscitur nuda essencia rei future, vel etiam ipsa res fore, per argumentacionem non per cognicionem intuitivam, verum est quod deus potest revelare creature racionali futura contingencia.

Fo. 58vᵇ. Dico quod deus potest futura revelare omnibus modis dicas in posicione; et dico, facta revelacione, quod ista revelata contingenter evenient, et non necessario propter revelacionem.

[2] Qu. 13–14, fos. 46rᵇ–53vᵃ.

cern with the relation of intellect to will, which stressed the latter without toppling over into voluntarism. And in striving to relate and not confound the modes of action, he opposed a doctrine favoured by many Ockhamists. But the foremost theme of the *Sentences* is the problem of *voluntas*, where FitzRalph's overriding concern was to safeguard human free will. Here he used his doctrine of realist intuition to limit the degree to which men must act according to the necessitating 'clear vision', and to restrict as far as possible the true 'revelation' in which we perceive God's predestinating will. Supporting his thesis at this point with the complementary argument on the vexed question of 'future contingents', he again modified his predestinarianism by asserting that God could in himself know the temporal future as eternally future and contingent.

To examine FitzRalph's *Sentences* is to be struck by the identity of the themes absorbing English theologians of his generation. The work is an important witness for its age; and it is on the foundation of this *Commentary* that an appreciation of the *De questionibus Armenorum* must rest.

v

FitzRalph's career in the 1330's and 1340's was active and itinerant. After some months in the household of Richard Bury, *c*. 1335, he departed for the Curia at Avignon, only to return early in 1336 to Lichfield, where the efforts of his patron had secured the deanery for him. But within a few months he had again left on chapter business for Avignon, where he was in fact to spend most of the decade 1334–44. On returning to England he remained at Lichfield for three years. But in 1346 the chapter of Armagh elected him archbishop and early in 1348, after wintering with Grandisson at Exeter, he sailed for his native land. In the summer of 1349 he was again in England, and the next year back at the Curia on royal business. He stayed there two years.[1]

It is not easy to guess precisely what dissatisfactions were stirring

---

[1] Emden, *Biographical Register*, II, 693; Gwynn, 'Richard FitzRalph at Avignon', *Studies*, XXII (1933), 591–607.

in the mind of the busy dean of Lichfield as he went about the interminable round of ecclesiastical lobbying for which his chapter judged him so well equipped. It is certain that long residence at Avignon is closely connected with his 'conversion' from philosophical studies, but this 'conversion', as will be shown, is in some respects more protested than real. Was the work contemplated in these years first conceived as an attack on the irrelevance of scholasticism? Or was it yet another apologia by an academic for abandoning scholarship for administration? Clearly in his official life other interests were coming to predominate. But at least one possible cause of intellectual distraction can be eliminated. Only in 1349–50 did FitzRalph plunge into the mendicant controversy. It was in that year, as he tells us, that he first began to concern himself with the doctrine of dominion, and the De questionibus Armenorum contains but one brief statement on the matter:

So far as I can judge, no man in a state of mortal sin has true lordship over other creatures in God's sight. He ought rather to be called a tyrant, a thief or a robber, though he may keep the name of king or prince or lord by reason of possession or hereditary succession, or the approval of the people subject to him, or by some other human law. But he has no true lordship until he repents, and until the grace of penance has restored him to a state that is acceptable to God.[1]

The Armenian Questions had certainly been completed by 1350, and so antedate FitzRalph's absorption in the quarrel with the mendicants. Indeed we can say of both FitzRalph and Wyclif that it is remarkable that two secular controversialists of such combative natures should have entered so late in their careers into the battle against the friars.

No consideration of the changing climate of opinion in the mid-fourteenth century can ignore the revulsion from scholasticism which FitzRalph experienced, and which he himself recounted in

[1] Summa domini Armacani in questionibus Armenorum (Paris, 1512), fo. 75v, ed. and trans. Gwynn, English Austin Friars, p. 67; and cf. R. L. Poole, ed., De pauperie Salvatoris (WS, 1890), p. 273.

the memorable autobiographical prayer which concludes the *De questionibus Armenorum*.[1]

The *Questions*, which were both a *pièce d'occasion* and an expression of his new convictions, were composed in the early 1340's, mainly at Avignon, and issued *c.* 1350. The occasion was the arrival at the Curia in 1339 of the Armenian prelate, Nerses of Manasgard. Missionary enterprise in the east was much in the mind of the Church, and Clement VI, noting the doctrinal differences between the west and the Armenians, asked FitzRalph to write an apology for Rome and a correction of the Armenian errors. The *Questions* were the result. But the work in fact falls into two parts, of which only the first (Books 1–13) deals with the Armenian disputes proper, the second part (Books 14–19) being concerned with theological problems long argued in the universities of the west, and on which indeed FitzRalph himself had dwelt when reading his *Sentences* nearly twenty years before. The later books, which can be compared with his *Commentary*, are the best evidence for the study of his change of opinion.

The nature of this 'conversion' is well known; it was an utter repudiation of the techniques and ambitions of the schools and an affirmation of the absolute and divinely revealed truth of Scripture. The autobiographical prayer, addressed in Augustinian language to God himself, was a paean of thanks for his saving mercy, which had preserved FitzRalph from the hands of his enemies and revealed to him the vanity of his past life. Once he had put his trust in the arguments of Aristotle; now he can only thank God for dispersing with the light of Scripture the cloud of error that encompassed him when 'with the frogs and toads' he was 'croaking in the swamps'. His rhetoric can hardly be translated.

---

[1] Though the contents of the *Armenian Questions* await detailed examination, the date of their composition and FitzRalph's 'conversion' are treated by Gwynn, 'Richard FitzRalph at Avignon', pp. 600–2, and L. L. Hammerich, *The Beginning of the Strife between Richard FitzRalph and the Mendicants, with an edition of his autobiographical prayer and his proposition Unusquisque*, Historisk-Filologiske Meddelelser, xxvi, 3 (Copenhagen, 1938), and esp. 24–5. As to dating, we incline towards Gwynn, who argues for 1341–2, against Hammerich, who supposes that the work was finished at Lichfield, 1344–7. On FitzRalph's conversion see also Pantin, *The English Church in the Fourteenth Century*, pp. 153–4.

Nec illis sex annis michi, Solida Veritas, abfuisti, sed in tuis sanctis scripturis—que de te Veritate incarnata a te atque propter te erant tuis populis promulgate—me veluti in quodam radioso speculo illuxisti, qui annis meis prioribus in philosophorum nugis me quasi ita in quadam tenebrosa caligine latitasti. Putabam enim antea per Aristotelica dogmata et argumentaciones quasdam profundas hominibus nonnisi vanitate profundis cum celi tui civibus Veritatis tue me penetrasse abyssos, donec tu Veritas Solida, in tuis michi litteris splenduisti, fugans huiusmodi mei erroris nubeculam, michi ostendens quomodo cum ranis et buffonibus in paludibus crocitabam.

Audiveram quippe, sed non noveram nisi te Veritate ductrice, contra te Veritatem garriencium philosophorum, pertinacium Iudeorum, simigentilium Grecorum, carnalium Saracenorum, atque indoctorum Armenorum tumultum, qui fraudulenter et callide decorticabant tuam scripturam....[1]

The *Questions* are the chief evidence for the truth of FitzRalph's words. But two further references bearing on the conversion to Scripture and the rejection of the schools may be noted. The first, which is not authenticated and must be treated with caution, is the *Sermo in opus Armachani* which precedes the *Sentences* in MS. Oriel 15. As has been noted,[2] the first two *quaestiones* which follow the *Sermo* are attributed to FitzRalph in this MS. alone, and are almost certainly not his. The *Sermo* also is unique, and must therefore fall under the same suspicion. But the contents are quite compatible with FitzRalph's opinions *c.* 1340. Taking the text 'Fluminis inpetus letificat civitatem dei', the writer speaks of the Earthly and Heavenly Cities which compete for man's allegiance. How then does God strengthen and console us? Through sacred Scripture and the *quadripartitum volumen* of the Lombard. And in his second book, the writer adds, the Master of the Sentences has exposed the errors of those who pervert the truth of God, the Manichaeans who believe that evil is eternal and the Pelagians who deny that we need the gift of grace—'and the minds of the faithful, purged from these and like errors by Sacred Scripture, he leads into the way of truth'. The Bible and Master

---

[1] *De quest. Arm.*, Book 19, ch. 35, ed. Hammerich, *op. cit.* pp. 20–1.
[2] See above, p. 75.

Peter are at one. Was this an 'intermediate' opinion maintained by FitzRalph in the years between his two big works?[1]

The second reference, though of a much later date and almost an aside, is fully authenticated. In 1357-8 he learnt that John de Marignollis, the Franciscan bishop of Bisignano, planned to journey to Avignon to answer the *Defensorium Curatorum*. In a truculent letter he warned the bishop that he would get the worst of a fight, and boasted that he would destroy his arguments 'as we have destroyed the sophisms of Ockham and Burley'.[2] Could his contempt for the schools be more pointed?

Yet FitzRalph's own words, so redolent of the *Confessions*, are but an imperfect guide to the course and extent of his 'conversion'. We do not deny that he underwent a profound experience; but to come to the later books of the *De questionibus Armenorum*, after reading the *Sentences*, is to enter no new world, even if it is to see the world in a different light. For these chapters treat of the reconciling of the truth of Scripture with the illumination of the 'clear vision', and the assertion of free will on men and contingency in future events—precisely those problems dealt with most strikingly and *con amore* in the *Sentences*. FitzRalph did not, could not, wipe out his past as if it had never been. After all he had been Chancellor of Oxford. That the old questions were now proved by the truths of Scripture is true, but even so not to the extent to which FitzRalph would have us believe.

In Book 14 he discusses the opinion of the Greek and Armenian philosophers who claimed that we cannot have the 'clear vision'

---

[1] MS. Oriel 15, fo. 11ᵇ. ...Hos enim philosophos Magister Petrus, et omnes alios philosophos mundum eternum mencientes, ac etiam Manicheos naturam mali eternam asserentes...Pelagianos graciam non esse necessariam ad servanda mandata asseverantes, manifestos hereticos in secundo libro sui voluminis, errore sacrilego involutos esse demonstrat; et mentes fidelium ab hiis et similibus erroribus per sacram scripturam utiliter purgatas in viam veritatis inducit contra aliud incommodum tactum in prothemate.

[2] G. Golubovich, *Biblioteca bio-bibliografica della Terra Santa*, IV (1923), 270: 'Neque vestrum, reverende pater, timemus adventum, ut vestris argumentis terreamur in aliquo, qui iam Anglicana sophismata, Okkam puta, Burley et aliorum qui sub apparentia veri tunicam falso secernerunt [sic] contexere, omnino destruximus.' Cf. Gwynn, 'Archbishop FitzRalph and the Friars', *Studies*, XXVI (1937), 66.

of God because it is his invisibility that is the proof of his omnipotence. FitzRalph's argument for the truth of such a vision, derived indirectly from Averroes, had been a distinctive feature of his *Commentary*, and it reappears in the *Armenian Questions*, though without the scholastic proofs and supported by the authority of Scripture and the neoplatonist Denis. FitzRalph declares that as Moses saw God face to face so do we; being mortal we lack the full clarity of the blessed, but we do have, though imperfectly, a clear vision of God.[1]

In his *Commentary*, it will be recalled, FitzRalph had to face the task of relating the truth of the Vision to free will in men, and of divine omniscience to human contingency. Neither of these aims had been abandoned when he came to write the *De questionibus Armenorum*, but their reconciliation had been complicated by a new factor, his new found conviction of the infallibility of Scripture. Wrongly interpreted, the doctrines of the 'clear vision' and of scriptural infallibility led to determinism, which FitzRalph would in no circumstances admit. In Books 15 and 16 he denies again that God's prescience and omnipotence destroy the contingency of the future, and that the infallibility of Scripture is incompatible with contingency. We would seem, remarks 'Johannes', his interlocutor in the *Armenian Questions*, to have the impossible choice either of conceding that both the future and the Word are contingent or of refusing mutability to both.[2] FitzRalph replies that each conclusion is false and rests on a double confusion, the logical error of supposing that no contingency can follow from a certainty, and the theological error of assuming that our acts are necessitated by infallible Scripture. For all the saints and the doctors confirm that we can never be deprived of

---

[1] *De quest. Arm.*, Book 14, ch. 27, fo. 118r. Patet insuper ex hiis que superius adducuntur, quod intentio istius sancti [*sc*. Dionysii] erat, quod in hac unione super intellectum cum haberetur, unde videtur deus nude seu incircumvelate; quia cum hec unio duplicem habet modum, unum apud viatores perfectos et alium apud comprehensores scilicet apud veros beatos, quorum primus est obscurus et caliginosus, licet sit nudus, quia est per fidem...non sequitur quod tu nitebaris inferre, scilicet quod beatitudo non consistit in nuda et clara visione divine essencie.

[2] Book 15, ch. 1, fo. 119r.

our free choice and 'liberty of contradiction'.[1] Without suggesting that FitzRalph substituted one for the other, we may say that logically the 'clear vision' plays the same role in his *Commentary on the Sentences* as scriptural truth in the *Armenian Questions*, in that both doctrines pose the problem of relating God's omniscience to contingency and free will.

Much of the argument of the *De questionibus Armenorum* consists simply of assertion supported by biblical references. FitzRalph admits that there was a time, and not so long before, when parts of Scripture seemed to be contradictory; but now he knows it to be concrete truth.

Fateor enim michi sepius apparuisse falsitatem et nonnunquam contrarietatem fuisse in multis locis scripture, ubi tamen clara veritas fuerat expressa sed etiam negligentius attendebam et aliquotiens ex prophetis propheticis vanis argumentationibus quas recentes habueram nimis leviter scripturam solidam iudicabam.[2]

And on a later occasion, when arguing publicly that the doctrine of Christ's poverty was unbiblical, he dared any friar to find a text to prove it—'dicebam quod si quis in evangelio id reperiret illi bibliam meam darem'.[3] Nevertheless FitzRalph was not a literal fundamentalist. Though he accounted it a virtue of the New Testament (not always shared with the Old) that its words could be taken in a literal sense, he did not forget that behind the Vulgate lay the Greek and Hebrew originals to which when in doubt we should return. If we find a text which seems unintelligible or unacceptable, he says, reference to the original will always dispel our doubts.[4]

But no reading of the *Armenian Questions* can disguise the fact

---

[1] Book 16, ch. 1, fo. 129r. Johannes: Utinam dictis facta compensares et inciperes a dissolutione mei primi obiectus de infallibilitate scripture. Ricardus: Videris ex logica astute arguere, et tamen peccas in logica que varios arguendi modos ostendit...deduxisti nunquam posse ex necessario sequi contingens, necque ex opposito, scilicet ex contingente sequi impossibile...unusquisque novit quod antecedens est necessarium primo modo prescripto, et forte consequens est contingens, iuxta opinionem multorum, si consequens sic sit de futuris que pendet a nostro arbitrio.

[2] Book. 19, ch. 19, fo. 157r.   [3] Gwynn, *Studies*, XXVI (1937), 57.

[4] Book 19, ch. 23, fo. 162(*bis*)r.

that much of the old Adam remained. It is not merely that Fitz-Ralph resumed the questions he had first tackled in his *Commentary*: for in great part his arguments are thoroughly scholastic, at times repeating almost word for word the phrases of his *Commentary*. Is God the cause of sin? He draws the traditional distinction between his authority as *auctor* and *causa* of things.[1] Are our acts necessitated by God? Noting that, if he determines our acts, any human evil is excusable, FitzRalph emphasises the vital argument, first made in his *Sentences*, that an event is in some sense future before it can be foreknown. Thus divine omniscience and prescience are preserved in a non-determinist form.[2]

Viewed in the light of his *Sentences*, therefore, FitzRalph's conversion seems less than absolute in manner or matter. Autobiography is always revealing, but what it reveals is not always an undistorted image of objective truth; nor, if it communicates emotion inimitably, is the cause of the emotion necessarily explained. For all the drama of his language, we must still guess why FitzRalph was converted to the doctrine of scriptural infallibility and rejected, or partially rejected, the doctrines of the schools. It was not the result of an academic quarrel, for there was no breach with old friends at Oxford. In the autumn of 1356 he almost certainly revisited the university and at Christmastide declared, in a sermon at St Paul's Cross, that he had sent copies of the *De pauperie Salvatoris* to friends at Oxford.[3] But if such personal explanations must be ruled out, there remain more general factors. Was FitzRalph influenced by the anti-intellectualism that was certainly an important strand in fourteenth-century thought?

---

[1] Book 15, ch. 13, fo. 124r.

[2] Book 16, ch. 5, fo. 130v. [Johannes]...si vero quisque dixerit prescientiam dei inevitabilitatem inducere, non quia sola prescientia sed quia prescientia omnipotentis, non video adhuc plene quomodo possit refelli. Ricardus: Illud stare non potest...est enim prius ordine seu causalitate, aut saltem ratione causali, quod res sit futura quam prescita, quoniam prescire rem nihil aliud est quam scire rem esse futuram...quoniam, si scitur futura esse, ipsa est futura, non econtra...et ob hoc hec prescientia dei in quantum huiusmodi nullius rei est causa, sed est conformitas dei scientis in quantum res subest illi differentie temporis ad rem futuram...prescientia dei, in quantum prescientia nullam inevitabilitatem potius quam tua, que semper in rebus prescitis posterior potest inducere.

[3] Gwynn, *Studies*, XXVI (1937), 57.

This is possible, though it is a feature more prominent, perhaps, in the second half of the century. It is also possible that, consciously or unconsciously, he was expressing his disapproval of the success of the Modern Pelagians. But it seems most satisfactory to follow Fr Gwynn in seeing the secret of FitzRalph's conversion in the long sojourn at Avignon. In his discussions with the Armenians he found himself dealing with Christians who differed widely from Rome in dogma and ecclesiastical organisation, and with whom he appeared to hold only the Scriptures in common.

It is worth comparing the intellectual crisis which FitzRalph experienced with those through which Wyclif and Bradwardine passed. In the case of Wyclif, of course, there was really no crisis; he was, unlike FitzRalph, a literal fundamentalist and his fundamentalism was the direct and inescapable consequence of his ultrarealism. Every word of Scripture was, and always had been, eternally true, in that it was an extension of the divine idea. Bradwardine, on the other hand, did undergo a most powerful conversion, in which Scripture played a vital part; for his revelation of God's prevenient grace came when meditating on the words of Paul. And his conversion was not the less profound for taking place, as it were, within the scholastic mould. Indeed in some ways it may have gone deeper than FitzRalph's; for there is no evidence that the latter's public life, his pastoral cares, above all his conduct towards the friars, was in the least affected by his 'philosophical' conversion. Perhaps Bradwardine's career as a royal clerk also seemed to keep its even tenor, but every line of the *De causa Dei* breathes the intense conviction of one to whom the truth of God has been uniquely revealed.

Whatever the nature of FitzRalph's conversion, the consequences were immediate—and ironical. For the *De questionibus Armenorum* became with the *De causa Dei* the work of the previous generation most frequently cited by Oxford scholastics of the second half of the century. For Wyclif it was the authoritative exposition of the doctrine of free will as was the *De causa Dei* of predestinarianism. When later he began to write on lordship it was inevitable that he should turn to the *De pauperie Salvatoris*; he had accepted Ardmachanus as an authority for many years.

CHAPTER IV

TRENDS IN SPECULATION
AT OXFORD, 1350-1370

I

THE activity of Oxford masters in the years between the publication of the *De causa Dei* and the emergence of Wyclif as the leading master in the schools is exceedingly difficult to trace. The evidence is scattered and fragmentary (Buckingham's *Questions* alone excepted), and its paucity apparently reflects a real decline in the intellectual vigour of Oxford. How far was the Black Death responsible for this? We know that it killed Bradwardine and Holcot; we can only guess at the number of young students, yet to make their names, whom it carried off. Certainly Wyclif's rise can only be understood in this context; and we have noted that he himself, save for some scathing comments, treats the men of these decades as if they had never been. However, an effort will be made to pierce the gloom, though the material is too slight to allow us to draw general conclusions from such disparate examples.

After nearly a century and a half of the closest association Oxford and Paris began to go their separate ways. This divorce is first apparent at the time of the outbreak of the Hundred Years War, and very likely connected with it.[1] If the history of Parisian thought in the later fourteenth century is only less unexplored than that of Oxford, the evidence of the *Chartularium* indicates that the *via moderna* continued to find adherents amongst Parisian

---

[1] Knowles, 'The Censured Opinions of Uthred of Boldon', p. 308. 'From about the middle of the century, however, a great change began to take place. While the University of Paris became increasingly nationalistic in outlook, the Hundred Years War and later the Great Schism isolated English thought and the two English universities both from Paris and from what may be called the theological climate of continental Europe.'

masters. The climax of the struggle between the new and the old logicians had been reached with the condemnations of terminism by the Faculty of Arts in 1340, and of Nicholas Autrecourt and Jean de Mirecourt by the theologians in 1346–7. But the *Chartularium* records at least four censures between 1351 and 1363 of terminist or radical propositions of precisely the same kind as had been condemned ten years before,[1] whilst, as has been noted,[2] the *Commentary on the Sentences* of Pierre de Ceffons, read in the late 1350's, vigorously defends the memory of *monachus albus,* Jean de Mirecourt. But most remarkable of all is Parisian ignorance (fully reciprocated at Oxford) of the work of English theologians, who had but recently been so prominent in the university of Paris. Even Peter of Candia, who studied at the Franciscan convent at Norwich and at Oxford, refers in his *Commentary* only to Parisian masters.[3] This newly acquired provincialism was certainly harmful to Oxford.

There the situation seems to have been different. The Arts faculty does not appear to have adopted terminism to any overwhelming degree, a surprising fact when one recalls the stature of Ockham and the strictures of Wyclif upon it. It was rather the theology of the Venerable Inceptor which found disciples at Oxford. That Ockham's logic was successfully combated, if not repelled, is probably due to the teaching of Walter Burley, a metaphysician of the old school. Burley[4] (1275–c. 1344) had an exceptionally long career; he was already a fellow of Merton in 1301, and is last heard of on business at Avignon in 1343, when he presented a revised edition of his *Expositio librorum Politicorum* to his old master at Paris, Clement VI. Burley was another protégé of Richard Bury, and the first edition of his *Commentary on the Politics* was dedicated to Bury and was composed at the instance

---

[1] Denifle and Chatelain, eds., *Chartularium,* III, 11–12 (1351), 21–3 (1354), 95–7 (1362), 108 (1363).

[2] Above, p. 40.

[3] We have seen the copy of his *Sentences* in MS. Balliol College, Oxford, 64; for Peter's work see F. Ehrle, 'Der Sentenzkommentar Peters von Candia', *Franzisk. Studien,* IX (1925), 1–106.

[4] Emden, *Biographical Register,* I, 312–14; Michalski, 'La Physique nouvelle', pp. 95–102; Boehner, *Medieval Logic,* pp. 44–51.

of another member of the Durham circle, Richard Bintworth, bishop of London.[1] He was well travelled and had read theology at Paris under Thomas Wilton as well as under Pierre Roger, the future Clement VI.

He was, therefore, already a middle-aged man of great experience when Ockham first began to write.[2] Burley was a decided realist, perhaps the leading one at Oxford. He was deeply influenced by Grosseteste, and it has been noted that his *Posterior Analytics* is simply a gloss on Lincolniensis; whilst he himself admits that he read the *Ethics* (another work dedicated to Pierre Roger) in accordance with Grosseteste's gloss.[3] Burley's realism is apparent in his tract on universals (where he is fulsomely called 'doctor evangelice veritatis'),[4] in which he attacks the central terminist argument that in simple supposition the term supposits merely for the mental concept and not for the reality of the thing signified.[5] It has recently been shown that in later life he revised his work expressly to combat Ockham's teaching, and that the *Tractatus de universalibus realibus* and the final version of his

[1] Anneliese Maier, 'Zu Walter Burleys Politik-Kommentar', *RTAM*, xiv (1947), 332–3; S. H. Thomson, 'Walter Burley's Commentary on the Politics of Aristotle', *Mélanges Auguste Pelzer* (1947), pp. 557–78.

[2] His commentaries on the *Posterior Analytics, Elenchi, De obligacionibus, Insolubilia, Notabilia, De suppositionibus,* and the first version of the *De puritate artis logice* are 'all free from any reaction to Ockham's teaching' and therefore pre-1319. Cf. Ph. Boehner, ed., *De puritate artis logice tractatus longior,* and revised edition of *Tractatus brevior,* Francisc. Inst. Public., text ser. 9 (1955), and Emden, *loc. cit.* L. Baudry, 'Les Rapports de Guillaume d'Occam et de Walter Burleigh', *AHDL,* ix (1934), 155–73, argued that Ockham and Burley were not absolutely opposed; but the researches of Maier, cited below, seem to disprove this. S. H. Thomson, 'An Unnoticed *Questio Theologica* of Walter Burley', *Medievalia et Humanistica,* vi (1950), 84–8, prints an interesting text, attributed to Burley, which supports the 'Pelagian' proposition that men could attain justification 'secundum legem naturalem sine fide infusa'. But the question appears to be incomplete, without either the arguments *contra* or the *resolutio* of the question; it is hard to know, therefore, what was Burley's own view.

[3] Michalski, 'La Physique nouvelle et les différents courants philosophiques au XIVe siècle', *Bull. int. de l'acad. pol. des sciences et des lettres* (Cracow, 1928), p. 96.

[4] MS. Gonville and Caius, Cambridge, 139/79, *Tractatus de universalibus realibus,* p. 42.

[5] Michalski, 'La Physique nouvelle', p. 122.

Commentary on the Physics contain undoubted refutations of the Venerable Inceptor.[1] Burley, alone of the Artists working at Oxford at this time, merits citation by name in Wyclif's works, and this in itself is a clue to his standing. Even so we must remember that Walter Burley was much older than most of his colleagues in the 1330's, a contemporary of the disciples of Henry of Ghent whom longevity prolonged into the age of the disciples of Ockham.

What then of the Oxford logicians of the middle of the century? For seldom in the history of the university can logicians have played so prominent a part. The notebooks, for example, of the Worcester monks who came up to Gloucester College at this time are filled with the tracts of Swineshead, Heytesbury, Mylverley, Billingham and their successors.[2] But a sampling of their contents does not confirm the view that terminism *à outrance* flourished at Oxford in these years. Treatises on universals abound (some of them actively realist), but the logicians seem unaware that matters of great moment turned on this issue; the distinction between the real and the term is explained, yet the existence of the real is hardly questioned.[3] How then is this to be reconciled with Wyclif's well known attacks on the 'doctors of signs', whom he represents as being very powerful at Oxford? Undeniably there was a current of 'modernist' opinion in the university, but terminism, we suggest, was not its principal feature. Wyclif is the chief witness for the contrary view, but his ultrarealism makes him an uncertain guide to contemporary thought; first, because he may dismiss as 'terminist' any shade of moderate opinion, and secondly because his own preoccupation with the existence of the

[1] A. Maier, 'Zu einigen Problemen der Ockhamforschung', *AFH*, XLVI (1953), 161–94; 'Handschriftliches zu Wilhelm Ockham und Walter Burley', *ibid.* XLVIII (1955), 235 ff.

[2] Cf. J. K. Floyer and S. G. Hamilton, eds., *Catalogue of Manuscripts Preserved in the Chapter Library of Worcester Cathedral*, Worc. Hist. Soc. (1906), MSS. F 73, F 116, F 118, Q 54. The Oxford logicians of the period are the subject of a study by J. A. Weisheipl, O.P., *Early Fourteenth Century Physics and the Merton 'School'* (Oxford D.Phil., 1957).

[3] See, for example, *De superficiali universalium noticia* of William Mylverley, the Mertonian logician (B.M., Royal MS. 12. B. xix, fos. 14–19), and *Universalia* of John Sharp of Queen's (B.M., Harleian 2178, fos. 107 ff.).

real makes him concentrate on a feature of his opponents' logic that was to them only secondary.

For a theme of at least equal, perhaps greater, interest to the Oxford logicians was the question of certainty and contingency in the future and of possibility and impossibility in events.

A most interesting manuscript of our period bearing on this problem is MS. Bodleian, Digby 176,[1] a collection of astronomical treatises belonging to William Rede, the Merton bishop of Chichester, and gathered by him, partly with gifts from his patron Nicholas Sandwich, and partly by purchase from the executors of Richard Camsale and Thomas Bradwardine, formerly fellows of Merton. The tracts, which are dated 1337–68, consist of astrologies, predictions and astronomical calculations. Those of Reginald Lambourne are particularly delightful. Lambourne, who had been fellow of Merton in Wyclif's time (both appear in the famous bursarial roll for 1356),[2] later retired to a monastery conveniently close to Oxford; and it was as Reginald, 'a simple monk of Eynsham', that he answered in February 1363 a friend's request to know what the stars foretold. His letter[3] is in fact an astrology, and a gloomy one at that, predicting nothing but bad weather and, on the political scene, only social strife between the people and the great lords of Church and State.

These predictions may do as much credit to Reginald's common sense as to his astronomy; but other tracts in this collection touch on much more serious academic issues. For do not astronomical predictions assume that the future is determined? In such treatises we see the old dispute between determinism and free will, which had long exercised the theologians, raised in the Arts faculty as well, with the difference that, in these cases, it was not the divine will but the stars which might be thought to necessitate the future. This question is examined in a tract in the Digby MS. (fos. 34–9), dated 1357, by another Mertonian, the celebrated John Ashenden;[4] and it is, therefore,

---

[1] Described in Powicke, *Medieval Books of Merton College*, pp. 167–8.
[2] Above, p. 11.
[3] MS. cit., fos. 50r–53v.
[4] Emden, *Biographical Register*, I, 56.

of some interest to note that at the conclusion of his astrology Ashenden enters a formal protestation of the contingency of his predictions.

These things, concerning the meaning of the aforesaid important conclusions, I have written for the use of those studying the science of astronomy, under the aforesaid protestation:

I here protest that it is not my wish to assert that the predicted effects will inevitably or necessarily occur in consequence of these predicted conclusions....But this I wish to assert, that these two conclusions will be signs signifying that these predictions will happen or will be future, in accordance with astronomy and the opinion of those astronomers whom I have cited in this treatise.[1]

Ashenden's words may appear somewhat equivocal, but a further passage in his tract indicates that he wrote in all sincerity and was not a determinist. For he attacks a *socius*, presumably a fellow of his own college, who, on commencing his biblical lectures, proved a determinist proposition (that the exact occurrence of the Day of Judgement is already fixed) by astronomy and other techniques of the Arts faculty. The master, identified in a marginal annotation as 'Aston' (*nota contra Aston*), is perhaps John Aston (fellow of Merton, 1365). Ashenden's words are an apt reminder that men trained in two different disciplines may be preoccupied with much the same problems.

But amongst other new and unheard of things bruited in these days, I greatly wonder at the words of a certain reverend master and fellow, who in that year began to lecture on the Bible at Oxford and who, at the beginning of his reading, as I am reliably informed, publicly asserted and determined in the Schools that there was a certain and determined number of years between the first Flood of water in the time of Noah and the second Flood of fire which is to come, namely

---

[1] MS. cit., fo. 38r. Ista scripsi de significacionibus predictarum conclusionum magnarum pro utilitate studencium in scientia astronomie sub protestacione premissa: protestor etiam adhuc quod mee voluntatis non est asserere quod effectus predicti significati per conclusiones magnas predictas evenient inevitabiliter seu necessario ex predictis conclusionibus magnis....Sed istud volo asserere, quod iste due conclusiones erunt signa quedam signancia predictos futuros effectus contingere seu futuros esse, iuxta sentenciam astronomie et iuxta sentenciam dictorum astronomorum, quos allegavi in hoc tractatu.

7900 years. And he said, as I gather, that he would show this from prophecy and Scripture by proofs of astronomy and philosophy.

I suppose that the aforesaid master wishes to speak of the...Last Judgement and the end of the world, when Christ will come to sit in judgement. But it follows that this master arrives at the same unacceptable conclusion as the Abbot Joachim and so many others, who have tried to determine exactly the date of the end of the world. [We know for certain how much time has elapsed since the Flood...but he presumes] to show and prove that there is a certain and determined, and even known, period until the end of the world, which is, in my judgement and with great respect to all, most rash and presumptuous.[1]

'Dixit se esse ostensurum, pro ut mihi erat intimatum, ex propheciis et scriptura sacra per astronomiam et philosophiam.' Here is valid evidence of the common interests of the two faculties, and a good example of a master employing in theological exercises arguments derived from his studies in the Arts faculty ('philosophia'). And is not Ashenden's tract evidence of the existence of determinism amongst the Artists—else why the need of his protestations of contingency?

Nor is this mingling of the two disciplines surprising, for members of the Faculty of Arts and the theologians were often tackling common problems, many of which could as well be determined 'logically' as 'theologically'. For example, the tracts on *consequentiae* and *obligationes* deal fully with the question of the

[1] Fo. 39v. Sed inter cetera nova inaudita, que hiis diebus proferuntur, multum admiror de quodam reverendo magistro et socio, qui isto anno Oxonie intravit ad bibliam; qui etiam, in principio lecture sue, pro ut mihi erat relatum a fide dignis, publice asseruit et determinavit in scolis certum et determinatum numerum annorum [esse] a diluvio universali aque, qui erat tempore Noe, usque ad diluvium ignis futurum, viz. 7900tos annos; quem quidem numerum annorum dixit se ostensurum, pro ut mihi erat intimatum, ex propheciis et scriptura sacra per astronomiam et philosophiam.

Suppono quod dictus magister vult loqui...de diluvio universali ignis predicto. Cum ergo illud diluvium universale ignis erit in finali iudicio et in fine mundi, quando, videlicet, Christus veniet ad iudicium: sequitur quod iste magister incidit in idem inconveniens in quod incidebat Abbas Joachim et alii, quam plures, qui nitebantur determinare certum et determinatum numerum annorum usque ad finem mundi...[presumit] ergo demonstrare et probare certum et determinatum et cognitum tamen tempus usque ad finem mundi, quod, meo iudicio, magne temeritatis est et magne presumpcionis, salva reverencia cuiuscunque.

possible and the impossible, the inevitable and the contingent. So William Heytesbury, the Merton logician, discusses in his *Sophismata* all aspects of the problem of necessity and future contingents.[1] Can the contingent follow from the necessary? How does the future differ from the present? Is the future equally possible and impossible? And even, is God contingently present in our acts? We can be certain that Aston was not alone in arguing biblical theses on the basis of 'astronomy and philosophy'.

It was in their concern with the problem of possibility and certainty rather than in their terminism, we suggest, that Wyclif conceived his dislike of the 'sign doctors'. Himself convinced that in metaphysics we can by enquiry know everything with absolute assurance and clarity, he could have no sympathy with those who argued that logic might be uncertain in its answers and knowledge indefinite. The modernist interest in 'possibilism' was anathema to Wyclif.

II

The evidence for theological speculation in these years is equally scanty.

MS. Merton College O. 1. 9[2] is a collection of theological *questiones*, arranged according to the four books of the *Sentences*, which originally belonged to Simon Lambourne, fellow of Merton 1347–61, and perhaps a relation of Reginald, the astronomer. References to the *De causa Dei* show that it must have been compiled after *c.* 1344; and we can be reasonably sure, therefore, that Lambourne was the first owner of the work, which he bequeathed to Warden Bloxham. Simon Lambourne was still alive in 1369, when he bought the sumptuous copy of the *De causa Dei* which the Merton Library still possesses,[3] so that the *Questions* may be dated *c.* 1345–70.

The interest lies not in the *Questions* themselves, which are a miscellany 'a variis doctorum scriptis', but in the citations from the *De causa Dei* which throw a welcome light on Mertonian

---

[1] *Hentisberi regulae, videlicet de sensu composito et diviso...item sophismata* (Venice, 1494), soph. 6, fos. 99r–105v.

[2] Coxe 284, described Powicke, *Medieval Books*, p. 187.

[3] MS. K. 2. 6, described Powicke, *op. cit.* pp. 159–60.

reactions to Bradwardine. These are definitely critical, particularly of his voluntarist assertion that God's will is immediate in secondary causes (that is, in human acts). The compiler refers many times (often in the same sentence in which Bradwardine's name occurs) to the condemnation of this thesis as a determinist error by Bishop Tempier in 1277.[1] The key question, 'Utrum voluntas dei sit causa prima et inmediata omnium que hic sint', contains may references to Bradwardine. As the writer admits, the relation of human to divine will is delicate. The voluntarists had argued, he notes, that if man's will can cause God's, men must exist before he has willed them, 'an impossible consequence, and against the Profound Doctor in c. 20 of his first book, where he says that the will of God is the cause of everything subsequently caused'.[2] But what is the logical conclusion of this proposition? If we concede that God is the direct mover of secondary causes, such as the human will, it follows that he is responsible for every act. Bradwardine may repeat, notes the compiler,[3] that all acts are substantially good; but by making God the immediate cause of everything, he bars the usual qualification, that he is not the cause of sin. This argument must lead in the end to the Averroist error, condemned in 1277, which subsumed all secondary causes in the primary and, in fact, destroyed free will.

This question includes a marginal notation in the same hand, which seems to refer to one of the opinions which Jean de Mirecourt had to recant in 1347 (that God actively wills us to sin).[4]

---

[1] MS. cit., fos. 66v, 96r, citing 'Doctorem Profundum in 2⁰ libro suo cap. 18' and 'Doctorem Profundum per scripta'.

[2] Fo. 95v. Item si creatura esset causa voluntatis divine, tunc creatura moveret creatorem divinum. Cum igitur prius naturaliter creatura sit quam ipsa aliquid moveret, sequitur quod prius naturaliter creatura foret quam deus ipsam esse vellet: consequens inpossibile, et contra Doctorem Profundum, in primo libro suo cap. 20, ubi dicit quod voluntas dei est causa omnium posterius causatorum.

[3] Fo. 96r.

[4] Fo. 93r. 'Sed est opinio dampnata a Roberto Parisiensi episcopo, quarta in ordine, quod deus facit aut velit voluntate beneplaciti quod aliquis peccet.' Does this refer to the condemnation of 1347, presided over by Robert de Bardis, Chancellor of the University? Cf. Stegmüller, 'Die zwei Apologien des Jean de Mirecourt', RTAM, v (1933), 194: 2nd apol. art. 4; 'quod deus facit quod aliquis peccet, et quod sit peccator, et quod vult voluntate beneplaciti quod iste sit peccator.'

The compiler of the Merton *Questions* saw clearly the implications of Bradwardine's thesis.

A fortunate survival from this obscure period is a portion of the *Commentary on the Sentences* of Nicholas Aston, fellow of Queen's and Chancellor of the university. Thanks to the researches of Fr S. L. Forte, we can now trace Aston's life and work with some confidence.[1] He first appears in 1350, already a senior fellow of Queen's and a bachelor of theology, and was Chancellor *c.* 1359–61. In June 1362 he is described in a letter from the king to the university as 'nuper cancellarius dicte universitatis'. Only a part of his *Commentary* now survives.[2] MS. Oriel College 15, fos. 210–22 contains twelve questions specifically ascribed to Aston: '12 questiones magistri Nicholai Aston Oxonie disputatae' (fo. 210r). But MS. Worcester Cathedral Library F 65, a theological miscellany dated 1350–70, also contains fourteen questions (fos. 42–63), written as a single treatise, eight of which are substantially identical with those in the Oriel MS. Fr Forte has shown that, of the total of sixteen questions, all but two can be confidently ascribed to Aston. Since Aston was a B.Theol. in 1350, his *Sentences* must have been read at that time.

Though apparently only a surviving portion of a larger work, his questions merit examination because they reveal a strong interest in those topics (determinism and free will, necessity and contingency, the question of possibility) whose attraction for other Oxford masters has already been noted. Indeed the techniques of the logician are so apparent that Aston's questions can be taken as a casebook example of the interaction of logical and theological arguments.

He is not a terminist, criticising 'a reverend master who says that things are nothing but substance and quality'[3] (who is either

---

[1] S. L. Forte, *A Study of Some Oxford Schoolmen of the Middle of the Fourteenth Century* (Oxford B.Litt., 1947), I, 35–44; II, 142–63; Emden, *Biographical Register*, I, 68.

[2] Thus MS. Oriel 15, fo. 215v[b]. 'quod inprobatur super primum librum articulo primo.' Fo. 211r[a]. 'Illud quod mihi videtur esse tenendum in illo dubio, dicam in 3° libro, tractando de incarnacione verbi et in fine quarti libri, tractando numquid antichristus incarnabitur.' Cited Forte, *loc. cit.*

[3] Fo. 211r[a].

Ockham or a disciple); but he is deeply interested in 'problems of necessity and possibility'. Is the past necessarily past, and is it God's will that has made it so? Or is it merely contingent, so that it might not have been?[1] Aston's reply is tinged with 'possibilism'. The first cause, he says, from which everything derives, must be absolutely free. It is possible, therefore, for God to will an object to exist now and not to will its past existence in the future; thus he has a double volition which is not necessarily contradictory.[2] The same interest in the 'extension of possibility' is shown in Aston's discussion of the necessity of the present ('Utrum id quod nunc est sit possibile quod non est nunc'). One can either argue, he says, that God wills the present as contingently as the future, so that he can cause existing things not to be, or that the future is contingent but the present irrevocable. His reply reduces the element of necessity in the universe to the absolute minimum: 'the third (solution) is that which I wish to hold, that everything except God is contingent'.[3]

Aston maintains his belief in contingency, whilst admitting that God must concur in every act. Do human actions then necessarily and always require God's co-operation? Scotus had thought that if secondary acts are contingent, the first cause must act contingently towards them. This Aston refuses to accept; God's necessary concurrence had been confirmed in the condemnations of 1277. But he denies that this destroys free will because, though his concurrence is infinite, its actual effect is not.[4] Are we to deduce, then, that the divine will determines future contingents? Theologians customarily say, notes Aston, either that God wills before he knows, or *vice versa*. But, after all, what is the point of these distinctions? The first was made to avoid admitting that God

[1] Fo. 214v[b]. Utrum omne preteritum necessario sit preteritum.

[2] Fo. 215r[b]. Ad questionem, supponendo primum agens esse principium summe liberum, et quod nihil agit ad extra, nec agere potest, nisi libere contradictorie...non ex hoc quod deus vult A esse presens, sequitur quod deus volet in futurum A esse preteritum. Stant igitur simul deus vult A esse presens et deus nunquam volet A esse preteritum.

[3] Fo. 219v[a]. Tercia est, quam volo tenere, quod omne quod non est deus est contingens ad utrumlibet, et omnis proposicio est contingens ad utrumlibet, excepta illa 'deus' vel convertibilis cum ea.

[4] Fo. 213v[b].

can be the cause of sin (by showing that he knew it before willing it); and the second was made by the extreme voluntarists to prove that nothing exists prior to God's willing it. Aston rejects this approach and, like Richard FitzRalph, proposes a solution that stems from God's knowledge of the *ydea* of things. God, he declares, has a simple and perfect idea of all effects, actual or potential, in which everything remains contingent; and the purpose of his will, as Bradwardine has said, is to select those future events which will occur from the possible futures that will not.[1] God, therefore, possesses an absolute freedom to will the future, which, however, cannot make him the cause of sin, for this is the immediate consequence of human volition, the *voluntas creata*. His will in respect of sin is neutral—'non velle nec nolle'—since the act, whether good or evil, never loses the possibility of not occurring, of being otherwise than it is.

Though the *questiones* on necessity and uncertainty and the 'logic of contradictories' are the most interesting of the surviving part of Aston's *Sentences*, one reference to another question is justified. In a question on the relation of grace to sin,[2] Aston discusses the proposition that, since God can grant or remove his gifts at will, their presence or absence does not necessarily depend on whether we are in grace or sin. For God, it has been argued,

---

[1] Fo. 213 v^b–214 r^a. Utrum certa previsio futurorum contingencium sit ex predeterminacione voluntatis divine. In ista materia sunt duo opiniones: / prima ponit deum scire prius futurum fore quam velle; et secunda econtra. Racio prime opinionis est talis; non videtur isti opinioni aliunde posse vitare deum esse auctorem peccati, nisi ponendo scientiam dei complexam futurorum preordinare voluntatem divinam respectu eorumdem. Sed contra illam pro parte articuli affirmativa sic arguo: doctores catholici omnes quasi sic ymaginantur quod essencia divina est quasi speculum clarissimum infinitum, nihil ab obiecto paciens, recipiens aut reflectens, sed active, et ex sua infinitissima claritate, distincte non confuse, ydeas omnium intelligibilium obiectorum proferens, in quod speculum intellectus divinus perspiciens hec omnia speculatur. Videns autem intellectus divinus determinacionem voluntatis sue, quoad distinctionem possibilium futurorum a non futuris, eam esse infrustrabilem et inpedibilem, certitudinaliter scit quod hoc erit per determinacionem voluntatis sue...item ad idem: sic distinctio possibilium futurorum a non futuris est per actum voluntatis divine, sicut tenet Doctor Subtilis, I Sent. dist. 39, et similiter Doctor Profundus, libro primo cap. 17 & 18, tenet illud idem.

[2] Fo. 215 v^a. Utrum positivum vel privativum formaliter opponitur peccato.

can deprive us of justification, though we continue to show merit; whilst, on the other hand, it is possible for sinners to be justified. Moreover, he adds, it has been said that, because Adam was deprived of grace before the Fall, there may possibly be a *medius status* between grace and sin, where the presence of the one does not involve the deprivation of the other.[1] This is, of course, precisely the argument put forward by Thomas Buckingham in *questio* 6 of his *Commentary on the Sentences*,[2] from which Aston is undoubtedly quoting. It is interesting to find a proposition so characteristic of the 'modernist' disputes of the 1330's repeated nearly twenty years later.

Finally, no discussion, however brief, of Oxford theology, 1350-70, can ignore the case of Uthred Boldon, the Durham Benedictine, certain of whose propositions were censured by Archbishop Langham in November 1368. Since the contents of Uthred's articles and the occasion of their censure have recently been printed and fully analysed,[3] we need only try to assess their value for the course of speculation at Oxford in these years.

In the first place, the articles are by far the most radical document which appears to have survived for this period, to be compared in their extremism only with the work of Wyclif and Bradwardine. In this sense they stand apart from the rest of the material here noticed; for they reveal a degree of Ockhamist influence, especially as regards the sanctifying nature of grace, which we have not succeeded in finding in other contemporaries at Oxford. It is legitimate to argue whether the tracts examined in this chapter are, or are not, 'modernist' or 'Ockhamist'; for these propositions totally lack the clarity, boldness, indeed truculence of

---

[1] Fo. 216r^a. Hic arguitur per auctoritates, quod gracia non formaliter opponitur peccato, sed est dare medium statum; aliter forte diceret aliquis quod gracia formaliter opponitur peccato. Sed contra arguitur sic: angeli ante casum et primi parentes in statu innocencie erant sine gracia et sine culpa mortali, et per consequens est status medius possibilis ut pena, quod aliquis homo sit qui nec sit filius regni nec perdicionis, igitur gracia et peccatum non formaliter repugnant.

[2] Cf. Buckingham, ed. cit., fo. 16v^b, and above, p. 43.

[3] D. Knowles, 'The Censured Opinions of Uthred of Boldon', *Proc. Brit. Acad.* XXXVII (1951), 305-42; *idem, Religious Orders in England*, II, 83-9; Pantin, *The English Church*, pp. 166-75.

Uthred Boldon's retorts to William Jordan and the friars. The episode only serves to underline how insufficient is the evidence for making generalisations about Oxford thought at this time. But at least the articles confirm the supposition that the supernatural quality of grace and the reality of the 'clear vision'[1] continued to be important topics of controversy and discussion. And Uthred's concept of grace was unquestionably, for all his glosses, thoroughly Pelagian,[2] whilst his development of the doctrine of the 'clear vision', though nobly intentioned for the benefit of the 'theologically depressed classes' (in Professor Knowles' phrase), led him to take up a position surprisingly vulnerable for so able a mind. For in widening the field of salvation to include all men Christian or pagan, adult or child, who chose to respond at the moment of death to the 'clear vision' of God, Uthred necessarily questioned the value and efficacy of the Church's sacraments and of the moral conduct of the individual in his life. He took no account of the inevitable implications of his thesis.

One of Uthred's articles, however, was a herald of the future rather than an echo of the past: his passionate belief in the impossibility of annihilation. Not only did he assert this, he retorted to the friars, but he had done so for a long time: 'this article I have very often held and argued, and here reason tells me that it is true'.[3] And a monk of Worcester, studying at Oxford at this time, thought it worth while to note down Uthred's proposition on annihilation as well as an attack by a fellow master on his concept of the 'clear vision'.[4] We cannot say definitely that Uthred

---

[1] Cf. Knowles, 'Censured Opinions', pp. 314–25.

[2] Uthred denied that the justified receive the infused habit of grace, defining the state of grace as a mere right relationship to God. This is a key question for distinguishing Ockhamists from orthodox; cf. Knowles, 'Censured Opinions', pp. 337–8, Uthred's articles 14, 17.

[3] *Ibid.* p. 334, Uthred's article 2. 'Quod deus non potest aliquod anichilare.' Hunc articulum sepius tenui et persuasi, et adhuc dictat mihi ratio quod sit verus.

[4] MS. Worcester Cathedral F 65, fo. 19v. 'Conclusio: si aliqua sit creatura creabilis a deo quam non potest deus in esse conservare, aliqua tamen potest esse creatura non plus ens quam illa data, quam non potest deus adnichilare.' Though anonymous, this conclusion follows one attributed to Uthred in this MS. and concerned with the 'clear vision'. Cf. Forte, *op. cit.* II, 112; Knowles, 'Censured Opinions', p. 316.

drew this opinion from Wyclif; but he does not claim it as his own, and it seems likely that we have here 'evidence of the commanding position of Wyclif at Oxford in philosophical matters'.

The occasion of the censure of Uthred Boldon's propositions throws a welcome light on the Oxford of Wyclif's youth. First, there is the obvious fluidity of doctrine; as Professor Knowles notes, the episode 'shows clearly how eclectic and personal theological teaching at Oxford had become, and how easily a master could leave the paths of traditional doctrine to pursue some favourite theory of his own'.[1] And these words surely apply as forcefully to metaphysics as to theology, and to Wyclif as much as to Uthred. Two decades of uncertain purpose or direction in speculation were ideally suited for the sudden efflorescence of a powerful, dogmatic and eccentric philosopher. Secondly, the first intervention by Canterbury in a scholastic dispute for many years was a portent. Pecham and Kilwardby had intervened on several occasions, but after the Thomist disputes had died away, the archbishops had left Oxford in peace—even during the Ockhamist controversies. Simon Langham's censure heralded a change; within a few years, with the rise of Wyclif and Lollardy, would come the interventions first of Courtenay and then of Arundel, with lasting effects upon intellectual life at Oxford.

Whatever new evidence comes to light is unlikely, we suggest, to upset the view that the period 1350–70 was one of grave decline in scholastic studies at Oxford. And it is this, rather than the importance of any particular current of opinion, which is to be remembered when assessing the nature of Wyclif's impact on the university. However, it seems clear that, with variants, the same topics which had been fought out in the schools in the great decades 1325–45 continued to be debated there. This continuity of themes, from 1325 to 1370, combined with the lack of distinction in the men of his own day, together explain what to the student of the early Wyclif is the most puzzling feature of all—the dismissal of his contemporaries (when they merit notice at all) as 'sign-doctors', and the repeated return to Bradwardine and Fitz-Ralph, philosophers of the previous generation. Wyclif appears to

[1] *Ibid.* p. 330.

have been justified in this; though his metaphysics were his own, in his theology he faced the same issues that had stirred 'Profundus' and 'Ardmachanus'.

Wyclif can have found little to excite or attract him in the Oxford of *c.* 1360. In comparison with the international centre of thirty years before, it must have seemed a university which pestilence, war and the play of chance had reduced to something very like provincialism.

PART II
THE 'SUMMA DE ENTE'

CHAPTER V

THE STRUCTURE OF THE
'SUMMA DE ENTE'

I

THE study of Wyclif's academic philosophy is seriously complicated by the difficulty of dating the composition of his treatises. Despite the careful investigations of the past seventy years the position is still very much as described by Professor Harrison Thomson in his important paper, 'The Order of Writing of Wyclif's Philosophical Works'.[1] Even when the editing of the Wyclif canon is complete, Thomson noted, we may not be absolutely sure that a satisfactory chronology has been arrived at.

We have, probably, no original MS. extant. Our earliest datable copies come from the 1390's. Most of the Wyclif MSS. come from the first two decades of the fifteenth century, one, very valuable, is dated 1433, and another 1449. The texts bear evidence of editing. It is almost certain that Wyclif did not publish any tractate before the lectures had been delivered and corrected several times. Cross-references may thus represent as anterior a work which was actually begun a matter of years later. This possibility raises difficulties which can only be solved, if at all, by a prolonged and minute study of the subject-matter, with the aid of a better knowledge of the philosophical disputes taking place in the Oxford of his day.[2]

All we can say with assurance is that Wyclif's works can be divided into those composed before and after c. 1373. In the first category lie his academic non-controversial studies in logic, physics, metaphysics and theology; in the second the polemical writings on doctrine and politics. Bridging the two are the tracts written against Kenningham, the Carmelite, which certainly

[1] In Českou Minulosti (Prague, 1929), pp. 146–65.
[2] Ibid. pp. 146–7.

belong to the period 1371–3;[1] and the biblical commentary,[2] which may have been begun when Wyclif was B.Theol., but which must have taken several years to 'read' in the Faculty of Theology. Contemporary allusions make it possible to date the later works without great difficulty; but, not surprisingly, the academic philosophy has no such references. The twenty-two treatises, therefore, which scholars agree Wyclif composed before his controversy with Kenningham and emergence into national politics remain dated only within the wide margin, c. 1356–73. Thomson carefully limited his aim to investigating 'the order of writing' of the philosophical works, and pointed out that the examination of cross-references is bound to be inconclusive where no original manuscripts survive.[3]

Our only other guide is knowledge of the accustomed order of composition in the schools. The treatises of both master and student were in general the product not of the vagaries of individual research but of the requirements of public disputation and lecturing. In the subjects pursued in the Arts faculty we can expect a progress from logic and logical disputation to metaphysics and physics or mathematics; whilst from the rigid distinction between the two faculties it follows that 'philosophical' works must be prior to any whose subject is pure theology. Since Wyclif incepted in theology as a bachelor in 1368–9,[4] his academic treatises can with some assurance be dated before or after these years according to subject-matter. It is interesting to see that the order of writing deduced by Thomson purely on the basis of internal references, corresponds precisely to such a grouping of tracts, arranged according to Wyclif's progress in the schools. So we have at least no reason to despair of arriving at a fairly reliable order of composition.

Yet these facts would seem to pose many difficulties in assessing the place and purpose of the great treatise commonly known as

[1] Printed FZ, pp. 453–80.
[2] B. Smalley, 'John Wyclif's Postilla super totam bibliam', Bodleian Library Record, IV (1953), 186–205.
[3] Thomson, 'The Order of Writing...', p. 147.
[4] See above, p. 15.

the *Summa de Ente*. This survives in one almost complete copy, MS. Trinity College, Cambridge, B. 16. 2, fos. 1–141, and in one partially preserved copy, MS. Vienna, Nat. Bibl. ccccvi (4307), fos. 158a–242b. It is not, however, an original composition, conceived and executed at one time, but an edited version of a number of treatises, composed by Wyclif over a period of years prior to *c.* 1372, and later arranged as a *Summa* in two books, containing seven and six tracts respectively. At this time a number of interpolations and many cross-references were added. Four of these tracts are known only in the two copies or partial copies of the *Summa* mentioned above. One is complete only in the Trinity manuscript; another is unique in the Vienna manuscript. But of several of the other tracts many copies survive.

Since we must now discuss the composition of the *Summa de Ente*, and the relation which the treatises incorporated therein bear to the rest of Wyclif's philosophical writings that were excluded, we now print a table of manuscripts of the individual treatises contained in the *Summa*. It is drawn from the printed authorities; and, no doubt, additions, particularly to those cited from Vienna, Prague and Cracow, will have to be made when a full catalogue of Wyclif MSS. appears. But the relative abundance or scarcity of texts of the individual treatises in the *Summa* gives some value to the list for purposes of comparison.

The table (incomplete though it may prove to be) illustrates satisfactorily the considerable variation in the numbers of surviving copies of the works contained in the *Summa*; and from it we can draw an interesting comparison, or contrast, between relative contemporary popularity and the value the different treatises may have for the student today. For example, we list nineteen copies of the *De Universalibus*, twelve of the *De Tempore*, thirteen of the *De Ydeis*. This wide distribution accurately reflects the importance of these treatises as an exposition of Wyclif's realism, and in this study they form the basis of our analysis of the principles of his metaphysics. The four preliminary tracts, Book I, tracts 1–4, on the other hand, are found only in the two codices of the 'edited' *Summa*. They are comparatively brief, and much less important than the two big metaphysical treatises of Book I, to which they form a 'logical introduction'. The remaining tract of Book I, *De ente praedicamentali*, is unique in the partially complete Vienna codex of the *Summa*. It is undoubtedly genuine; but the manuscript is late (1433),[1] and the work itself appears to be a restatement of earlier opinions, and certainly composed after Wyclif had taken his doctorate in theology.

With the treatises of Book II, on the other hand, importance seems to be matched by rarity. We know of only two copies of Book II, tracts 1–3; and as regards Book II, tract 6, we can add to the unique complete text in the Trinity MS. only some two chapters in MS. Prague University 1762 (IX. E. 6). But these works are of the utmost value in establishing Wyclif's attitude to the theological controversies of his day (and, in particular, to those discussed in Part I of this study). Yet their importance for the historian was not, apparently, matched by an equal interest amongst Wyclif's contemporaries, who were much more excited by his metaphysical novelties. So we may contrast the meagre survival of these works with the seven listed manuscripts of the *De Trinitate*, an exercise (in our opinion) much less rewarding, in which the unity of the Trinity is demonstrated by realist principles.

MSS. of tracts in the 'Summa de Ente'[2]

BOOK I

Tract 1, *De ente in communi*

Trinity Coll. Camb. B. 16. 2, fos. 1 r–5 v.
Vienna, Nat. Bibl. ccccvi (4307), fos. 158 a–167 a.
    Ed. Thomson, *De Ente*, pp. 1–61.

---

[1] Thomson, 'The Order of Writing', p. 153.
[2] The majority of the treatises are to be found either in the National-Bibliothek, Vienna, or in the University Library, Prague. For the Vienna MSS. listed below, roman numerals refer to the description in M. Denis, *Codices manuscripti theologici Bibliothecae Palatinae Vindobonensis* (2 vols. in 5 parts, 1793–1802), vol. I; arabic numerals refer to *Tabulae codicum manuscriptorum...in Bibliotheca Palatina Vindobonensi*, ed. Academia Caesarea Vindobonensis (7 vols., 1864–75). References for Prague MSS. are to J. Truhlar, *Catalogus codicum manuscriptorum latinorum qui in C.R. Bibliotheca...asservantur* (2 vols., 1906). The

Tract 2, *De ente primo*

Trinity Coll. Camb. B. 16. 2, fos. 5v–9r.
Vienna, Nat. Bibl. ccccvi (4307), fos. 167b–177a.
Ed. Thomson, *De Ente*, pp. 62–112.

Tract 3, *Purgans errores circa veritates*

Trinity Coll. Camb. B. 16. 2, fos. 9v–12r.
Vienna, Nat. Bibl. ccccvi (4307), fos. 177b–184a.
Ed., from the Trinity MS. only, in Dziewicki, *De Ente*, pp. 1–28.
For the Vienna MS., which supplies lacunae in the Trinity MS., see
S. H. Thomson, 'A "lost" Chapter of Wyclif's *Summa de Ente*',
Speculum, IV (1929), 339–46.

Tract 4, *Purgans errores circa universalia*

Trinity Coll. Camb. B. 16. 2, fos. 12v–14v.
Vienna, Nat. Bibl. ccccvi (4307), fos. 185a–190a.
Ed., from the Trinity MS. only, Dziewicki, *De Ente*, pp. 29–48;
cf. also Thomson, *loc. sit. supra*.

Tract 5, *De Ente praedicamentali*

Vienna, Nat. Bibl. ccccvi (4307), fos. 190b–242b.
Ed. R. Beer, *De ente praedicamentali* (*WS*, 1891). The tract is described
in Denis, vol. I, pt. 2, col. 1512, as 'de ente particulari'.

Tract 6, *De universalibus*

Trinity Coll. Camb. B. 16. 2, fos. 15r–36r.
Lincoln Cathedral C. 1. 15, fos. 293–324 (R. M. Woolley, *Catalogue of
the manuscripts of Lincoln Cathedral Chapter Library* (1927), p. 124,
no. 159).
Vienna, Nat. Bibl. ccccvi (4307), fos. 62b–114b.
Vienna, Nat. Bibl. cccxc (4523), fos. 58a–132b.
Prague University 535 (III. G. 10), fos. 70a–104b.
Prague University 773 (IV. H. 9), fos. 1a–52b.
Prague University 993 (V. H. 16), fos. 1a–78a.

relevant catalogues for other MSS. are given in the text. MS. Trinity College,
Cambridge, B. 16. 2 is described in M. R. James, *The Western Manuscripts in the
Library of Trinity College, Cambridge* (1908), I, 513, no. 378. The basis of this list
is W. Shirley, *Catalogue of the Original Works of John Wyclif* (rev. edn by J.
Loserth, 1924), pp. 2–3, which is the source of information, unless otherwise
stated. Where this list is supplemented, the authority is given.

Prague University 1555 (VIII. F. 1), fos. 1a–39a.

Prague University 1588 (VIII. G. 6), fos. 1a–57a.

Prague University 1605 (VIII. G. 23), fos. 1a–84a.

Vienna, Nat. Bibl. 5204 (*olim* Philos. 420, not in Denis), fos. 1a–65b.
(See Thomson, 'Unnoticed Manuscripts and Works of Wyclif',
Journal of Theological Studies, XXXVIII (1937), 140.)

Prague University, Lobkovice 153, fos. 3a–71a (see Thomson, *loc. cit.*
pp. 29–30).

Escorial e. 11. 6, fos. 104a–124b (*Catálogo de los códices latinos...del
Escorial* (Madrid, 1910–16), II, 38; and see Thomson, *loc. cit.* p. 27).

Venice, San Marco Cl. VI. 172, fos. 27c–78c (see Thomson, *loc. cit.*
p. 28).

Gonville and Caius 337/565, fos. 1–47 (M. R. James, *The Western
Manuscripts...of Gonville and Caius College, Cambridge*, I, 380; and
see Thomson, 'A Gonville and Caius Wyclif Manuscript',
Speculum, VIII (1933), 197–204).

Bibl. Vat., lat. 4313, fos. 1–31b (see I. H. Stein, 'Two Notes on Wyclif',
Speculum, VI (1931), 465).

Pavia University 311 (139. G. 46), fos. 1–35 (L. de Marchi and G.
Bertolani, *Inventario...della R. biblioteca universitaria di Pavia*
(1894), I, 170; and see Stein, *loc. cit.* p. 466).

Stockholm, Royal Library 9, fos. 87–134 (B. Dudik, *Forschungen in
Schweden für Mährens Geschichte* (Brunn, 1852), pp. 201–2; ed.
Dziewicki, *Johannis Wyclif Miscellanea Philosophica* (*WS*, 1901),
I, li).

Cracow, Jagellonian Library 1855, unspecified foliations (W.
Wislocki, *Catalogus codicum manuscriptorum bibliothecae universitatis
Jagellonicae Cracoviensis* (Cracow, 1877–81), p. 441; and cf.
Thomson, 'Some Latin Works Erroneously Ascribed to Wyclif',
Speculum, III (1928), 383).

Tract 7, *De tempore*

Trinity Coll. Camb. B. 16. 2, fos. 37r–46 (*bis*)r.

Vienna, Nat. Bibl. ccccvii (4316), fos. 85a–125a.

Prague University 1555 (VIII. F. 1), fos. 87a–113a.

Prague University 535 (III. G. 10), fos. 31a–69b.

Prague University 773 (IV. H. 9), fos. 94a–113b.

Trinity College, Dublin, C. 1. 23 (T. K. Abbott, *Catalogue of
the Manuscripts...of Trinity College, Dublin* (1900), p. 35,
no. 242).

Lincoln Cathedral C. 1. 15, fos. 325–40 (Woolley, *loc. cit.* p. 124, no. 159).

Prague University, Lobkovice 153, fos. 75a–109a (see Thomson, 'Unnoticed Manuscripts and Works of Wyclif', *Journ. Theol. Studies*, XXXVIII (1937), 30).

Venice, San Marco Cl. VI 172, fos. 1a–27c (see Thomson, *loc. cit.* p. 28).

Pavia University 311 (139. G. 46), fos. 48b–49d, 51a–d, 50a–d, 52a–57d, 59a–d, 58a–d, 60a–61d, 38a–42a (Marchi and Bertolani, *op. cit.* p. 170. The leaves have become disordered; see Stein, 'Two Notes on Wyclif', *Speculum*, VI (1931), 466).

Gonville and Caius 337/565, fo. 48v (Prologue only; see Thomson, 'A Gonville and Caius Wyclif Manuscript', *Speculum*, VIII (1933), 198).

Stockholm, Royal Library 22, fos. 1–33 (Dudik, *op. cit.* pp. 198–9; ed. Dziewicki, *Johannis Wyclif Miscellanea Philosophica* (*WS*, 1901), I, xlix).

BOOK II

Tract 1, *De intellectione Dei*

Trinity Coll. Camb. B. 16. 2, fos. 47r–54r.
Prague University 1762 (IX. E. 6), fos. 1–15v.
Ed., from the Trinity MS. only, Dziewicki, *De Ente*, pp. 29–112.
See I. H. Stein, 'Another "lost" Chapter of Wyclif's *Summa de Ente*', *Speculum*, VIII (1933), 254–5.

Tract 2, *De scientia Dei*

Trinity Coll. Camb. B. 16. 2, fos. 54r–70v.
Prague University 1762 (IX. E. 6), fos. 16r–51r (see Stein, *loc. cit.*).

Tract 3, *De volucione Dei*

Trinity Coll. Camb. B. 16. 2, fos. 71r–92r.
Prague University 1763 (IX. E. 6), fos. 55v–96v (see Stein, *loc. cit.*).
Ed., from the Trinity MS. only, Dziewicki, *De Ente*, pp. 113–286.

Tract 4, *De Trinitate* (or *De personarum distinctione*)

Trinity Coll. Camb. B. 16. 2, fos. 92r–116r.
Vienna, Nat. Bibl. ccclxxviii (1337), fos. 182a–243b.
Vienna, Nat. Bibl. ccclxxxiv (1387), fos. 47a–74b.

Vienna, Nat. Bibl. ccccvii (4316), fos. 1a–79a.
Vienna, Nat. Bibl. ccccx (3925), fos. 237a–271a.
Prague University 1615 (VIII. G. 32), fos. 83a–143b.
Prague, Bibl. Metrop. 1543, fos. 13a–57a.

The seven known MSS. of the *De Trinitate* are described by A. du P. Breck, 'The Manuscripts of John Wyclif's *De Trinitate*', *Medievalia et Humanistica*, VII (1952), 56–70.

Tract 5, *De Ydeis*

Trinity Coll. Camb. B. 16. 2, fos. 116r–122v.
Vienna, Nat. Bibl. ccclxxviii (1337), fos. 244a–258b.
Vienna, Nat. Bibl. clxxxi (4002), fos. 42a–52a.
Vienna, Nat. Bibl. cccxc (4523), fos. 133a–156a.
Prague University 1555 (VIII. F. 1), fos. 73b–87a.
Prague University 535 (III. G. 10), fos. 119a–137b.
Prague University 773 (IV. H. 9), fos. 114a–130b.
Prague University 993 (V. H. 16), fos. 79a–100a.
Escorial e. 11. 6, fos. 97b–103c (*Catálogo...del Escorial*, II, 38; and see Thomson, *Journ. Theol. Studies*, XXXVIII (1937), 27).
Prague University, Lobkovice 153, fos. 167a–187a (see Thomson, *loc. cit.* p. 30).
Pavia University 311 (139. G. 46), fos. 42b–47d, 72a–76b (Marchi and Bertolani, *op. cit.* p. 170; I. H. Stein, 'Two Notes on Wyclif', *Speculum*, VI (1931), 466).
Stockholm, Royal Library 9, fos. 33–52 (Dudik, *op. cit.* p. 199; ed. Dziewicki, *Johannis Wyclif Miscellanea Philosophica* (*WS*, 1901), I, xlix).
Cracow, Jagellonian Library 1855, unspecified foliations (Wislocki, *op. cit.* p. 441).

Tract 6, *De potencia Dei productiva ad extra*

Trinity Coll. Camb. B. 16. 2, fos. 123r–141r.
Prague University 1762 (IX. E. 6), fos. 51r–55v (chaps. 1–2 only).

From the Trinity MS., chaps. 12–14, fos. 135r^b–138v^b, are printed by Dziewicki, *De Ente*, pp. 287–315.

II

The overwhelming preponderance of Bohemian manuscripts (now in the libraries of Vienna and Prague) is clear at a glance. Wyclif's realism, as well as his radicalism, found there a ready acceptance, and his philosophical works were copied countless times in the early fifteenth century. Unfortunately the destruction of manuscripts that followed the condemnation of Wyclif's teaching by the Council of Constance was by no means confined to his later and controversial writings. At Prague in 1410 over two hundred codices were burned by order of Archbishop Zbynek. In England too there was much destruction. Happily some owners of works of Wyclif were content merely to erase the evidence of his authorship. Nearly all the surviving English manuscripts of his academic treatises are, or have been rendered, acephalous.[1]

Nevertheless it is with an English manuscript that we are principally concerned. MS. Trinity College, Cambridge, B. 16. 2[2] is a sumptuous codex, written in a fine late fourteenth-century English hand, and having some fine illuminated initials. It was given to the college by Nevile (Master 1593–1615), but of its previous history nothing is known. It contains the following works, all by Wyclif.

Summa. Fos. 1–141.
Sermones. Fos. 142–352 (ed. J. Loserth, 4 vols., *WS*, 1887–90).
De sermone dominicali in monte (i.e. *Opus Evangelicum*, ed. J. Loserth, 2 vols., *WS*, 1895–6).

The first work, as we have noted, consists of twelve treatises, all of which are to be found, independently or in groups, in other manuscripts. It was first described by Bernard[3] in his *Catalogi* (1697) as 'Joannes Wicliff, de ente universali et attributis divinis': an accurate description of its contents. In John Lewis' life of

---

[1] Examples of erasure of Wyclif's name in Oxford manuscripts are given by Miss Smalley, 'John Wyclif's Postilla super totam bibliam', p. 188; and, for the *De incarnacione Verbi*, by L. Minio-Paluello, 'Two Erasures in MS. Oriel College 15', *Bodleian Library Record*, IV (1953), 205–7.

[2] James, *The Western Manuscripts*, I, 513. Described also in *Iohannis Wyclif Sermones*, ed. J. Loserth (*WS*, 1886), I, xxxv–xxxvii, and A. du P. Breck, 'The Manuscripts of John Wyclif's De Trinitate', *Medievalia et Humanistica*, VII (1952), 58–60. See also Dziewicki, ed., *De Ente*, introd. pp. vii–viii, and Thomson, ed., *De Ente*, introd. pp. x–xiii.

[3] Edward Bernard, *Catalogi librorum manuscriptorum Angliae et Hiberniae* (Oxford, 1697), p. 96 of second series of pagination.

Wyclif (2nd edn, 1820), it is called simply a 'MS. volume of tracts'.[1] It is in Shirley's catalogue[2] of 1865 that the work begins to acquire a name. In his Introduction, Shirley prints (pp. xiv-xvi) a description of the Trinity codex, supplied by Bradshaw, the University Librarian, who cautiously follows Bernard and Lewis in describing the first work as 'containing some of Wyclif's Philosophical Treatises, arranged in two books'. But by page 2 of his catalogue the work is entitled *De ente sive Summa Intellectualium*. Now the Trinity manuscript is acephalous, as Shirley himself states in a note (p. 2 n. 2), in which he explains how he came to adopt this double title. The first part was drawn from the partial text of the *Summa* in MS. Vienna, Nat. Bibl. ccccvi (4307) (to be described hereafter), where Book 1, tract 2, begins (fo. 167v), 'Incipit tractatus secundus libri primi de ente primo in communi'. The second part was deduced from Bale,[3] who lists a *Summa intellectualium lib. I* by Wyclif, 'a title which', states Shirley, 'seems to correspond to the present collection of treatises'.

Neither of these deductions is sound. The first title (*De ente primo in communi*) is that of tract 2 itself,[4] and not that either of Book 1 (for which it would be not inappropriate), or of the whole work (for which it would be most misleading). And the second can be no more than a guess. If Bale's cryptic reference is indeed to this manuscript, the title is his own; and, on the other hand, the catalogues of some monastic libraries point, as will be shown,[5] to the existence of other philosophical *Summae* of Wyclif. In truth the work has no title, and we would not quarrel with the one Bernard bestowed on it. But later writers on Wyclif (especially the Wyclif Society editors) accepted Shirley's description without his cautionary qualification. Dziewicki, for example, the editor of four tracts of the *Summa* (*WS*, 1909), refers to 'Wyclif's great philosophical "Summa Intellectualium", called also "De Ente"'.[6]

---

[1] J. Lewis, *The History of the Life and Sufferings of the Reverend and Learned John Wiclif D.D.* (new edn, 1820), pp. 185-6.

[2] W. Shirley, *Catalogue of the Original Works of John Wyclif*.

[3] J. Bale, *Scriptorum illustrium maioris Brytannie...Catalogus* (Basle, 1559), p. 452, 'Summam [*sic*] intellectualium lib. I'.

[4] Cf. Thomson, ed., *De Ente*, p. 62.   [5] See below, pp. 127-8.

[6] Dziewicki, ed., *De Ente*, p. v.

Subsequent writers have generally called it the *Summa de Ente*; and as a matter of convenience we continue to do so. But we must recognise that this title is not the author's, and is only partially accurate; for the *Summa* is as much, if not more, concerned with the 'divine attributes' as with 'being'.

Of this acephalous work, an edited version of a number of treatises, two copies survive. One is complete (or perhaps lacks a single tract); the other is truncated. The first, MS. Trinity Coll. Camb. B. 16. 2, fos. 1–141, is divided into two Books of six tractates each. At the head of the pages stand running titles, 'li. primus tr. 5, de universalibus', 'li. secundus tr. 2, de scientia dei', and so forth. It ends (fo. 141r) 'explicit tractatus Magistri J.W. de potentia dei'. The second, MS. Vienna, Nat. Bibl. ccccvi (4307)[1] is a codex containing the following treatises:

Sharp, tractatus de anima, fo. 1.
Wyclif, de compositione hominis, fo. 38 (dated 1432).
Wyclif, de universalibus, fo. 62 (dated 1433).
Wyclif, de incarnacione verbi, fo. 115 (dated 1433).
Wyclif, de ente in communi, fos. 158–167.
Wyclif, de ente primo in communi, fos. 167–177.
Wyclif, purgando errores circa veritates, fos. 177–184.
Wyclif, purgando errores circa universalia, fos. 185–190.
Wyclif, de ente praedicamentali, fos. 190–242.

The date of copying of three of these treatises is given as 1432–3, and the whole MS. may be taken as of this period. But it was Beer[2] who demonstrated that the present MS. consists of two parts, a separate work beginning on fo. 158. The four following tracts are a text of the *Summa*, Book I, tracts 1–4. They have the same running titles—'liber primus, tractatus primus', 'tractatus secundus', and so on; and the unique text of the *De ente praedicamentali*, as Beer noted,[3] is described (fo. 190) as 'tractatus quintus'. It is interesting to note that in the Trinity MS., though the *De*

---

[1] See Denis, *op. cit.* I, part 2, col. 1510 (which is incomplete); *Tab. cod....in bib. pal. vind.* III, 236 (also incomplete); Thomson, ed., *De Ente*, introd. pp. xiii–xv.
[2] R. Beer, ed., *De ente praedicamentali*, introd. pp. vi–ix.
[3] *Ibid.* p. viii.

Universalibus is numbered as the fifth treatise in Book I, there is a gap of a column and a half at the end of tract 4, and that here the four remaining leaves of the quire have been cancelled.[1] It may, therefore, have been the intention of the scribe of the Trinity MS. to insert later a text of the *De ente praedicamentali*, adding a fresh quire of the requisite length.

But Beer also showed that fos. 158–242 of the Vienna codex are but the trunk of a complete version of the *Summa*.[2] For they include many references to subsequent tracts now only to be found in the Trinity MS.: 'ut probatum est secundo libro, tractatu de ydeis'; 'ad primum dicetur libro secundo, tractatu primo, capitulo quarto'; 'ut patet secundo libro, de intelligencia dei'; 'vade ad II^m capitulum 2^i libri, tractatus 3^i, de volucione'. From this we can conclude that, in the Vienna manuscript, as originally constituted, the *Summa* consisted of a first Book of seven tracts and a second Book of six tracts. It should be added that, according to this reconstruction, the copy of the *De Universalibus*, on fos. 62–114 of this manuscript, is independent of the portion of the *Summa*, contained on fos. 158 ff., and is not the 'missing sixth' treatise which followed fo. 242. But, with the *De ente praedicamentali*, uncertainty is not confined only to its right to be included in the *Summa de Ente*. The treatise itself is difficult to place in Wyclif's career. For, though predominantly logical and metaphysical, it contains two chapters (17 and 18) taken verbatim from the *De volucione Dei*,[3] which, we shall argue, can be dated to the period of Wyclif's reading the *Sentences*, 1370–2. The work seems to be an occasional piece, recapitulating propositions advanced by Wyclif over a number of years.

But, whilst a comparison of the Vienna and Trinity manuscripts shows that the treatises they contain are an edited and not a random collection (for the Trinity MS. includes throughout

---

[1] Cf. Beer, *op. cit.* p. ix. In MS. Trinity Coll. Camb. B. 16. 2, fo. 36 is followed by four cancels, forming the end of a quire.

[2] *Ibid.* p. viii.

[3] Compare Dziewicki, ed., *De Ente*, pp. 203–21 (*De volucione Dei*, chs. 9 and 10) with Beer, edn cit. pp. 158–78. See Thomson, 'The Order of Writing', p. 153. For these reasons it seemed best to base the analysis of Wyclif's metaphysical position on *De Universalibus* and *De Tempore*.

cross-references of the same kind as we have noted in the *De ente praedicamentali*), it has yet to be proved that Wyclif was their editor. We know at least that he did write a philosophical *Summa*. A catalogue of books in the library of Durham College, Oxford, which has been dated to *c.* 1390–1400, includes in a list of *libri logice* a 'Summa Wyclyffe de dono Magistri Roberti Rypon';[1] and the library of the Austin canons at Leicester also possessed a 'Summa mag. Jo. Wycliffe in logica et philosophia sua'.[2] But it is uncertain whether these describe our *Summa*. The Durham College catalogue, for example, is divided into theology, philosophy and logic, and Wyclif's *Summa* is listed under the third category.

Some further light is thrown on the problem by references to a *Summa* of Wyclif in the notebook of a student in the Arts faculty at Oxford, *c.* 1400. This collection (which is of considerable interest, and is discussed more fully later) contains a long summary on logic and metaphysics entitled 'Quedam abstracta a Summa Doctoris Evangelici Iohannis Wicliff'.[3] The writer refers to a treatise, which may be the *De ente praedicamentali*. Thus we find:

Ulteriorem processum illius require in 2º capitulo predicamentorum Summe Magistri Wicliff.

Ista brevis summa sufficit pro presenti; si autem alicui in ista materia ulteriorem processum placuerit indagare, ad secundum capitulum Summe Magistri Io. W. recurrat, et ibidem inveniet processum valde diffusum in Predicamentis.

Istam materiam, si profundius volueris perscrutare, in Summa Magistri Io. W. capitulo 2º super Predicamenta.[4]

Since the summary of the unknown Artist deals, at these points, with topics discussed in the *De ente praedicamentali*, chapter 2, it is possible that it is to this work, and perhaps to the *Summa* as we

---

[1] W. A. Pantin, 'Catalogue of the Books of Durham College, Oxford', in *Formularies which bear on the History of Oxford, c. 1204–1420*, ed. H. E. Salter, W. A. Pantin, H. G. Richardson, *OHS*, new ser. IV (1942), I, 243.

[2] M. R. James and A. Hamilton Thompson, 'Catalogue of the Library of Leicester Abbey', *Transactions of the Leicestershire Archaeological Society*, XXI (1939/41), 17.

[3] MS. Corpus Christi College, Oxford, 116, fos. 132r–140r. See also below, pp. 224 ff.

[4] MS. cit. fos. 132r, 132v, 133r.

know it, that the writer refers. Again, when he notes a reference to the *De materia et forma* (an early tract not included in the *Summa de Ente*), there is no mention of any *Summa*: 'Hec Wyclyf in tractatu suo, De materia et forma, etc.'[1] It is clear, therefore, that Wyclif wrote a *summa* 'in logic and philosophy', and that this may very possibly be the work with which we are here concerned. On the other hand, it is arguable that some of these references may be to one of the three books of his *Tractatus de logica*.

But an important objection remains. How can the *summa* 'in logic and philosophy' of the late fourteenth-century catalogues be identified with the *summa* now extant, Book II of which is pure theology? Wyclif's metaphysics and theology are, of course, interdependent, but this hardly explains the discrepancy. The absence of any reference to the theological tracts may be pure chance. After all, the Oxford commentator was an Artist, unconcerned with theological disputes; and, if he ignores these works, he equally fails to mention the *De Universalibus* or the *De Tempore*. But the treatises in each of the two Books of the *Summa de Ente* are indeed the product of different periods of Wyclif's career; and those in Book II are as unquestionably the work of a member of the Faculty of Theology as those in Book I are of a teacher in the Arts faculty. It is, therefore, not impossible that we are dealing with two *Summae*, or with two stages in the compiling of a *Summa*: Book I representing Wyclif's principal treatises on metaphysics, and Book II those composed after he had incepted in theology.

III

We know of twenty-two treatises,[2] academic and non-controversial, composed by Wyclif before *c.* 1372, of which the *De incarnacione Verbi* is admitted to be the latest. Thirteen of these (if we include the *De ente praedicamentali*) were incorporated in the *Summa de Ente*. But why was the *Summa* composed, and what

[1] MS. cit. fo. 133 v.

[2] To the twenty works listed by S. H. Thomson in 'The Order of Writing of Wyclif's Philosophical Works', *Českou Minulosti*, pp. 146–65, must be added Thomson's discoveries of the *Insolubilia* and *Commentary on the Physics*, for which see below, p. 139.

relation have the tracts embodied in it to those that were excluded? To attempt this question, we must examine any clues to the date of the individual works. These are few enough. With undated treatises from the medieval schools we shall look for internal evidence of academic disputes; for early references to the tract by other masters; and at the form and content of the work itself. At first glance the *Summa* seems to yield little. There is a single reference to an academic quarrel that can be dated with confidence: a passage in Book II, tract 6, *De potentia dei productiva ad extra*, which has been accepted (since Knowles recently drew attention to it) as referring to the condemnation of Uthred Boldon's proposition on annihilation by Archbishop Langham in November 1368.[1] There are also early references to two treatises by Wyclif himself. For the passing reference in the controversy with John Kenningham, the Carmelite, *c.* 1372, to the tract 'Materia de notitia Dei'[2] almost certainly denotes the *De scientia Dei*, which forms Book II, tract 2, of the *Summa de Ente*. In the same passage Wyclif also refers to *De Ydeis*, which is incorporated as the fifth tract in Book II.[3]

The argument from form and content must always be tentative and circumscribed. Certainly the treatises in Book I defy dating. We know of no contemporary references before those just noted, by which time not only they but also the theological treatises in Book II must have been composed. They are the product of an Artist, entirely concerned with logical and metaphysical aspects of realism. Our evidence, therefore, is entirely negative: these works are pre-theological. But one slight qualification may be noted. At the close of *De Universalibus*, chapters 13–15, there are passages on necessity, on foreknowledge and free will, and on annihilation which clearly touch on issues of theology. One might suspect a later addition, did not all copies of the treatise appear to include this material. It seems rather that the work as a whole comes at the end of Wyclif's career in the Arts faculty. But this still gives a

---

[1] M. D. Knowles, 'The Censured Opinions of Uthred of Boldon', *Proceedings of the British Academy*, XXXVII (1951), 327 and n. 1. Cf. Dziewicki, ed., *De Ente*, p. 287; and see above, p. 109.

[2] *FZ*, p. 464.   [3] *FZ*, p. 464.

range of possible composition for the treatises in Book I of almost a decade, *c.* 1360–8. Beyond this we can only follow Thomson in his attempt to deduce an order of writing. His conclusion is to place the metaphysical tracts of the *Summa* among the later compositions of Wyclif as master of arts.

The theological treatises of Book II may yield more evidence. Their place in the Wyclif canon is not obvious. But the two datable references noted above are suggestive. Tract 6, *De potentia Dei* must be post-1368, whilst Wyclif's remark seems to date the *De scientia Dei* to before *c.* 1372–3. These were, of course, precisely the years in which Wyclif incepted in the Faculty of Theology; and we therefore put forward the suggestion, which does not appear to have been made before, that the treatises in Book II of the *Summa de Ente* derive from Wyclif's reading the *Sentences* in these years.

As an incepting bachelor he had to comment on the Bible and the Lombard. To 'read' the whole of Scripture was a heavy task, and we may suppose that his lectures on the Bible took several years to deliver before being incorporated into the *Postilla super totam bibliam*, completed before the outbreak of the schism.[1] Of his *Commentary on the Sentences* no trace has been found. The importance attached to these lectures may seem surprising; they were, after all, usually (but not in Wyclif's case) the product of a young man in his late twenties, who might be expected to produce maturer work. Often this did happen. The *Summa Theologica* is rightly regarded as superseding Thomas' *Commentary*; and the young Thomas Buckingham, as we have seen, was a very different man from the cautious chancellor of Exeter. Nevertheless, the *Commentaries on the Sentences*,[2] perhaps because they provided the one occasion for a wide survey of all the principal questions of pure theology, kept their importance, at any rate for other theologians.

A more difficult problem is to decide what precisely is a late medieval *Commentary*.[3] Far from being a straightforward topic by topic discussion of the Lombard, they had become a mere collection of *quaestiones*, grouped roughly according to the four

[1] Smalley, 'John Wyclif's Postilla super totam bibliam', pp. 196–7.
[2] See P. Glorieux, 'Commentaires sur les Sentences', *DTC*, XIV, 1860–84.
[3] For fourteenth-century *Commentaries* see *ibid.* cols. 1875–7.

Books of the *Sentences*, and with the emphasis strongly on the first Book. They might be reduced to very few questions indeed. Richard FitzRalph's *Commentary* contains twenty-seven, but Buckingham's only six. The *Sentences* of Thomas Claxton, O.P., is one of the few Oxford *Commentaries* of the end of the century to have survived. His long *Commentary* on Book I[1] contains only eight questions.

This fluidity of structure makes our suggestion more tenable. We can assume that Wyclif's *Commentary* was never published as delivered. Clearly there was no compulsion to do so. Thomas Bradwardine had waited about fifteen years after reading the Lombard before publishing the *De causa Dei*; and of many Oxford men of the fourteenth century we only know that they incepted as theologians from their holding offices confined to graduates of the senior faculty. This is notably true of some of the logicians (Swyneshead and Heytesbury, for example) who, no doubt, considered their arts lectures as their contribution to learning. We have but one reference to Wyclif's *Sentences*: William Wodeford's description in the *De sacramento altaris* of their exchanging notebooks at the time both bachelors were reading the Lombard, and of the development of Wyclif's teaching on the Eucharist.[2] But the significance of this passage for our present purpose is precisely that Wodeford heard, and did not read, these words. We cannot claim that the treatises in Book II, in their existing state, are part of Wyclif's *Commentary*; they are not arranged in 'question' form ('*utrum* theologia sit scientia', and so forth); nor do they have the three parts of *affirmatio*, *oppositio* and *resolutio* that an academic *quaestio* properly requires. They are tracts designed to be read, not a version of the spoken word. Apart from the interesting but uncertain argument from dating, it is on their content that the matter must be judged.

Book II of the *Summa de Ente* consists of six treatises, and between four of these there is a close connection both in content and manuscript association. They are amongst the least frequently copied of Wyclif's works, only two manuscripts being

---

[1] MS. Gonville and Caius 370/592.
[2] For discussion and references see below, pp. 190 ff.

known to us. Book II, tracts 1–3 (*De intelleccione Dei*; *De scientia Dei*; and *De volucione Dei*), were long believed to be unique in MS. Trinity Coll. Camb. B. 16. 2. But, in a valuable note, I. H. Stein[1] pointed to the existence of a second copy of these treatises in MS. Prague, University Library 1762 (IX. E. 6). In both manuscripts they appear in the same order and, in the case of the Trinity MS., on a single group of quires. The correspondence was marked; and Dr Stein was able to note that it was now possible to restore the text of chapters 12 and 13 of the *De volucione Dei*, which had been partially lost by a cancel in the Trinity MS.[2] But the Prague MS. contains a further item; and in noting that the number of 'unique' treatises in the *Summa* had now been reduced from four to one, Dr Stein did not realise that she had herself handled a part of the text of the fourth 'unique' tract. For, at the explicit of the *De scientia Dei* (fo. 51r), there follows not the *De volucione Dei*, but the incipit of Book II, tract 6, 'Consequens ad dicta est tractare de potencia productiva dei ad extra'. The text of the *De potencia Dei* continues for two chapters to the middle of fo. 55v.[3] Though there has never been any serious doubt that this work was from Wyclif's hand, the appearance of part of a second text is a welcome addition.

It also confirms what a study of the text insistently urges, that the content of Book II of the *Summa*, and especially tracts 1–3 and tract 6, are interrelated and contemporaneous. They have a common theme, and one that is eminently 'sentential'. Their subject is divine knowledge and will, grace and predestination, contingency and free will, divine power and its limits, the eucharist and annihilation. The substance of these treatises could only have been delivered by a theologian; and we have argued that one tract was composed after 1368 and another before *c.* 1373. The implication is at least very tempting.

[1] I. H. Stein, 'Another "Lost" Chapter of Wyclif's *Summa de Ente*', *Speculum*, VIII (1933), 254–5.

[2] *Ibid.*; cf. Dziewicki, ed., *De Ente*, pp. 229–30.

[3] I have to thank the Cultural Secretary of the Czech Embassy for obtaining for me a microfilm of this MS. Truhlar does not mention this fourth item. The text breaks off at 'nec alterum altero', ten lines before the end of ch. 2 in the Trinity MS.

How far can these arguments be applied to the other treatises in Book II, *De Trinitate* and *De Ydeis*? They are distinguished from the rest, in that they led an independent existence, and were read as self-contained works; they also appear to have been better known. *De Trinitate*[1] is a defence of realism as applied to the Trinity; the Godhead is not a fourth Person but a universal containing the essence of the three Persons. The nature of the Trinity was, of course, a subject necessarily treated in a *Commentary on the Sentences*. *De Ydeis*, on the other hand, is one of the most copied, most widespread and most frequently cited of Wyclif's works. But its appearance in Book II of the *Summa* may seem suspicious. It is mentioned in Wyclif's determination against Kenningham[2] and so, if 'theological', can only have been composed very soon after inception; and was not the question of Ideas in the province of the metaphysician? Yet *De Ydeis* in fact deals with the relation of God to creatures, and the application of this theory is theological enough. Moreover it was quite in order for a realist theologian to discuss divine emanations and ideas in his *Sentences*. We see, therefore, no reason to doubt that this work finds its correct place in both manuscripts[3] of the *Summa de Ente*, that is in Book II. But, though composed, we believe, at the same period in Wyclif's career, tracts 4–5 do not have the same intimate relationship shared by the other four.

To sum up: if we exclude those passages which (we argue below) are probable interpolations, we can say that all six tracts of Book II of the *Summa de Ente* treat questions of pure theology in an academic and non-controversial manner; one in which even eucharistic doctrine is regarded simply as an aspect of the problem of annihilation, and which is without reference to the subjects that dominated Wyclif's thought from *c.* 1375/6. Some four years

---

[1] Cf. A. du P. Breck, 'The manuscripts of John Wyclyf's *De Trinitate*', *Medievalia et Humanistica*, VII (1952), 56–70.

[2] FZ, p. 464.

[3] Though no longer extant in the truncated text of the *Summa de Ente* in MS. Vienna, Nat. Bibl. ccccvi (4307), its original presence is attested by the cross-references in the tracts in Book I: 'ut probatum est secundo libro, tractatu de Ydeis'. See Beer, *Johannis Wyclif De Ente praedicamentali* (*WS*, 1891), p. 1; and above, p. 126.

separate Wyclif's inception as master from the beginnings of his embroilment in ecclesiastical controversy, time enough for his facile pen to produce a respectable amount of academic theology. What survives from this period, we suggest, is contained in Book II of the *Summa*, whose contents correspond remarkably with what one would expect to find in the first book of a *Commentary on the Sentences* of this period. Is it not possible that we have here the body of Wyclif's 'lost' *Commentary*?[1]

This argument is at variance with the generally accepted statement that his Sentential lectures have been preserved as the treatise *De incarnacione Verbi*.[2] This conclusion appears to rest on the authority of its editor, Edward Harris, who printed an entry of 1454 from the treasurer's accounts of Oriel College. In this year the college bought the celebrated MS. 15, containing amongst other works copies of FitzRalph's *Sentences*, cited above, and of the *De incarnacione Verbi*. The purchase was recorded as follows: 'Sol. pro libro empto a Johanne More continente Armacanum, Holkot et Wyclyff super sententias xlii^s.'[3] The evidence is hardly conclusive. The entry (in the college accounts, not in the book itself), was made seventy years after Wyclif's death, and more than eighty after he had lectured on the *Sentences*. And the fact that the two largest works in this manuscript are indeed the *Commentaries* of FitzRalph and Holcot might easily lead the treasurer, or his clerk, to describe the whole book simply as 'super sententias'.

We do not feel, therefore, that this invalidates the argument in the preceding paragraphs. But there is one solution which could reconcile the two. Harris correctly notes[4] that the treatise obviously belongs to Wyclif's early non-controversial theology. Now the theological treatises of the *Summa* consider the problems traditionally discussed in the first two books of the Lombard. It is therefore possible that *De incarnacione Verbi* is the product of

---

[1] The incipit of the *Commentary* attributed to Wyclif in Stegmüller, *Repertorium commentariorum in sententias Petri Lombardi*, I, 249, is in fact that of the *De mandatis divinis*.

[2] Workman, I, 332; Gwynn, *Austin Friars*, pp. 211–12.

[3] E. Harris, ed., *Johannis Wyclif De benedicta incarnacione* (*WS*, 1886), p. xx. On the original owner of this MS. see below, p. 242.

[4] *Ibid.* p. viii.

Wyclif's lectures on Book III of the *Sentences*, which treats of God the Son. Certainly the number of references to the third book of Peter Lombard and his commentators is suggestive, whilst the matter of the work alone is too narrow for the notion that it is the substance of the whole of Wyclif's *Commentary* to be entertained. If the same arguments of form, noted before, can be brought against this proposal, the same arguments of content can be arrayed in its favour.

IV

It remains to consider when this series of treatises, composed over a number of years, was gathered into the *Summa de Ente* as we now have it. The edited *Summa* as surviving in the Trinity MS. cannot have been written before the mid and, more likely, the later 1370's. For it contains at least four passages which are patently interpolations, and in which the argument is abruptly broken off to admit anticlerical and anti-papal outbursts.

Twice the powers of papal provision are attacked. In Book II, tract 2, *De scientia Dei*, noting that the words grace and judgement are inadequate to describe the processes of God's will, Wyclif states that it has been said that no human law is valid unless confirmed by God's eternal law. But he continues, warming to his task (and with a play on *gratia* as grace and favour), we should not dream of describing as gracious the conduct of a ruler towards subjects whom he forcibly bends to his will. Nor should we so describe the acts of the Pope who, far from giving his flock of his bounty, takes from them that which is theirs and dispenses what is Christ's. It cannot be a 'grace' to grant a cure from his patrimony; for if the recipient is worthy, he has merited his reward, whilst grace, strictly speaking, must precede merit.[1]

---

[1] MS. Trinity Coll. Camb. B. 16. 2, fo. 63r[a]. Unde videtur michi multa usurpative dicta de gratiis hominum factis suis inferioribus, ut delinquentes in dominos exacciones dicuntur ponere se in suis gratiis, quando subiciunt se extortionative potestati eorum; et certum est quod non faciunt illis gratiam si minus iniuste extorquent quam poterunt ad eorum indigenciam. Nec Papa facit gratiam suo curato, cui dispensat bonum de patrimonio Christi, quia si ista bene fiant, recipiens prius naturaliter meretur ubique, quia dispensacione indiget sic facere ad augmentum sui meriti et illa excludunt gratiam. Ideo grates sunt reddende homini et non gratie.

Secondly, the *Summa* itself ends with a passage of sustained vituperation against papal provisions and reservations, which are stigmatised by Wyclif as an unjust dominion. No earthly Vicar of Christ, he declares, can deprive a man of what is lawfully his by the practice of reservation, nor condemn one who has not already merited damnation; for all these powers belong to God and not to his vice-gerent:

And it may be said that it is man's lot to be punished to his own benefit, as was blessed Job; and since there are many ministers of the church who are good enough, so that they may 'fittingly' be made poor by removing their 'burdens' (which they have gathered through their merits), it seems possible to deprive such men of their benefices, without their having merited this loss. But we say here that anyone who should so deprive another is indulging not in condemnation but in peculation. . . .

Thirdly, it may be said that it is in the power of the Supreme Vicar to make, as it were 'mentally', a first reservation of benefices, before bestowing them on some worthy person; or to make conditions on bestowing them; or to transfer them from ignorant hands to someone more fitted—else he would not possess the plenitude of power over the whole treasure of the church. But we say that this does not follow, if the Vicar of Christ decides to reserve (and not 'mentally') such benefices for money, favour, or something pertaining not to the glory of God, but to the profit of himself and his accomplices. Nor by such reservation does he acquire a right to reserve to himself or to dispense to others.[1]

---

[1] MS. cit., fo. 141r^a. Ex ista conclusione cum suis mediis videtur corelarie sequi, quod nullus vicarius Christi terrenus potest per viam reservacionis vel quovis alio modo dampnificare hominem habentem ius ad aliquod bonum dei vel possessionem licitam in eodem, si dampnificatus previe non demeretur. Patet ex hoc quod deus omnipotens non potest adnichilare vel dampnificare creaturam peccantem, nisi preexigens sit causa, igitur multo magis eius vicarius hoc non potest: antecedens patet ex predictis. Et si obiciatur de probatione inhabilitatis personarum ad preposituras ecclesia[stica]s, quas personas post recepcionem inhabilitatis licet deponeretur [*sic*], confirmatur conclusio; sed tunc demeritum est in causa deposicionis. Et forte multi tales, licet videantur habere huiusmodi bonum dei, tamen non habuerunt nec possiderunt, sed habuerunt usum illicitum suppositum in conclusione.

Et si secundo obiciatur, quod stat hominem puniri ad augmentum sui, ut patet de beato Iob, cum igitur multi sint ministratores ecclesie satis boni, quibus expediret esse pauperes, tollendo tribulaciones propter sua merita cumulanda:

It is not merely the inappropriateness of the passage in its context (a summary of the objections to annihilation) which marks it out as an interpolation; but also the inclusion of a reference to the question of dominion, a subject otherwise, with one exception, unmentioned in the *Summa*. And this exception is itself contained in a suspect passage. For in further discussion on the impossibility of annihilation, Wyclif adds a theological objection to his main metaphysical argument. God cannot transfer to any creature the power to create 'creancia', and much less the power to destroy; and just so, he adds, we should avoid the blasphemy uttered by our prelates today, who claim to 'create' ministers to whom they grant favours, by the 'grace' of temporal power.[1]

Two passages in the *De volucione Dei* may also be interpolations. Discussing predestination, Wyclif asks whether we are entitled to resist evil acts, which seem to be ordained of God. He has, indeed, Wyclif replies, allowed many tyrants, lay and ecclesiastical, to hold power as a punishment for the sins of the community, as witness the current abuses whereby Pope and Sacred College compete for the incomes of rich churches. It can happen, he adds, that the main defect is in the head of the body. People, in fact, get the prelates they deserve, as is shown by the parlous condition of

videtur quod aliquos tales esset possibile privare beneficiis sine demerito precedente. Hic dicitur quod taliter privans non simpliciter dampnificat sed lucrificat....

Et si tertio obicitur, quod stat capitalem vicarium Christi mentaliter previe reservare beneficia antequam conferat dato digno, vel aliter solum condicionaliter conferre, vel tercio conferendo post notam ignoranciam magis digno (cum aliter non haberet plenitudinem potestatis super totum thesaurum ecclesie): dicitur quod non sequitur, si non mentaliter cogitat talia beneficia reservare propter peccuniam, favorem vel aliquid non cedens ad ho[no]rem dei sibi vel suis complicibus cumulandum, igitur propter talem reservacionem adquirit ius vel reservat sibi ius ad taliter despensandum [sic] etcetera.

Explicit tractatus Magistri J.W. de potentia dei.

[1] MS. cit., fo. 134v[b]. Unde videtur vel cohibenda equivocacio vel verbum blasphemie illud quod prelati nostri dicunt hodie se creare ministros quibus dant gratias, et sic forte est de gratia potestatis temporalium pretense ab eisdem. Cavendum est ergo catholico ne quomodolibet attribuat creature potentiam creandi.

the Church.[1] A second, though much less specific, passage may also be noted. Can we do evil that good may result? Wyclif rejects the idea. It is just such a nefarious doctrine which has been propagated in his own time, and, until men arise who know it to be false, the Church will never be secure.[2]

The deduction seems clear. The treatises of the *Summa* all date from the purely academic period of Wyclif's career; technical and non-controversial, and not looking beyond the audience of the schools, they are a most unsuitable medium for anti-papal propaganda—even if we had not already concluded that they were composed before their author became embroiled in public dispute. The *Summa*, therefore, contains the individually composed works, spiced with some topical allusions. And by whom were these added, if not by Wyclif? It is conceivable, of course, that the *Summa* is the work of two editors, one responsible for the cross-references, the other for the interpolations. But following the axiom that editors are not to be predicated beyond necessity, it seems reasonable to accept that the treatises underwent a single editing, and that their editor was Wyclif himself. At least there is no positive evidence that it was another; the Lollards were rarely schoolmen, and the manuscript gives no hint that Purvey or some other Oxford disciple was involved in its appearance. We suggest that in the mid 1370's, perhaps realising that he had nothing further to offer in the field of pure philosophy, Wyclif gathered together the fruits of some ten or twelve years' teaching in the form of an edition of 'collected essays', which summed up his contribution to scholastic theology, and that, in doing so, he made a few topical interpolations.

The basis of their selection is indicated by a comparison of those

---

[1] Dziewicki, ed., *De Ente*, pp. 269–70. Mala communitas meretur habere malum prelatum....Et sic forte in penam peccati utriusque partis sunt hodie manifestissimi abusus patrimonii Christi, ut pinguiorum ecclesiarum redditus nunc papa vel cardinales...avare sibi accumulent pro fructibus corporalibus inhiantes....Et potest contingere quod principalis defectus sit in capite: cuius esset, remote speculando, de talibus periculis providere.

[2] Dziewicki, ed., *De Ente*, p. 257. Et antequam sint tales qui in praxi cognoverunt quod non sunt facienda mala ut bona eveniant, nunquam solidabitur ecclesia a procellis tribulacionum inconcussa.

works included with those that were not. Of the twenty-one treatises listed by Thomson as prior to the *De incarnacione Verbi*, thirteen (counting the *De ente praedicamentali*) are incorporated in the *Summa de Ente*. First amongst those excluded stand the four volumes of logic: the three books *De Logica*[1] and the unprinted *De Insolubilibus*.[2] In their stead and acting as a logical introduction, we presume, there are the four short treatises, Book I, tracts 1–4; for, though the logic of universals is clearly germane to the *Summa*, formal logic is outside its scope. Secondly there is the *Commentary on the Physics*.[3] The identification of this work, described as *Dubia super materia librorum Physicorum Aristotelis secundum sentenciam magistri Jo. Wycliff*, confirmed an old entry in the Syon library catalogue,[4] and was one of the most important of Professor Thomson's discoveries. A full analysis is much to be desired. But its exclusion from the *Summa* is self-explanatory; a large commentary on sixty folio leaves could obviously not be assimilated into another work, to the theme of which it was in any case not central. Two other works appear to have been omitted because their material was either superseded or already embodied in other treatises. *De actibus anime* is so early a composition that it does not deny the possibility of annihilation;[5] and *De composi-tione hominis* (possibly a primer to more advanced study) is a conflation of Wyclif's opinions on universals and the Trinity and Incarnation, which he had expressed more fully elsewhere.[6] So

[1] Dziewicki, ed., *Johannis Wyclif Tractatus de logica*, 3 vols. (*WS*, 1894–9).

[2] Discovered by Thomson in MS. Vienna, Nat. Bibl. 5204, fos. 76r–96v; see S. H. Thomson, 'Unnoticed Manuscripts and Works of Wyclif', *Journal of Theological Studies*, xxxviii (1937), 139–44.

[3] MS. Venice, San Marco Cl. vi. 173 (2625), fos. 1–58, fully described by Thomson, 'Unnoticed Manuscripts', pp. 144–8. The text may be a *reportatio*; thus fo. 1v^b, 'hic sunt quedam summarie collecta ex dictis magistri Jo. Wy. super primum Phisicorum'. I have to thank the Italian Institute, London, for help in obtaining a microfilm.

[4] 'Wyclyf super tres libros methereorum et super 8 libros phisicorum Aristotelis.' M. Bateson, ed., *Catalogue of the Library of Syon Monastery, Isleworth* (Cambridge, 1898), p. 244.

[5] Ed. Dziewicki in *Johannis Wyclif miscellanea philosophica* (*WS*, 1901), I, 1–127; and cf. Thomson, 'The Order of Writing', p. 164.

[6] Ed. R. Beer, *Johannis Wyclif De compositione hominis* (*WS*, 1884), cf. Thomson, 'The Order of Writing', p. 152.

only *De materia et forma*[1] seems to remain as a possible candidate for inclusion.

The contents and arrangement of the *Summa de Ente* reveal a clear and comprehensive purpose. Book I exposes the elements of Wyclif's realism and the metaphysical basis of his theology. Wyclif was the greatest name that the Faculty of Arts at Oxford had produced since Ockham and Burley. Like the Venerable Inceptor he approached the problems of theology with a mind steeped in logic and metaphysic; and the first Book of the *Summa* is a declaration that true philosophy, the knowledge of things human and divine, must be founded on principles of metaphysics. In the second Book, he treats, in the context of these preconceptions, the range of questions in contemporary theology, which we have seen debated in the Oxford of his youth.

[1] Printed in Dziewicki, ed., *Misc. phil.* I, 163–242.

CHAPTER VI

WYCLIF AND ULTRAREALISM[1]

I

W YCLIF's realism,[2] in its early purity, is expounded in Book I of the *Summa de Ente* and, in particular, in the treatises *De Universalibus* and *De Tempore* which comprise two-thirds of it. The large number of surviving manuscripts proves their popularity; and there is also evidence that they were regarded as complementary. It is remarkable how often they are found together (or in association with *De Ydeis*); frequently one follows directly on the other —as in the Pavia and Venice MSS., and with MS. Prague University 535 (III. G. 10).[3] They are, or have been, contiguous in all the English manuscripts (except that in Trinity College, Dublin, which has *De Tempore* alone); for it is clear that the Caius MS. of *De Universalibus* was originally bound with *De Tempore*.[4]

---

[1] In chapters VI–VIII of this study all MS. references, unless otherwise stated, are to the text of the *Summa de Ente* in MS. Trinity College, Cambridge, B. 16. 2 (hereafter T), described above, pp. 123 ff. MS. Prague University 1762 (IX. E. 6) (hereafter P) has been used for some superior readings and to correct some obvious blunders in the text of Book II, tracts 1–3, in T.

[2] As noted by Gwynn, *Austin Friars*, p. 211, and McFarlane, *John Wycliffe*, p. 30, Wyclif's early philosophy awaits systematic investigation; but see Lechler, pp. 223–87; Workman, I, 103–50; Gilson, *La Philosophie au moyen âge*, pp. 618–20. For the main features of his realism the texts printed in *FZ*, pp. 453–80, 'are still the most convenient introduction' (Knowles, 'Uthred of Boldon', *Proc. Brit. Acad.* XXXVII (1951), 310 n. 1). These disputes are examined below, pp. 161 ff. An old appreciation, now for the most part superseded, is by Dziewicki, *Miscellanea Philosophica* (*WS*, 1901), I, v–xxvii. A valuable essay is that of S. H. Thomson, 'The Philosophical Basis of Wyclif's Theology', *Journal of Religion*, XI (1931), 86–116, which uses the unpublished *De Universalibus* and *De Tempore*, which are further examined in this chapter.

[3] See above, pp. 119–22.

[4] MS. Caius 337/565, described in M. R. James, *Descriptive Catalogue...of Gonville and Caius College* (1907), I, 380–1. Wyclif, *De Universalibus* occupies fos. 1–47r. The formerly blank leaves, fos. 47r–48v, have been filled, first with a summary of *De Universalibus*, and secondly (fo. 48v), with the chapter head-

Why did Wyclif's metaphysic appeal so immediately and powerfully to his contemporaries? A casual jotting by an unknown Oxford student of the 1360's gives us a clue. About this time a monk of Worcester, possibly the one who copied the *quaestiones* of Nicholas Aston, now found in the same manuscript, noted down three propositions made by Wyclif in a determination in the Schools. Two of these, on the absolute perfection and potency of God, are unexceptional and unremarkable; but the first is fundamental to his teaching: 'That the existence of God can be proved by infallible proof by a pure philosopher.'[1] Here we have the two vital features of his metaphysics, that we can obtain absolute certainty of knowledge, and that the basis of ultimate truth, including divine truth, lies in 'pure philosophy'— that is in metaphysics and not in theology.

Idealism is as old as Plato and, of course, it permeates the whole fabric of medieval thought; but in the form advanced by Wyclif and in the context of Oxford scholasticism at this time its appeal was renewed and effective. We shall have occasion to mention later the names of some who, like Thomas Netter of Walden, were wholly, indeed passionately, opposed to Wyclif's doctrinal aberrations, and yet were bowled over ('stupebam', says Netter)[2] by his teaching in logic and metaphysic. And the attraction of his argument lay surely in its promise of certain and infallible

ings of *De Tempore*, beginning 'Tractatus de tempore capitulariter sic habet....'. At the foot of fo. 48 v is the catchword 'Incipit in tractando de tempore', which gives the incipit of *De Tempore*. Fo. 49 begins a new quire with a new hand; and it is therefore clear that in this MS. *De Tempore* originally followed *De Universalibus*. I have to thank Professor C. N. L. Brooke for help in collating the quires.

[1] MS. Worcester Cathedral Chapter Library F. 65, fo. 33 r, in S. L. Forte, *Some Oxford Schoolmen* (Oxford B.Litt. thesis, 1947), II, 136.

Proposiciones Wyclif in determinacione sua

PRIMA. Deum esse probari potest per infallibilem demonstracionem a puro philosopho.

SECUNDA. Deus est tante bonitatis, perfeccionis et potencie infinite quante aliquis sine formali repugnancia potest esse.

TERCIA. Quamvis ex processu Philosophi deduci potest deum esse potencie infinite, processui suo tamen repugnat ipsum esse potencie infinite intensive.

[2] *Thomae Waldensis Carmelitae anglici Doctrinale antiquitatum fidei Catholicae ecclesiae*, ed. B. Blanciotti (Venice, 1757–9), I, 1; and see below, p. 224.

knowledge. Even if, as is very likely, there were realist logicians in the university, the prevailing school had emphasised, had rejoiced in exploiting, the range of possibility in logical argument. And suddenly there appeared a master, influenced by no current of contemporary opinion, who swept aside all talk of possibility with the assertion of 'infallible proofs from pure philosophy'; it is little wonder that his pupils were impressed. It is easy to over-estimate the importance of logical and quasi-theological daring of the kind against which Wyclif so strongly reacted. It is also easy to dismiss it as of no serious significance. A recent account[1] of a *lectura Oxoniensis*, composed by a pupil of Henry of Oyta (who apparently studied at Oxford in the years of Wyclif's doctorate), illustrates very clearly the distinctive features of possibilist logic and theology. Symbolically it also includes a determination by Wyclif implicitly limiting God's extraordinary power in respect of reprobation and demerit.[2] A list of twelve propositions proved by the disputant in the Oxford schools included such startling conclusions as:[3]

2ª conclo. Proprie loquendo, nullus deus praescius futuri potest revelare futura contingentia creaturae racionali.

9ª conclo. Satis est conveniens, tota lege Christi stante, quod plures sint summe sacerdotes in ecclesia militante.

10ª conclo. Non est aliter Christus in sacramento eucharistiae quam in pane puro, ligno, vel lapide.

Though the basis of such assertions was not heretical sympathies but 'plain linguistic casuistry', we can hardly ignore the deliberate use of 'a terminology calculated to dazzle, to surprise, to make a point'. We probably ought to make a generous allowance for deliberate undergraduate provocation; but as Fr Trapp remarks, it is the product of a 'logistic' theology in an age which imper-turbably 'carried the play of logic into the most sacrosanct precincts of dogma'.[4] At any rate Wyclif himself was perfectly

---

[1] D. Trapp, 'Unchristened Nominalism and Wycliffite Realism at Prague in 1381', *RTAM*, xxiv (1957), 320–60, and especially 322–4, 338–49.
[2] *Ibid.* p. 349.   [3] *Ibid.* p. 344.
[4] *Ibid.* pp. 344, 349.

conscious of this opposition between himself and the 'modern logicians', whom he attacked precisely for their reluctance to admit any absolute truths. We can, he says, describe certain propositions as absolutely true, because truth depends not on the terms of the proposition but on the fact that what is asserted has its principle in being. Since nothing exists that cannot be known, the Moderns are wrong to restrict necessary consequence to negative propositions only.[1]

Wyclif's extreme realism seems to have been self-acquired; at least neither he nor any of his opponents calls him the disciple of any master. Augustine made the realism of the neoplatonists a part of Christian philosophy, from which it was in no way displaced by the reception of Aristotle. Wyclif imbibed his platonism from Augustine himself, from Anselm and from Averroes; but for him the tradition was summed up in the work of Robert Grosseteste.[2] It is true that Lincolniensis is cited by all Oxford masters of the fourteenth century (and notably by FitzRalph, as we have seen); it was a part of local patriotism. Wyclif, therefore, in no sense discovered Grosseteste; but in his writings he saw, and rightly, the old Augustinian realism before it had been modified by the Thomist revolution. All Wyclif's work is a testimony to the influence of Lincolniensis, but in a remarkable passage in *De Trinitate* he includes an impassioned eulogy of his hero: 'Vir iste sanctus et catholicus, eminenter commendatus, in philosophia mundana et divina excellentissime imbutus, multo perspicacius et limpidius quam nos....'[3] Would that the Moderns, he says, would listen to the words of such a man, who sought to reconcile and expound the teaching of the ancient doctors in their catholic sense, and who did not seek to revile the dead, trampling on their writings and exalting their opponents, as is the too frequent

---

[1] Thomson, ed., *De Ente*, p. 72. Unde venerabilis Anselmus...sic dicit: 'Iam potes videre quomodo summam veritatem in meo Monologion probavi non habere principium vel finem per veritatem oracionis....Quippe veritas oracionis non semper posset esse, si eius causa non semper esset.'...Ex isto patet error logicorum modernorum, qui ponunt solum proposicionem negativam esse necessariam, et affirmativam inpossibilem.

[2] On his use of Grosseteste see above, p. 26.

[3] Fo. 110v[b].

custom today.[1] Here breathes the spirit of the true conservative; and no doubt Wyclif saw himself as the last of the *antiqui*, repeating the ancient message to a barbarous age. But it is by no means impossible that as a student he had himself been attracted to the New Way. There are a number of hints in the *Summa* that he had once been less than a full-blooded realist, that he had, for example, regarded the singular as prior to the universal.[2] And on one occasion, at least, he suggests that as a young man he had not even been a realist at all: 'et sic quando fui iunior involvebam ignoranter universalia'.[3] We should not read too much into these asides, but they do reveal a period of uncertainty before Wyclif became wedded to ultrarealism. Is the rigour of his doctrine really the fanaticism of the convert?

II

As a question of pure logic, the dispute between realists and terminists turned on the meaning of 'supposition'. When we speak of an object, do we refer to the conventional sign which denotes that object, the *signum*, or to the reality that underlies it? Indeed is there any independent reality outside mental concepts and the meaning which the mind imposes on external objects? To this the realists replied that behind every particular object lay an ultimate reality, superior to all singulars but contained in their essence; and, baptising Plato's doctrine of ideas, they posited a hierarchy of ideas (*universalia, ydee*) flowing, as it were in a stream,

[1] Fo. 111r[a]. Hec Lincolniensis. Utinam moderni scribentes attend[er]ent ad verba sensus huiusmodi boni hominis, cuius intencio fuit con[cor]dare antiquos doctores, colligendo sensus eorum catholicos et exponendo eos ad sensum primum ac favorabilem, non autem arguendo contra homines mortuos ad sensus equivocos ut scripture eorum subpeditentur, [et] ut scripta sunt [sic] arguencium exaltentur; sic enim faciunt hodie culpabiliter nimis multi.

Grosseteste is coupled with Democritus, Plato and Augustine as the greatest of the metaphysicians; cf. Thomson, 'Philosophical Basis', p. 106, citing *Trialogus*, ed. G. V. Lechler (Oxford, 1869), p. 84.

[2] Fo. 26v[a].

[3] *De Universalibus*, ch. 10, MS. Gonville and Caius 337/565, fo. 25v. The relevant leaf in the Trinity MS. has been cancelled. Cited also by Thomson, 'Philosophical Basis', p. 89.

from the Supreme Being to the singular object. As interpreted by Augustine and the best of the Christian neoplatonists, there was little danger that the gulf between the natural and the super-natural would be compromised, but in the writings of the Arab commentators neoplatonism undoubtedly acquired a pantheist tinge. This element can be found in aspects of Wyclif's realism,[1] for instance in his belief that the Word of Scripture was God Himself, an emanation of the Supreme Being 'transposed into writing'. Terminists like Ockham, on the other hand, started from the existing particular, which for them was the only reality. When, said the Venerable Inceptor, we 'supposit' a term for some object, we refer to our concept, *signum*, of a particular singular and not to any underlying meaning, *significatum*, that is, the essence of a superior idea. Ockham did not deny that one can legiti-mately speak of universals, but insisted that they remain concepts without extra-mental reality. There is no universal being, *humanitas*, present in but fundamentally distinct from singular man, *homo*. No doubt the resemblance seen by Fr Boehner[2] between Ockhamist logic and logical positivism is open to attack, but there are obvious and interesting comparisons to be made between the two movements.

Wyclif's rejection of terminism was rooted in his belief that truth could only be known in the real, *res*. In his opinion the Ockhamists limited the range of ascertainable truth by making it dependent on logical convention; the meaning and 'reality' of an object became what our mind chose to impose upon it.[3] But from conventional signs, he declared, could only come conven-tional truths. And it was precisely in the *res extra*, whose existence the Moderns denied, that truth was to be found; for to restrict knowledge to what can be derived from sense-data (which was, in fact, the terminist argument), was to limit oneself to the imperfect and perishable. The sensible particular may be forgotten, says

---

[1] Cf. Lechler, p. 254. The charge is refuted by Thomson, 'Philosophical Basis', p. 101.

[2] P. Boehner, *Medieval Logic* (Manchester, 1952), pp. x–xiii.

[3] Fo. 16v[b]. Omnis species logica vel diccio pertinens est signum vel terminus vel conceptus, ut asserunt; ergo in nulla specie est res extra....

Wyclif, but the universal perceived in it can never be.[1] He therefore follows Grosseteste in stating that truth depends on the *res
signata* and not on our concept of it. But he does not regard
universals as knowable only through their singulars, for men have
an innate knowledge of *res* which is not derived from sensible
objects.[2] Such knowledge reaches ultimately to God himself, and
every man has the chance to know him and what is necessary to
salvation.[3] Indeed the danger in Wyclif's system is not that it
removes God from the realm of rational speculation, but that he
may become involved in the hierarchy of being. For God is the
Final Cause, the principle in which all universals are reconciled; so
that if we know anything, states Wyclif, we know that God
exists.[4] Reality and Godhead are interdependent.

Plato and Aristotle, he recognised, differed as to whether
universals were substantial, and he tried to reconcile their views.
Aristotle's conception was, of course, not Plato's at all.

For it seems impossible that any universal term should be the name of a
substance. For firstly the substance of each thing is that which is
peculiar to it, which does not belong to anything else; but the
universal is common, since that is called universal which is such as to
belong to more than one thing.[5]

But in fact Aristotle himself is not entirely consistent on the
matter, and Wyclif succeeds in forcing the two into some sort of
agreement. Plato, he says, conceived prime substance as self-
sufficient and independent, but naturally seeking to inhere in
secondary substances; whilst Aristotle saw substance as essence
inhering first in its accidents and then seeking out prime sub-

---

[1] Thomson, ed., *De Ente*, p. 14. Bene potest ut quilibet homo oblitus sensibile
primo cognitum ab eodem, sed commune, quod primo cognoscit, nemo
obliviscitur.

[2] Thomson, ed., *De Ente*, pp. 18–19.

[3] Thomson, ed., *De Ente*, pp. 17–18. Cuilibet homini inest possibilitas ad
noscendum divinitatem et alia necessaria ad salutem...ut totum universale
est nobis nocius quam eius pars subiectiva...et deus prius quam universitas
creata.

[4] Thomson, ed., *De Ente*, p. 103.

[5] *Metaphysics*, Book Z, ch. 13, trans. W. D. Ross, *Works of Aristotle*, vol. VIII
(2nd edn, Oxford, 1928), unpaginated.

stance.[1] But secondary substance, according to Wyclif, only subsists in relative habits which, whether universal or singular, are
distinct from their subject, since universals are only present in an
object in respect of what is universal in its essence. So it is clear,
in his view, that the Philosopher was not denying that universals
were substantial, but was simply distinguishing between universal
and particular substance. In none of his works, says Wyclif, does
Aristotle deny the existence of universals *ex parte rei*.[2] At other
times, where the words of the Philosopher defy a satisfactory
interpretation, Wyclif simply dismisses them as inaccurate. We
have no cause, he says, to believe his story that Plato taught that
ideas, though substantial, cannot be communicated to secondary
substance; indeed if this were so, there would be neither place
nor purpose for universals.[3]

Wyclif therefore returns to an old-fashioned Augustinianism;
and his authority is Robert Grosseteste. Lincolniensis had distinguished, and Wyclif agreed with him, five kinds of universal.
First and supreme is the idea, the eternal exemplar present in God.
Secondly and thirdly stand universals existing in the heavenly
bodies and the powers that move mind and matter, and those that
inhere in individuals (which are Aristotle's species and genera).
The fourth and lowest order that can truly be called universal
subsists in accidents whose universality is apprehended by the
mind, for, as Grosseteste stated, it is meaningless to talk of univer-

---

[1] *De Universalibus*, ch. 11, fo. 28v[a]. Unde ut Plato consideravit substanciam,
habet racionem per se stantis quod maxime competit substanciis secundis;
Aristoteles autem videtur considerare substanciam ut est essentia per se substans
accidentibus, quod maxime competit prime substancie.

Ibid. ch. 2, fo. 17v[b]. Et in tali equivocacione de minoritate laborant Plato et
Aristoteles, ut dicit Commentator, 7 Metaphysice 7, Aristoteles ponendo
singulare magis substanciam quia pluribus predicacionibus substat: Plato
econtra ex prioritate nature et ampliori communicacione dicit universalius
habere racionem magis substancie vel essencie.

[2] Fo. 171[a]. Hic dicitur quod nusquam in libris Aristotelis, quos nos habemus,
negat ipse universalia ex parte rei, sed utrobique sentenciat oppositum...
principalis intencio Aristotelis in dicto capitulo est dividere hoc nomen substancie in terminos singulares et terminos communes, sed intendit quod
substanciarum quedam est substancia singularis et quedam substancia universalis.

[3] Fo. 17v[a]. ...preservando tamen a sentencia quam Aristoteles imposuit
Platoni, quod est dare universalia separata ab individuis.

sals in respect of terms and signs.[1] This stark and *simpliste* definition goes to the heart of Wyclif's metaphysics, and the multitude of his metaphysical tracts are in essence only an elaboration of this concept. There existed a hierarchy of being, streaming down from the Supreme Cause in whom subsisted the ideas of all particular being. What then is knowledge? The act of knowing involves both the apprehension of the real, *res*, and the use of the term, *signum*, employed by the mind for predication. To know, therefore, is a process both logical and metaphysical and it is, Wyclif states, in the combination of these two modes that Aristotle has with a 'marvellous subtlety' so notably excelled.[2] But logic alone is not enough, indeed logical truth, founded upon 'signs', is the lowest order of truth; logic is a tool for approaching reality.

Wyclif devotes some attention in *De Universalibus* to the opinions of his opponents. These, it seems, were mainly conceptualists; or perhaps they were the only school with whom he thought it worth arguing. He believed their views to be dangerous because, after a fashion, they did admit the existence of universals; but either they denied extra-mental reality to such universals or they supposed them to be realised by intellection. Wyclif argued that the first of these explanations deprived universals of being, and the second made them impermanent and the product not of the hierarchy of being but of human act. Thus some philosophers had posited a *universale logicum* and a *universale metaphysicum*; but the one represented in reality a disguised con-

---

[1] Fo. 17r[b]. Primo quod est dare quinque maneries universalium, ut declarat Lyncolniensis, primo Posteriorum, capitulo septimo: primum et suppremum genus est racio vel ydea exemplaris eterna in deo; secundum genus est racio communis creata in causis superioribus ut [in] intelligenciis et orbibus celestibus; tercium genus universalium est forma communis fundata in suis individuis et illa, inquit Lyncolniensis, sunt genera et species de quibus loquitur Aristoteles; quarto, forma communis in suis ac[ciden]tibus apprehensa ab intellectu infirmo est universale; sed quintum modum universalium, pro signis vel ac[ciden]tibus intelligendi, dimittit Lyncolniensis ut sibi impertinens.

Cited also in Thomson, 'Philosophical Basis', p. 98.

[2] Fo. 17r[a]–r[b]. Sic Aristoteles mirabili subtilitate complectitur in logica tam noticiam signorum quam noticiam signatorum etc. Cum enim logica sit medium [sic] inter gramaticam et metaphysicam, oportet ipsam participare condicionibus utriusque, tractando principaliter de rebus cum sit medium ad metaphysicam, et secundarie de signis cum sit finis gramatice.

ceptualism and the other, by making the universal a product of
intellection, denied to it any distinctness or separateness from its
subject.[1] In Wyclif's eyes this was a confusion of terms, for
universality was not a quality but a substance inherent in the
essence of the subject. A similar proposition had been advanced in
this form: since the sensible is known in particular objects, we can
deduce that their qualities only exist at the moment of apprehension, that is, that they are created or imposed by intellection.
Wyclif again refuted this line of reasoning as a conceptualist
error. Metaphysicians, he says (plainly distinguishing these from
the terminist *logici*), recognise that all things known to us in their
effects are first known to God and are communicated by him as
universals to the individual objects wherein our senses know them.
And it is the failure to understand this that has caused Ockham
and other 'doctors of signs' to deny the reality of universals.[2]

Further sections in this treatise again show Wyclif occupied
with the problem of conceptualism. One suggested definition, he
noted, was that a substance was singular, but universal as apprehended 'universally' in the mind: so that once more 'universality'
became a mental product—an opinion which, somewhat curiously, he states to have been attributed to Thomas and Giles of
Rome. A second interpretation went to the other extreme, supposing universals to be so absolutely distinct from singulars as to

[1] Fo. 17v[a]. Unde Eustacius distinguit inter universale logicum et universale
metaphysicum, et Commentator dicit quod intellectus est qui agit universali-
tatem in rebus; ex quo sequitur quod est universalitas in rebus, licet non
separata, nec haberent universalia istud esse secundum, nisi [in] anima esset.

[2] Fo. 17v[a]. Unde notandum pro modis loquendi philosophorum quod
sensibile formaliter intellectum dicit tria....Cum igitur illud posse non venit
ad actum nisi per operacionem sensus, dicunt nimirum quod tunc solum est
sensibile in actu, id est potencia sensacionis reducta ad actum, quando sensus
accidentaliter apprehendit.

Fo. 17v[a]–v[b]. Metaphysici tamen sciunt quod natura communis prius
naturaliter intelligitur a deo, ut communicata multis suppositis, quam in effectu
communicatur eisdem; et sic universalitas vel veritas metaphysica non dependet
ab intellectu creato, cum precedit ipsum, sed dependet ab intellectu increato,
que ex eterna noticia intellectualium producit omnia in effectu; et ignorancia
huius sensus fecit Ockham et multos alios doctores signorum ex infirmitate
intellectus declinare ab universali reali.

The final clause is quoted also in Thomson, 'Philosophical Basis', p. 108.

be incapable of communication with them; and this, he added, and again very doubtfully, seemed to have been the view of Walter Burley. The proper definition, Wyclif concludes, is a mean between these two extremes, which admits that the universal is the singular but is formally distinct from it.[1]

The responsibility for propagating the error that the universal has no essence outside its singular, and is essentially identical with it, Wyclif places upon Averroes.[2] Such reasoning he dismisses with contempt; any fool knows that it is invalid: 'scitur a brasiatricibus Oxonie non valere'. Here he is unusually severe upon Scotus to whom he attributes two arguments (which one might think mutually contradictory). His first accusation against the 'Doctor Subtilis' is that, though a realist—'constans universalium explanator'—he had denied that universals were substantial, arguing that no individual substantial object can be substituted for the term 'universal'. His second was that Scotus had declared universals to be each of their inferiors, and so not even formally distinct from them.[3] And elsewhere in *De Universalibus* Wyclif taunts him with outright terminism, classing him with the Modern Doctors, who state that general terms, abstracted by the mind, cannot be predicated even of the subjects in which they

[1] Fo. 18v[b]. Sed post percepi precipuos philosophos perturbari et variare verbaliter in ista sentencia, ut aliqui dicunt quod omnis substancia est singularis, et ut universaliter apprehenditur est universalis. Sed opus dicitur humanum, et res visa, intellecta vel aliter extrinsice denominata ab humanitate, visione et intelleccione extra opus; et ista sentencia imponitur Sancto Thome, Egidio et multis aliis. Secunda via dicit quod universale non est aliquod suorum singularium...et illius opinionis videntur fuisse Magister W. Burlay et multi alii.... Ego autem per medium incedo, concordando extrema, et concedo cum prima opinione, quod omne universale est singulare et econtra, licet distinguantur formaliter abinvicem.

[2] Fo. 19r[b].

[3] Ch. 7, fo. 21v[a]–v[b]. Alii autem dicunt quod non potest demonstrari pronomine talis communis veritas, et per consequens nec aliquod universale, eo quod omne pronomen signat singulariter meram substanciam, et sic pronomen non foret pronomen sed nomen appelativum sicut terminus communis secum convertibilis; et istius sentencie videtur esse Doctor Subtilis, quamvis fuerit constans universalium explanator; ponit enim super distinccione 2[a] Primi Sentenciarum, qu. 7[a], saltem sentencialiter, quod universale est singulum suorum inferiorum, sicut superius allegatum est a Commentatore, Boecio et Anselmo. Sed, ut dixi superius, ista contencio verbalis est nimis inutilis.

supposit.[1] In other words, instead of saying that Scotus identifies universals and their singulars, Wyclif now accuses him of refusing to admit any logical relation between them. Nor is Scotus alone in being charged with denying the substantial nature of universals. Henry of Ghent too is rebuked for saying that prime matter is insubstantial, because it does not act directly but only through the particular objects in which it inheres.[2]

The metaphysical system, developed in *De Universalibus*, can therefore be called thoroughly platonist, yielding nothing either to terminism or to conceptualism. Truth exists in being, and being radiates from the First Cause through a hierarchy of universals to every particular object. In fact it is impossible to conceive the particular without the universal, for each is mutually causal one of the other.[3] And it is through and as universals that God first knows created things, for his knowledge and volitions require a subject in which to inhere, whilst everything that he can know or will is present as an exemplar in himself. So it is fitting that God should know universals prior to and more fully than individual creatures; above all, it is in the essence that the universal inheres and not in the term, *signum*, of the known object.[4]

Realism indeed becomes for Wyclif almost a test of orthodoxy. Twice he breaks off the argument to declare that the Joachite

[1] Ch. 11, fo. 29r[a]. Moderniores autem doctores imbrigabilius dicunt, ut doctor subtilis dicit super dist. quinta primi Sententiarum, quod terminus ultimate abstractionis, cuiusmodi sunt tres termini supradicti, non recipit predicacionem huiusmodi personalem.

[2] Fo. 29r[b].

[3] Fo. 26r[b]. Non est possibile deum creare naturam particularem angeli, nisi creet multas naturas per ordinem se habentes, cum natura particularis non potest esse sine distincta natura superiori, cum omne inferius ponit formaliter suum superius. Nec econtra est possibile quod natura universalis sit sine natura particulari... quia, secundum Aristotelem 2° Physicorum, consonum est nature quod aliqua causent se reciproce in diverso genere causandi.

[4] Fo. 22r[b]. De scientia vero dei, de eius volucione ac ordinacione cum ceteris actibus deo intrinsicis, videtur ut dixi superius, quod eorum terminacio necessitat ad ponenda universalia preter signa, nam loquendo formaliter deus habet tot voluciones quot volubilia;...et per consequens, sicut deus prius quoad consequentiam et undique principalius vult hominem esse quam Petrum esse, videtur quod oportet ponere humanitatem priorem personalitate Petri ad quas voluciones huiusmodi terminantur; non enim terminantur ad signa.

heresy arose through ignorance of the nature of universals.[1] The divine nature, he states, is not a fourth Person but, as it were, a species present in its singulars from which it is formally distinct, though essentially the same. And just as Joachim erred through ignorance, so Peter Lombard was inspired by the truth of universals:

Thus it was by the eternal ordinance of the Holy Spirit that the faithful doctors of the church, gathered together to treat the dispute between Abbot Joachim and master Peter Lombard, were so instructed in the truths of universals that they saw that a personal action within the divinity was not to be attributed to the divine nature, just as a universal nature cannot be predicated in this way, since acts are acts of persons. So it seems to me very likely that, should the question be determined today according to this decree, the opposite conclusion of the Oxonians and other abhorrers of universals, that the divine essence, as a distinct Person, generates and is generated, would very easily be demolished.[2]

Thus realism is the road to truth, in seeking which God shall not desert us; a knowledge of universals is the pre-eminent step on the ladder of wisdom, by which we search out hidden truth; 'and

---

[1] Fo. 28v^b. Inde oppositum videtur esse determinacio ecclesie in principio decretalium dicentis [sic] 'dampnamus et reprobamus libellum abbatis Ioachim, quem edidit contra magistrum Petrum Lumbardum de unitate seu essencia trinitatis'...quod si Ioachim ita dixit, non dubium quin ex ignorancia universalium dixit falsissimum et summe hereticum.

[2] Fo. 27r^b. Unde ex eterna ordinatione Spiritus Sancti fuit, quod fideles doctores ecclesie congregati ad tractandam discensionem inter abbatem Ioachim et magistrum Petrum Lumbardum, ad tantum instructi sunt in veritatibus universalium, ut viderent nature divine non esse attribuendam ad intra actionem personalem formaliter, sicut nec natura universalis recipit formaliter predicacionem huiusmodi accidentalem, cum actiones sint suppositorum. Unde a mihi verissimili [sic T and MS. Caius, fo. 28r] videtur [sic Caius. Omits T] si dictus articulus esset hodie determinatus secundum decretum, Oxoniensium et aliorum abhominatorum [Caius, abhominancium] universalium facillime destrueretur [MSS. destruerent] oppositum, quod essentia divina generat et generatur, cum sit persona sic se habens.

The last sentence quoted is obviously corrupt, and can be emended in more than one way; but its sense is clear enough. The reference is to Fourth Lateran Council, ch. II. I have to thank Professor C. R. Cheney for pointing this out to me.

this, I believe, is the reason why God does not permit the school of universals utterly to fail'.[1]

The control which Wyclif's realism exercised over his theology is conveniently illustrated in chapters 13–14 of *De Universalibus*, which discuss the problem of annihilation and necessitation. These questions are more fully treated in other parts of the *Summa* (and later in this study);[2] but we may suitably note here the degree to which in *De Universalibus* Wyclif accepts the fact that his theological opinions largely depend on metaphysical premisses.

Fundamentally all depends on the single principle of the indestructibility of universals. Wyclif could not openly deny that they were created, without entangling himself in Aristotle's teaching on the eternity of the world and matter; but he so glosses creation as effectively to admit that they were eternal. Universals might be 'created'; but they were neither 'generated' nor 'moved'.[3] This opened the way to the rejection of the possibility of annihilation.[4] God's freedom to annihilate substance, states Wyclif, has customarily been defended as belonging to his omnipotence; and this reading clearly cannot be reconciled with his own affirmation of the nature of universals.[5] He rejects this argument as irrelevant. We must, he says, recognise that creation is the realisation of pure intelligible being; annihilation, therefore, supposes the destruction not only of realised substance but also of the intelligible being in which, by analogy, all creation

[1] Fo. 24r[b]. Ideo noticia universalium est gradus precipuus scale sapientie ad indagandum veritates absconditas; et hec credo est racio quare deus non permittit scolam de universalibus in toto deficere.

[2] For further treatment of these topics in the *Summa de Ente*, Book II, tracts 2, 3 and 6, see below, pp. 187–9, 196–214.

[3] Fo. 29v[b]. Tunc accedendo ad dubium, dicitur quod, loquendo formaliter de universali ut dicit rem universalem, conceditur quod omne universale extrinsecum est creatum; non tamen apparet michi nunc quod generatur vel movetur, nisi extensive equivocetur in terminis.

[4] In ch. 13, MS. cit. fos. 31r[b]–33r[a].

[5] Fo. 31r[b]. Tercium dubium est si adnichilacio sit incompossibilis positioni universalium supradicte. Et videtur multis, cum absolute necessarium sit quod deus potest adnichilare, si sentencia supradicta de universalibus sit sibi incompossibilis, tunc foret summe heretica et summe impossibilis; arguunt enim quod deus non esset omnipotens, nisi posset adnichilare.

inheres.[1] So to annihilate a single object with its intelligible being is to destroy all created things. The novelty of this proposition, formulated long before Wyclif came to concern himself with eucharistic doctrine, was hardly mitigated by an appeal to FitzRalph, who had simply put the orthodox view that God naturally sought to conserve and not to destroy.[2]

The section in Chapter 14 on liberty and necessity reveals the same overwhelmingly metaphysical approach. The riddle of predestination and contingency absorbed all theologians of the age; but Wyclif stands apart in that his position as a theologian was in large part already determined by the rigour of his metaphysics. For if the ideal exemplar present in the First Cause contains the essence of all events, has not God a knowledge which embraces past, present and future in a single act of comprehension?[3] And how then can there be mutability and contingency in the future? In this phrase, 'apud deum sunt omnia que fuerunt vel erunt presencia', lies the key to much of Wyclif's theology. He does not, however, develop the theme at this point, but refers the reader to the tracts on predestination and foreknowledge in the second Book of the *Summa*.[4]

---

[1] Fo. 31v^a–v^b. Solutis ergo istis quatuor evidenciis faciendo evidencias ad partem oppositam, suppono primo, quod sicut creacio est produccio de puro esse intelligibili et sic de nichilo in effectu ad esse effectuale extra deum, sic adnichilacio, si foret, esset cessio creature in pure nichil in effectu, sic quod preter existenciam creature haberet purum esse intelligibile; ex quo videtur primo, quod deus non possit adnichilare aliquam creaturam, nisi adnichilaret totam universitatem creatam, quod tamen non potest propter Christum et beatos; ideo videtur, quod non potest adnichilare, nam omnis creatura habet esse creatum in primo creato anologo [*sic*].

[2] Fo. 32r^b. Et istam sentenciam tenet dominus Ardemakanus, libro primo De pauperie Salvatoris, cap. xiiii°, dicens quod adnichilacio foret non accio sed conservacionis desicio, quod repugnat [*sic*] nostro Domino. Cf. *De paup. Salv.* in R. L. Poole, ed., *De dominio divino* (*WS*, 1890), pp. 299–300.

[3] Cf. Lechler, pp. 252–5.

[4] Fo. 34r^b. Omnia ista et eis similia patent ex hoc infallibili principio, quod apud deum sunt omnia que fuerunt vel erunt presencia, et sic si aliquid fuit vel erit, ipsum est pro suo tempore; unde 'benedictus est dominus temporis' qui elevavit nos supra tempus, ad videndum istam veritatem preclaram et alia que sequuntur; super hoc enim dependent materie de predestinacione et prescientia et omnimode [*sic*] tota materia de necessitate contingencium futurorum.

The reference is clearly to *De scientia Dei* and *De volucione Dei*.

III

The association of *De Universalibus* with *De Tempore* is not fortuitous; they are found together because they are complementary. The first treatise asserts that being is universal; the second that it is eternal. But ultrarealism poses its own special problems. Essences are present as pure intelligible being in divine exemplars, but at least accidentally in particular substance also. All substantial form, therefore, possesses something of the eternal and universal. Wyclif did not shirk the consequences of this premiss, which is indeed the foundation of his metaphysics. A few years later, in his controversy with Kenningham, the Carmelite, he put it as follows:

There are three parts [*nidus*] [to my argument].... The first, which is logical, is that by which we know real universals as genera and species, whose meaning is more often confirmed by Scripture; the second and higher, which is natural, is that by which we know all material substantial form to be accidentally related to its essence;...and the third and highest, which is metaphysical, is that by which we recognise the presence of the eternity of God, in the fulness of his power, in every moment, past or future... and it is by knowing this to be true that we resolve the complex problems of free will, necessity and contingency, and by which we sustain the literal truth of Scripture against the fulsome criticisms of the Sophists.[1]

We are here concerned with the relation of eternal being to its particular manifestation. All that we know in this world as local and temporal exists as indestructible *res* or *ydee* outside time, and their realisation in one form (which may, or may not, occur), cannot effect their continuing existence in the other. Wyclif therefore postulates two time-schemes: the first, eternal or extratemporal, which he calls *duratio*; the second, particular or successive time as apprehended by men, which he calls *tempus*. The distinction, not in itself original, did not involve an absolute division between the two moods; rather, he saw the realising of an object as its conversion from existence in duration to existence in 'successive' moments of consecutive and calculable length.

---

[1] *FZ*, pp. 453-4.

Such time is, in Wyclif's phrase, 'a kind of delay perceived by the imagination from the sensation of movement'.[1]

But, though all substances exist both 'duratively' and temporally, the two moods cannot commingle. Substance as known to us is mutable and corruptible: as intelligible being it is immutable and imperishable. Wyclif's argument, therefore, is simply the application of realist notions to the problem of time. Just as the universal is unaffected by change in the singular, so duration is untouched by temporal change; for to say otherwise would be to admit change, or the possibility of change, in the intelligible being that exists 'duratively'. Similarly subjects which are local and divisible as creatures of time exist in duration as indivisible substance. For example, we speak of the movement of things, or of their parts and qualities; but in duration they have neither parts nor qualities and cannot be moved, since we cannot speak of place in the context of infinity nor of movement (an accident of time) in eternity. In the same way we cannot know duration except in temporal forms, and duration cannot be realised without the qualities of mass and place involved in temporal existence.[2] So between the eternal form and temporal reality there is a correspondence and a relation, but not an identity; and temporal terms can only be used with qualification of enduring essences (as when

---

[1] *De Tempore*, ch. 1, fo. 37r[a]. In tractando de tempore sunt aliqua ex dictis superius capienda: primum quod tempus sit de genere accidencium, sicut enim philosophi supponunt motum esse tanquam notorium [*sic*]...tempus non est substancia sensibilis vel insensibilis assignanda, sed quedam mora ab ymaginativa concepta ex sensacione motus eciam ymaginacionis, nullo alio motu in particulari sentito.

[2] Fo. 37v[a]. Confirmatur ex hoc quod tunc foret eterogenia [?] composita ex duracionibus disparium specierum, quod est contra naturam forme in simplici essencia consistentis...et per consequens partis mundi corrupcio variaret mundi duracionem, et per consequens suum esse.

Ibid. Nam quorsumcunque corpus aliquod moveatur, in quotquot minucias divisum fuerit, manet continue eadem substancia...set manente eodem corpore, manet et eadem sui duracio; ergo nullius corporis duracio situaliter est extensa....

Ibid. Duracio essencie non requirit situacionem corpoream parcium sicut motus; patet eciam quod nulla forma universalis extenditur nec aliqua singularis, nisi cuius principium intrincicum est punctale...situs autem per se extenditur quoad molem et tempus [quoad] successionem.

we speak of God's attributes without supposing them to be finite
or measurable).

As time is a unit of measurement, it is in some measure the
creature of our intellects; weeks and months are human measures.
But this is not to say, declares Wyclif, that men have invented
time, which is like all things a divine creation and would exist
even if there was no man to measure it.[1] It is a human instrument,
but its use is confined to the limits of the created world which
mark the furthest extension of the measurable. And at this ultimate
point, at the moment of creation, time and duration meet. The
world possessed durative being before the creation and will continue to possess it after the Day of Judgement; but the first
moment of Creation was also the beginning of temporality.
Time and Creation, therefore, are reciprocally causal, for without
Creation there could be no first moment, and its purpose is to
cause the first moment. At this point God, the world and Creation
are united, and time as we know it began.[2]

It is plain that *tempus*, which is inseparable from the world,
cannot have preceded its creation; and it is from their necessary
connection that Wyclif proves the impossibility of a second
creation. If, he argued, there were more than one world, there
would have to be, since time is an accident of world, more than
one time-scheme. Characteristically it is with reference to
Grosseteste that he defends the uniqueness of the Creation. If,
said Lincolniensis, we concede the existence of a world prior to
the Creation, we must also concede the existence of 'time past'
before time began. For we can no more comprehend the idea of

[1] Fo. 38v[b].
[2] MS. Lincoln Cathedral Chapter Library, C. I. 15, fo. 329r[b]. Primum
instans et mundi creacio reciproce se individuant ut se causent, sic quod primum
instans, quod est prima mundi duracio, est finis proximus gracia cuius est illa
creacio.

Ibid. Videtur mihi probabile quod primum instans mundi individuatur a
creacione eius subita tamquam a principio proximo et completo...patet deum
et mundum et eius creacionem esse tria principia principaliter individuancia
primum instans.

The relevant leaf in the Trinity MS., containing the end of chapter 4 and the
beginning of chapter 5, has been cancelled, of which the stub remains between
fos. 39 and 40 (modern foliation).

time before time than we can the idea of space beyond the limits of space.[1] The unique quality of the Creation is reflected in the fact that it alone is effected without previous existence in duration.[2] Generation implies the existence of its subject in eternity, but the Creation supposes nothing more than the completed act itself; and since time depends upon creation, all moments of time are also unique.

Wyclif's concept of time helped to moderate some of the more extreme consequences of his metaphysics. Though un ultrarealist, he did not wish to deny the singularity of the individual subject. The individual is distinguished by its uniqueness; it is not another individual. The universal, on the other hand, is distinguished precisely by its communicability. Even so the singular is at least *a* universal as the universal is *an* individual. To emphasise the supremacy of the universal without denying the reality of the singular Wyclif posits time as that which individuates things. A subject, he says, not only exists in time but has its particular existence by virtue of the operation of time; whilst being attains individuation through the operation of time, which gives distinct existence to substance. If time did not particularise, we would have to accept Plato's theory of the time cycle, that all things will in the end return to their former state;[3] but, in fact, he argues, even if the same subject is repeated, the two occurrences are individuated by time.

This doctrine raised a crop of problems. It has been asserted,

---

[1] *Ibid.* fos. 329 v[b]–330 r[a]. Unde Lyncolniensis in quodam tractatu de emanencia creaturarum a deo...sic scribit in fine: desinant huiusmodi admirari cur mundus non sit antiquior quam dicit Scriptura, et cur non prius incepit, quia non potest intelligi incepisse priusquam incepit ab intellectu comprehendente totum tempus preteritum terminatum, sicut non potest intelligi mundum esse alibi quam sit ab intellectu qui comprehendit extra mundum non esse spacium....

[2] Trinity MS. ch. 5, fo. 40r[b]. Creacio in hoc convenit cum generacione et aliis translacionibus subitis, quod singulum talium est indivisibile et a quodam non esse ad existenciam actualem, set discrepat in hoc quod omnis alius motus presupponit existenciam sui subiecti durative...creacio autem non sic.

[3] Fo. 41r[a]. Tunc opinio Platonis haberet magnum colorem, de reditu earundem formarum in numero in magno anno 36 milium annorum.

Curiously this is the very argument raised by Kenningham to refute the ultrarealists. Cf. *FZ*, p. 56.

Wyclif noted, that if each moment causes a new individuation, we must accept Heraclitus' axiom that all is in flux, and that nothing therefore can be known absolutely and permanently. Each new individuation must identify a new substance. His answer is that all difficulties are solved by realist metaphysics; for, though time individuates singulars, their species remain constant, unaffected by temporality.[1] Moreover time does not create particular objects anew; every material substance known to us and created by God must be temporal, but time does not thereby become a necessary constituent of generation. For this would be to make it a necessitating quality, determining events and so repugnant to human free will.[2]

But ultrarealism, as propounded by Wyclif, was bound to carry overtones of determinism, as can be seen in *De Tempore* itself. For the repudiation here quoted is at once followed by a discussion of necessity which virtually negatives the previous statement. No creature can avoid the future unless God permits him to do so, and every future is necessary *ex supposicione*, and so will necessarily happen in its due season. Neither time nor anything else can destroy our freedom of choice; and yet, Wyclif adds, if we could see the unfolding of the course of events, as they are eternally present to God, we should know that those whom he has known to be predestined can never be separated from his love.[3]

---

[1] Fo. 41r^a. Set contra illud tripliciter: primo videtur quod quelibet forma substancialis materialis sit successive, quia proporcionaliter ut succedit novum tempus succedit nova causa individuacionis, et per consequens nova individuacio...maior argumenti primi patet ex hoc quod alietas temporis in quo regeneratur forma materialis faceret alietatem forme materialis.... Sed ista conclusio est descisa ab Augustino, ab Aristotele, 2^a De Generacione in fine, quod propter diversitatem temporis non redeunt eedem substancie in numero sed specie.

[2] Fo. 41r^a–r^b. Tempus non potest causare mundum, tercio ex hoc quod iuxta hanc viam omnia inevitabiliter evenirent, quia inevitabile est quin iste mundus succedet, et ad eius successionem requiritur cuiuslibet istarum parcium successio in tempore suo, sic quod non in alio poterunt generari; quod videtur repungnare [*sic*] libertati arbitrii.

[3] Fo. 41v^a. Conceditur tamen quod nullum futurum potest creatura evitare vel impedire in virtute propria sine speciali dei ordinancia, et tamen illa potest multa impedire. Verumptamen conceditur quod est necessarium ex supposicione quodcunque futurum contingere tempore suo.... Unde si essemus rapti

In this respect necessity does impinge on free will. But the determinist note here sounded, we may remark, owes nothing to theology (though it was profoundly to affect Wyclif's theological system). It was the direct consequence of conceiving matter as a hierarchy of universals, a stream of being which informs substance and by which individual substance is subsumed into a higher order.

The place given to time in Wyclif's metaphysics is crucial. In relation to the particular it is that which individuates; but in respect of itself it is not infinitely divisible into distinct moments. Thus paradoxically we reach the conclusion that time is itself extratemporal, and not a mere quality of substance (as some Ockhamists had contended). And at the end of *De Tempore*, as in the final chapter of *De Universalibus*, we find asserted the principle which recurs in all Wyclif's thought, that time is a unity, knowing neither past nor future but eternally present. At this level, as a *res perpetua*, it becomes an aspect of universal and indestructible being, an idea unaffected by the particular moment.[1] Time has itself become 'durative', embracing all tenses in one 'present'. Time has become an idea.

IV

Wyclif's propositions on time and being first came under attack in the years 1371-3, at the time of his inception in the Faculty of Theology. Our first reaction is one of surprise that this had not happened earlier. Tracing the development of his opinions, we see him led from premisses curious rather than heterodox to a metaphysical determinism; and at the time we meet him embattled in controversy, Wyclif had come to apply these to the text of Scripture. The result was his advocacy of an unusual brand of fundamentalism. Yet his opponents all agree that it was a shock

cum Paulo, videntes totam ordinacionem dei in decursu temporis deo totaliter presentis, tam certi essemus de necessitate cuiuscunque futuri quam certus ipse fuit, quod 'neque mors neque vita nec angeli etc. poterit eos quos scivit esse predestinatos non posset seperare [sic] a caritate dei', ut dicit Ro. 8; nec hoc repugnat summe contingencie vel libertati arbitrii, ut patet alibi.

[1] Fo. 46v[a]. Non igitur correspondet diversitas ex parte rei verbis diversorum temporum, et hic miror quare sic opinantes abhorrent omne preteritum vel futurum esse in tempore suo, cum omne preteritum vel futurum inplicat esse in eodem instanti.

to discover him slipping into unorthodoxy; 'the crop of heresies which he had sown was not at first apparent', as the *Fasciculi Zizaniorum* states.[1] More compelling is the deep respect, and even affection, in which Wyclif was held by his contemporaries. William Wodeford, the Franciscan, was on intimate terms when they read the *Sentences* together as young Bachelors; and when in 1381 he recalled the episode it was, after all the painful events of the intervening decade, with disappointment and sadness but still with respect. There was a laudable aversion to recognise the most prominent lecturer in the Oxford schools as a potential heretic. After all, how seriously did one have to take academic disputes? It is true that Uthred Boldon had just had an unpleasant brush with the authorities, and had been retired by his superiors to a small dependency of his mother house; but his career was not permanently damaged, nor was his reputation for orthodoxy and loyalty. And John of Gaunt clearly had no qualms about employing Wyclif on diplomatic business after his skirmish with Kenningham, nor in retaining him as a writer of broadsides long after he had come under much heavier fire.

John Kenningham,[2] the first publicly to criticise Wyclif's metaphysical eccentricities, was like so many English Carmelites an East Anglian, from the village of Kenningham near Norwich. He entered the Carmelite house at Ipswich, and was master in theology at his Order's school at Oxford when he began to attack Wyclif; he later became Provincial and confessor to John of Gaunt. The texts of his pamphlet war with Wyclif were included by the compilers of the *Fasciculi Zizaniorum*. We have four of Kenningham's determinations against Wyclif, one full-

---

[1] *FZ*, p. 1.

[2] Called 'Cunningham' by Shirley (*FZ*, pp. xvi ff.), who has been followed by most other historians. But see Emden, *Biographical Register*, II, 1077; K. B. McFarlane, *Cambridge Review*, LXXVII, 553 (noticing Knowles, *Religious Orders in England*, vol. II): '"Cunningham", which had no contemporary justification, was invented by an unscrupulous Scottish antiquary, Thomas Dempster, to add yet another name to the list of his country's theologians.' His career and controversies with Wyclif have been much discussed. Cf. *DNB*; *FZ*, *passim*; Workman, II, 120–2; Gwynn, *Austin Friars*, pp. 228 ff.; Knowles, *Religious Orders*, II, 70; McFarlane, *John Wycliffe*, pp. 59, 63. We attempt here only to relate this dispute to Wyclif's system as developed in the *Summa*.

dress reply by Wyclif and a second short tract, which is really a codicil to the first.[1]

Kenningham appeared at a crucial moment in the development of Wyclif's thought. Having incepted in theology in 1372–3, Wyclif must by statute have lectured on the *Sentences* and part of the Bible in the previous two years. It has long been agreed that his dispute with Kenningham must have occurred about this time; and it has been remarked that the Carmelite first refers to his opponent simply as 'reverendus magister meus' and only in the third tract as 'reverendus magister meus et dominus' (as a theologian should correctly be addressed).[2] Apart from this the substance of their dispute shows it clearly to belong to the years *c.* 1372–4. On the one hand, the arguments of Wyclif's earlier treatises had been hardened and extended; and on the other hand there is no mention of eucharistic doctrine or the theory of dominion by grace, which so preoccupied him from *c.* 1376.

Wyclif's metaphysics start from the cardinal assumption that everything possesses intelligible being eternally known to God by ideal exemplars; from which he deduced that all actual things have also an ideal being that knows neither past nor future, but only a 'present' and unchanging essence: whatever is newly created has been and always will be. This can be found in his logic and in *De Universalibus* and *De Tempore*. By 1372–3 not only did Wyclif hold the opinions expressed in these works the more extremely, but he had come to apply them to the text of Scripture. The word of God was divinely inspired; more, it was the material form of the eternal Word, itself a divine exemplar existing prior to the composition of the Scriptures in historic times. Each syllable of Scripture is true because it is a divine emanation: Wyclif had come to accept literal fundamentalism. In the determinations of Wyclif and Kenningham the questions of the eternity of intelligible being and of the literal truth of Scripture are equally prominent.

It is impossible to say precisely when Wyclif first began to apply his realism to Scripture. There is the well-known preface to *De Logica*: 'Motus sum per quosdam legis dei amicos certum

[1] FZ, pp. 4–103, 453–80.   [2] FZ, p. 43.

tractatum ad declarandam logicam sacre scripture compilare....'.[1]
And this work is thought likely to be his earliest. But what
evidence have we that the prefatory note is not a later addition?
At any rate the subject is conspicuous by its absence in the *Summa
de Ente*: that is, with one exception. Chapter 15 of *De potencia dei
productiva ad extra* consists (fos. 138v^b–140r^a) of an unheralded and
impassioned address on the necessity of scriptural study, the evils
resulting from its ignorance and neglect, and the writer's dismay
at the levity with which it is customarily regarded. Unheralded,
no doubt, because it shows every sign of being an interpolation.
As the penultimate chapter in the final tract of the *Summa*, it is
sandwiched between the discussion on annihilation (chapters 12–
14) and the final chapter with its long anti-papal coda, which (we
have argued)[2] is also a patent addition to the original text. The
connecting thread is, of course, the literal and 'eternally present'
truth of Scripture, so shamefully derided by the Moderns.

Racio autem quare scriptura sacra et specialiter evangelii est hodie
parvipensa est triplex: prima quia non considerantur conclusiones
scripture in suo robore, sed tamquam levia dicta cum quibus legifer
posset facillime despensare ordinando oppositum. Secunda causa est
inpertinencia et extraneacio glosarum quas dant moderni, non ponde-
rantes verba scripture usque ad elementa, sed dicentes quod auctor
scripture ex indifferencia posuit nunc casum pro casu, tempus pro
tempore, et ita de aliis non videret ex auctoritatibus scripture innui
quod apud deum sunt omnia presencia.... Tercia causa quare moderni
tam modice intendunt legi evangelii est spiritualitas premii intendentis,
cuius valor non percipitur a discruciatis intendentibus voluptuose aut
infantiliter sensibilibus....[3]

The truths of Scripture are more certain, more necessary than
any other.

Non igitur est putandum a catholico quod fuit [*sic*] tante contingencie
in veritatibus conneccionum et aliis conclusionibus scripture ut moderni
pretendunt, sed in quotlibet est absoluta necessitas prior, utilior, con-
veniencior et demonstrabilior quam conclusionis veritas doctrinalis in
sciencia mathematica demonstrate.[4]

[1] Ed. M. H. Dziewicki (*WS*, 1893), I, I.
[2] Above, p. 136; and, for the chapters on annihilation, below, p. 186.
[3] MS. Trinity Coll. Camb. B. 16. 2, fo. 140r^a.   [4] MS. cit. fo. 139v^b.

The evidence is clearly in favour of a late date for *De potencia Dei*: after 1368 (from a reference to Langham's censure of Uthred Boldon);[1] and before *c.* 1373 (cited in *De incarnacione Verbi*.[2] And if the original material was delivered as part of Wyclif's lectures on the *Sentences*, the work can be dated even more precisely: *c.* 1369–71. The inference is that the new concern for Scripture came at the end of his years as an Artist—a supposition that is also inherently credible.

The text of the controversy between the two masters, printed in *Fasciculi Zizaniorum*, is the best known introduction to Wyclif's early opinions, and there is no need for a simple narrative of their arguments. Indeed this would be difficult, since Kenningham's first tract begins with the battle already begun. He intends, says the Carmelite, to support what he has said in his 'last determination' against Wyclif and to develop arguments touched on in his first article but curtailed by insufficient time.[3] His use of the word *actus* indicates that the attack was delivered in person in the schools. Wyclif's determination follows in reply. But the loss of Kenningham's opening words is not serious, and his criticisms can be outlined with confidence.

Time and again he returns to what he rightly considers his opponent's central argument, that created things possess a triple order of being, as intelligible in God, potential in secondary causes and actual in their own genera.[4] But how had Wyclif arrived at the conclusion that all intelligible being is present in God? By saying, Kenningham replies, that everything which is absolutely necessary is essentially the divine essence, and that therefore intelligibility of being is necessarily present in God. This he denies; even if inherent in God, it is not identical with but caused by him. But Kenningham in his reply himself advances a proposition which Wyclif could never accept; refusing to distinguish between a creature and its being, he equated the

---

[1] Above, p. 129.
[2] S. H. Thomson ('The Order of Writing', p. 150) identifies the passage 'ut patet in materia de adnichilacione' in *De benedicta incarnacione* (ed. Harris, *WS*, 1886, p. 78) as referring to *De potencia dei*, ch. 14 (Dziewicki, ed., *De Ente*, p. 309).
[3] *FZ*, p. 4.   [4] *FZ*, p. 76.

intelligible being of a creature with its intelligibility—a purely conceptualist notion.[1] Wyclif was bound to reject this identification, which deprived being of real existence in God and of its quality as 'eternally present'. God, he declares, intuits being as a single reality which was and is and will be, and whose existence therefore can never cease.[2] To Kenningham this was to distort the word 'present' so grossly as to rob it of all recognised meaning. In his eyes 'present' could only mean what is in and apprehended by the mind or what exists at a given moment; in fact as he saw it 'present' and 'now' are interchangeable, whether we understand 'now' as an immediate intuition or an objective reality.[3] But for Wyclif, of course, present existence as understood by his opponent was only one aspect; for actual existence results when a subject is informed with intelligible being through divine exemplars.

Wyclif's metaphysics assumed being to be necessary and eternal; indeed, Kenningham sourly notes, he takes for granted that his opponents concede that anything that existed did so necessarily, and necessarily is and will be. For example, Wyclif had declared that the words of Christ must be perpetually valid, else he could be accused of falsehood. The Carmelite denies that he or any other scholar had ever suggested that Christ had told an untruth, but it did not necessarily follow that what was true for one moment had to be true at another. There was no need, therefore, to accept Wyclif's position that the past is equally the present and the future, for the fulfilment of a known future act simply results in its becoming a past act; that is to say, past and future are determined relatively to ourselves and one does not cause the other.[4] Every future act, in Kenningham's opinion, is necessarily

---

[1] *FZ*, p. 74. Et ratio est: ego non distinguo inter creaturam et suum esse, et ideo voco esse intelligibile creaturae ipsam creaturam intelligibilem....

[2] *FZ*, p. 9.

[3] *FZ*, p. 11. Praesens vero obiective, sive in ratione cognoscendi, dicitur illud quod clare cognoscitur et immediate, non cognitione abstractiva sed intuitiva.... Subiective autem praesens dicitur quod nunc est, vel in tempore praesenti, non includens respectum, nisi solam coexistentiam secundum tempus vel instans.

[4] *FZ*, p. 97.

contingent; even a prophecy, which is the affirmation of the certainty of a future event, cannot necessitate that event. So if Christ himself should make a revealed prophecy, it would remain a contingent statement until the moment of its actual occurrence.[1] Can we then speak of necessary being at all? Kenningham admits that the perfection of divine knowledge ensures that all things are intuitively present to God; but they are present as apprehended by him and not as actually existing in him. Wyclif regarded this as contradictory; his opponent could not allow that things are present to God and at the same time refuse existence to them.[2] The one point he conceded to Kenningham was that there is an apparent danger of identifying divine intuition with the reality of the intuited object. All the same, he declared, God knows perfectly, if by a simple apprehension, not only what exists but what may exist; and whatever he knows must to that extent have being.[3]

The Carmelite pressed home his attack on the doctrine of necessary being. Wyclif had said that everything that has possible being must be: everything which is possible, replied Kenningham, must necessarily *possibly* be[4]—a very different proposition. His opponent, he believed, had been led into the double error of supposing all being to be eternal, and so all contingent truth to be equally eternal;[5] whilst his realism had led him to posit a multitude of ideas known to God, whereas it is God himself who is the perfect and unique idea. Kenningham in fact was not a realist at all. He had to admit that many philosophers supported Wyclif's arguments; Augustine had certainly adhered to the platonists on the matter of ideas, but even his opinion was not conclusive, and 'only out of respect for the holy doctor' did Kenningham refrain from criticising them. In so Augustinian an age this is an interesting remark.

It will now be clear why it is that, in the determinations of both masters, the questions of the intelligibility and continuity of being

[1] FZ, p. 98.
[2] FZ, p. 465. Ulterius distinguit Doctor de praesenti; concedens quod res est Deo praesens, et tamen non est. Sed revera nec grammatica nec logica nec physica potest capere istum sensum.
[3] FZ, p. 463.   [4] FZ, p. 76.
[5] FZ, p. 65.

and of the literal truth of Scripture are inextricably mixed. For the second depends upon the first, as Kenningham underlined when he entitled his heaviest attack on Wyclif's fundamentalism *De ampliatione temporis.*[1] And what is amplification? It is the logical term used to describe the fullest extension of a subject in range and quality; and the 'amplification of time' is simply Wyclif's doctrine of the unity of time in an eternal present. When applied to the text of Scripture his theory of being led him to conclude that each word is literally true, because present in God, and his theory of time to conclude that Scripture must be eternal. The Bible and the writings of the Saints, he had said, are revered by the Church not because they are ancient but because they are eternal or, to use his own phrase, because of their 'eternal antiquity'. Kenningham retorted that no writing can be prior to its author, since books and their authors are creatures of time.[2] But Wyclif was arguing on quite different lines. Scripture is truth, he declared, and truth and being are convertibles; so Scripture has being, which is of its nature imperishable.[3] It is its natural eternity which ensures its literal truth. This is precisely the argument which six years later Wyclif elaborated in *De veritate sacrae scripturae*, that the literal interpretation alone yields the catholic sense of Scripture. As the immutable word of God it can have but one interpretation: it is as invariable as God himself.[4]

It is hardly surprising that Kenningham objects to such cavalier treatment of the Bible. In the first place it makes plain nonsense of many passages; how can a phrase torn from its context like 'daemonium habes', be absolutely and eternally true? Again Wyclif's theory is determinist and makes human acts valueless; the Donation of Constantine, for example, was pointless if inevitable. His opponent had reached this ridiculous position, the Carmelite said, through his theory of the extension of terms to cover the past and future of an act as well as its present reality. For instance Wyclif had tried to reconcile the eternity of contradictory qualities in the same subject by saying that one quality

---

[1] *FZ*, p. 43. [2] *FZ*, p. 43. [3] *FZ*, p. 454.
[4] R. Buddensieg, ed., *De veritate sacrae scripturae* (*WS*, 1905), I, 123–4.

is true of one moment and its opposite of the next. Even if this were so, replied Kenningham, it would not prove that 'what was is now', an axiom better described as a confusion rather than an 'extension' of words, and which could more accurately be put as 'everything is always and everywhere.'[1] And what are we to make of scriptural phrases like Amos' 'non sum propheta'? If Wyclif followed his theories to their logical conclusion, he would have to construe the words as 'I never was a prophet and never will be'. Wyclif did find a reply to this attack; prophecy, he said, is not an act or habit but a passion which does not cease to exist when it is not moving its subject.[2] But the Carmelite, one feels, got the best of it.

Moreover there is unquestionably force in Kenningham's accusation that Wyclif had not only misapplied a logical term but had contradicted his own rules. Only the terms of a proposition can be extended, he had said; but time, replies Kenningham, is not a term but a fixed point, a particular moment which cannot exist at any other moment. If Wyclif, therefore, was prepared to treat time as a term, then he had no business to quarrel with the 'doctors of signs' he had so frequently abused.[3] The retort was shrewd; for it is surely paradoxical that a philosopher who placed so great an emphasis on the reality of things, and not on their conventional significance, should be reduced to what was little more than word-chopping. It is curious that Wyclif's fundamentalism followed from his belief in the eternal being of each sentence of Scripture; a sense of the very fulness of meaning resulted in a rigidly literal interpretation.

---

[1] *FZ*, pp. 26–7; et sic esset nedum extensio sed confusio verborum (*FZ*, p. 27).

[2] *FZ*, pp. 458–9.

[3] *FZ*, p. 64. Apparet enim quod tota vis huiusmodi locutionis stat in signis, quod innuit Magister meus se velle vitare; cum tamen in hoc discrepat positio sua ab aliis, quod ampliat significationem huius verbi 'est'; quia tempus extra non ampliat, eo quod amplitudo eius non subiacet potestati illius, nec ampliat aliquam veritatem signatam, cum omnis talis sit causata a Deo, et ab eo solo limitata; nec aliam creaturam incomplexam ampliat eadem ratione. Ergo solum signum quantum ad significationem recipit huiusmodi ampliationem et sic Magister meus sibi ipsi facere videtur iniuriam, vituperando doctores signorum.

We can only admire the way Kenningham marshalled his attack. Courteous but firm, he was sure enough of his ground to poke fun at his adversary.

How hard it is to find support against the opinion of so great a doctor! For my arguments are only reed stems with which to beat upon that 'Nest' which is beyond the world of temporal things, as much use as the stones which boys hurl at the Pleiades. As the starry Heavens differ from a spider's web, so do my arguments compare with the opinion of my master. Truly the imposing words of a doctor so famed for learning and eloquence almost defeat me; for I know that neither Aristotle nor the great Augustine spoke thus, though both suffered much from contradictors.[1]

The 'almost' is perfect. Wyclif in fact was in an exceedingly vulnerable position and without any clear idea, as his determination shows, of how to escape.

Yet the attack had apparently come as a surprise which he was inadequately equipped to meet. This surely is the strongest criticism of Oxford philosophy in the 1350's and 1360's. That a man of powerful but eccentric opinions could progress to the extreme position which Wyclif had reached by 1372 without being attacked is an eloquent comment on the vitality of the Faculty of Arts. And even his near-rout by Kenningham did not destroy his reputation as a metaphysician. Thomas Netter himself tells us that he was swept away by Wyclif's logic; and so probably was Uthred of Boldon, if we may judge from his passionate denial of the possibility of annihilation.[2] Of course, the one who suffered most was Wyclif himself. His mind, which was gifted but unsubtle and easily led to extremes, needed trenchant and continuing criticism as a curb on its wilder flights. If there had been more masters of Kenningham's ability, and above all if Wyclif had had to face criticism of that kind ten years before, there would have been far less chance of his taking up so untenable a position. But Oxford in the 1360's contained no one capable of standing up to him. It was its tragedy as well as Wyclif's.

[1] FZ, p. 67. Cf. Gwynn, Austin Friars, p. 229.
[2] See above, p. 110.

CHAPTER VII

REALISM AND THE THEOLOGY OF THE 'SUMMA DE ENTE'

I

WYCLIF was entering middle-age when he took his doctorate. He was also a logician and metaphysician of pronounced and obstinate opinions, which we could expect to influence his theology; and this is the case. The subject of this chapter, the working of God's power as developed by Wyclif in the second book of the *Summa de Ente*, can only be understood if we bear in mind his career as master of arts.

He did not cease to be a realist on incepting in theology and to the place of ideas in God's activity[1] he specifically devotes a complete treatise, *De Ydeis*,[2] together with a single concluding chapter (ch. 15) in *De Universalibus*. His basic premiss is given in the opening statement of *De Ydeis*, that the idea is the eternal exemplar emanating from God by which he produces realities outside himself. The existence of these exemplars necessarily supposes his eternal knowledge of things, since everything intelligible to him must be known by him.[3] It is upon this doctrine of ideas that Wyclif bases

[1] On the relation of realist metaphysics to the divine attributes in Wyclif's system, see Lechler, pp. 250 ff.

[2] Comparison having showed that the text of *De Ydeis* in MS. Stockholm, Royal Library 9, fos. 34–52 was, in places, fuller than that in MS. Trinity B. 16. 2, the citations from *De Ydeis* in this section are taken from the Stockholm MS. I have to thank the Library staff for supplying a microfilm of the text.

[3] Stockholm MS., fo. 34r. Tractando de ydeis primo oportet querere si sint, supponendo quid nominis tale, quod ydea signat racionem exemplarem eternam apud deum secundum quam deus est productivus rei ad extra. Videtur ergo quod talia sint ponenda quia ipse deus intelligit omne intelligibile, illud intelligibile est; ergo est dare quotlibet intelligibilia eterna quibus sic convenit ratio ydee.

See Thomson, 'Philosophical Basis', pp. 96–8, where this incipit is also quoted. We may note that, whatever his conclusions, Wyclif *starts* from very conven-

his theories of knowledge, and it is this doctrine that gives meaning to his triple distinction of being as actual, possible and intelligible. For being exists because known to God; yet what he knows may not at every moment be actual. So we may possibly intuit what does not, and perhaps cannot have, present existence—for example, objects which have eternal being but for us remain only intelligible, or which have an eternal essence but only a temporal existence. But God, who is completely self-sufficient, contains within himself the essence of all things, which in their highest form participate in his essence and are communicated to creatures by ideal exemplars.[1]

In De Universalibus, chapter 15, Wyclif analyses ideas as real universals.[2] He recalled the arguments of conceptualists who, like Giles of Rome, had (in his view) suggested that universals were 'what was thought of universally'; and stated that Ockham's final position was that singulars as understood by God were ideas.

So master Giles seems to find support in Saint Thomas for the opinion that 'every man' is a universal in so far as it is universally conceived; and so the Moderns, ashamed because of Scripture not to admit universals except as terms, say that the sum of all men is the genus and species of Man, just as man is 'the universal clerk' in the circumstances in which he is perfectly knowledgeable. But the third definition was that of the Venerable Inceptor Ockham who in his last days argued that a singular as understood by God is an idea, and that by the same token there seems to be no objection to treating genus and species according to whether they be understood by God or by men.[3]

tional premisses; his words echo Augustine, 83 Quest. qu. 46: 'Sunt namque ideae principales formae quaedam, vel rationes rerum stabiles atque incommutabiles, que ipsae formatae non sunt, ac per hoc aeternae ac semper eodem modo sese habentes, quae in divina intelligentia continentur.'

[1] Stockholm MS. fo. 36r. Sed in deo qui non habet quicquam ab alio sunt omnia secundum esse intelligibile eadem essencia; ideo ista est plena et non partialiter distributa. Et hic dicit communis scola, quod creaturae in quantum huiusmodi sunt encia secundum participacionem, eo quod summum esse inest deo formaliter et communicatur creaturis secundum raciones exemplares.

[2] For which see Lechler, pp. 225–32.

[3] Trinity MS. ch. 15, fo. 34v[b]. Unde dominus Egidius videtur asserere ex sentencia Sancti Thome, quod omnis homo in quantum universaliter conceptus est proporcionaliter universale; et moderniores, erubescentes ex sensu scripture non ponere aliqua universalia preter signa, dicunt quod multitudo omnium

Of course, not even such a modified conceptualism was acceptable to Wyclif. He argued first, that in such a system the terms singular, genus and species would lose their individuality (since God would know things simply as 'an idea'), and secondly, that such ideas, far from giving meaning to their subjects, would be posterior to them and take their significance from them. In fact the definition which Wyclif assigned to Ockham refused any independent being to ideas, which were relegated to being 'the manner in which God knows' an existing object. The perverse consequence of such reasoning, Wyclif stated, was to allow an idea to whatever exists but to deny it to the divine nature, which can never have actual being. It was simply to misunderstand the reality of being, *quid rei*, that is, the essence of ideas.[1]

Wyclif defines ideas as the means by which God creates what is outside himself, the divine nature in action; and if ideas are in God, both the idea and that which it informs are eternal in him. He admitted that the conceptualists jibbed at this conclusion, or would only concede it by glossing 'eternal' in an unacceptable way—by saying, for instance, that ideas are eternally *understood*. He himself would have none of these half-measures; if a subject has being, it has an imperishable idea. He could, therefore, find no justification for those who admitted the necessary existence of ideas but not their necessary actuality; those who had such an opinion, he said, confused the idea with what it informs, *ydeatum*. For it is obvious that a subject may have actual existence at one moment and not at another, but the reality of its idea has an

hominum est genus humanum et species humana, sicut homo est universalis clericus in casu quo perfecte cognoscat multas sciencias. Tercio vere Venerabilis Inceptor Ocham posuit in ultimis diebus suis quod res singularis ut intellecta a deo est ydea, nec videtur ratio quin per idem sit genus vel species secundum modum intelligendi dei vel hominis.

[1] *Ibid.* fo. 35rᵃ. Istis premissis descendo ad materiam de Ydeis. Scribit enim Venerabilis Inceptor Ocham, super primi [*sic*] Sententiarum, dist. 35 qu. 5, quod ydea non habet diffinicionem quid rei sed tantum quid nominis, que est ista; ydea est aliquid cognitum a principio effectivo intellectuali ad quod ipsum activum aspiciens potest aliquid in esse reali producere, et sic ut dicit, quelibet creatura est ydea, sed nulla natura divina est ydea. Primo videtur istum capciosum logicum et subtilem in primo verbo contradicere sibi ipsi; si enim ydea habet diffinicionem quid rei, immo cum omnis creatura sit ydea, si creatura habeat diffinicionem quid rei tunc ydea sic habet.

independent existence. However, he added in a somewhat back-handed compliment, he did not believe that Ockham himself was responsible for so erroneous an interpretation, and the Moderns who had lately advanced it were partly influenced by other philosophers.[1]

God acts, therefore (he repeats in *De Ydeis*), through ideas, which are rationally but not essentially distinct from himself. And these we can regard as universals, for just as individual men are united in their species, so we are united in the uncreated unity of God. But there were others besides terminists and conceptualists with whom Wyclif was forced to disagree. He allowed that some theologians (he names Bradwardine and Bonaventure) had admitted that God was an idea, but had denied the existence of individual ideas; whilst others, like Aquinas and Scotus, had posited as many ideas as there were rational distinctions. But Wyclif found here no fundamental dispute, and only verbal discrepancy. For the first group were emphasising that there can be no essential distinction between ideas as they inhere in God: the second that every conceivable being has its own rationally distinct idea.[2] So there could be no danger of having to admit that God, through participation in ideas, acquires the attributes of creatures, for his essence remains inviolate.

Wyclif continued in *De Ydeis* and in *De Universalibus* to defend platonic idealism against the alleged criticisms of Aristotle and the open attacks of the Modern theologians. Whatever the Philosopher may have said, he writes, he had no justification for accusing Plato of treating ideas as absolutely distinct from God.

---

[1] Trinity MS. fo. 35r^a. ...sed non credo ista fuisse verba vel sentencia Venerabilis Inceptoris Ocham sed alicuius qui partem cepit ab eo et partem ab aliis sanctis doctoribus.

[2] Stockholm MS. fo. 41r. Unde Doctor Profundus, libro primo, ponit quod omnis ydea est verbum et per consequens materia divina, et idem tenet Bonaventura et multi alii doctores negantes multas esse ydeas. Alii autem profundius speculantes, concedunt esse quotlibet ydeas secundum rationem, sed non essentialiter distinctas, ut beatus Augustinus, Doctor Subtilis [*Trinity MS.* Solempnis, *i.e. Henry of Ghent*] et Sanctus Thomas et quotlibet alii illos sequentes. Nec est contradictio inter sensus istorum, licet verba discrepent; nam primi dicunt quod nulla est ydea a deo distincta, suple [*sic*] distinctione essenciali....Ideo quotquot sunt creature possibiles tot sunt ydee.

In the first place, our masters declare that Aristotle understood that Plato wished to say that eternal ideas are essentially distinct from God, and that he clearly refutes this. But it is certain that neither Plato nor anyone else could believe this—even if he got his terms muddled (which I do not think Plato did, for he was a fine philosopher). And the blessed Augustine often commends Plato for his exposition of ideas. So it is very likely that Aristotle, through using his own logic, which differed from Plato's, mistakes his meaning and misconstrues his words, as he often did with ancient philosophers.[1]

Wyclif refused to believe that Aristotle could ever consciously have impugned the platonic system, which alone could explain the eternal knowledge of God which is perfect and invariable, since he knows all things not in the vagaries of temporal existence but in their ideas present in his intellect. He was therefore opposed to the suggestion, which in his view appeared to have been put by both Grosseteste and Thomas, that ideas though 'real' do not inform their subjects but merely demonstrate the existence of a relationship between God and creatures. If this were so, he replies, ideas would still require an object in which to inhere, but the object would be the intelligible being of the creature, which is in fact its idea. 'Rational' ideas, therefore, suppose the presence of a 'real' idea in their subjects; and so the argument becomes circular. Ideas of their own nature must inform their subjects.[2]

And does every conceivable thing possess its idea? Wyclif makes the customary exception of sin and the sinful, as being not

---

[1] *Ibid.* fo. 44r. Ad primum dicunt nostri quod Aristoteles concepit Platonem velle dicere quod est dare ydeas eternas essentialiter distinctas a deo, et hoc inprobat satis plane; sed certum est quod nec Plato nec aliqua [alia] creatura posset hoc credere, licet terminos balbuciendo protulerit, quod non credo Platonem fecisse, cum fuit valde philosophus. Et beatus Augustinus commendat sepe Platonem exposicione ydearum; ideo est verisimile quod Aristoteles propter loycam [*sic*] propriam, in quantum varians a Platone, non capit sensum Platonis, sed equivocat secum in verbis, sicud sepe fecit cum antiquis philosophis.

[2] *Ibid.* fo. 48v. Quidam dicunt quod ydea formaliter loquendo est relacio rationis, sicud videtur Lincolniensis et sanctus Thomas sententiare, ut superius allegatur. Sed illud videtur mihi minus probabile, cum omnis relatio que non est ydemptitas requirit extrema [*Trinity MS.* in actu] vel in esse intelligibili presupposita ad eam; sed extrema rationis ydealis, ex parte creature, foret creatura in esse intelligibili, que est illa ydea, et per consequens presupponeret ydea seipsam.

substantial but mere privations of the good; bereft of being, they cannot possess ideas.[1] Otherwise everything which has species and genera has its idea. Wyclif notes that Aquinas criticised Plato for confining the operation of ideas to species; in Thomas' opinion, God must have a distinct knowledge of every possible creature.[2] Giles of Rome on the other hand had gone somewhat beyond Thomas in saying that even privations like sin are ideally known to God, at least as *ydee cognicionis*. Nevertheless Wyclif rested content with a more limited definition; it seems probable, he says, that in God are the ideas of all creatures, but of creatures alone.[3]

II

The intimate relation of Wyclif's metaphysical idealism and his concept of the operation of God's power is fully illustrated in *De sciencia Dei*, the second tract of Book II of the *Summa* and, in some ways, the most important of all the treatises in this work. The exposition of the working of divine knowledge in chapters 1–5 of this tract is central to our understanding of Wyclif's theology.

God's knowledge of externals, he states, is a formal relation of himself to things known. And since his knowledge is perfect and undivided, there is nothing which God can 'understand' which he does not also 'know'.[4] But it did not follow from this that, because he knows all things, they must all exist. As Wyclif had said to Kenningham—in a specific reference, we have presumed, to *De sciencia Dei*[5]—everything necessarily has

[1] Stockholm MS. fo. 52r.

[2] *Ibid.* fo 52r. Unde sanctus Thomas, parte tercia, dicit quod hereticum est hoc negare; ideo reprehendit in hoc Platonem quia non ponit ydeas citra sensus quia, ut dicit, ex hoc [sequitur] quod deus non habuit distinctam noticiam et intencionem singularium, cum tamen penetrat ad distinctissimam noticiam possibilem creature.

[3] *Ibid.* fo. 52r.

[4] Trinity MS. fo. 54rᵃ. Ex dictis superius satis liquet quod scientia, qua deus scit se ad intra, est divina potencia; scientia vero, qua scit res ad extra, formaliter loquendo, est relacio dei ad scitum vel aggregatum ex natura divina et relacione ad res scitas.

Ibid. Sed omne intelligere dei est suum scire cum respectu cuiuscunque scibilis habet necessario absolute unum scire actuativum.

[5] *FZ*, p. 464. See above, p. 129.

intelligible being and so is known to God; but existence, and his knowledge of existence, is contingent.[1] And following Thomas, he declares that God knows first not the individual creature but its idea as intelligible being, and only secondarily its actual existence.[2]

Wyclif's analysis of divine knowledge was determined by his prior conviction of the eternity of being.[3] The old Oxford quip, he says, that 'God knows what he has known'[4] is perfectly true, and in appreciating this we can explain his knowledge of existence. Nothing outside God can ever cause him to know, since divine knowledge is God himself. It is clear that this must be so of what he knows necessarily and non-contingently, but it is true also of his knowledge of creatures. As intelligible beings, present in him as ideas, they cannot cause him to know; and even as existing objects with whom he has a relation they are not causal. For though, as objects which exist here and now, they are posterior to his knowledge of them (and so would appear to be the 'final' cause of his knowing), as intelligible being they have always existed and have been eternally known to God. Wyclif's distinction between what is temporally and what is eternally prior is like that which all theologians made in discussing salvation—that, though merit is temporally prior to beatitude and so appears to be its cause, in the eternal order the meritorious act is the consequence of acceptance by God. So Wyclif declared that his knowledge and power to cause are aspects of the doctrine of eternal being; for, if all creatures are eternally present in God, their temporal existence cannot move him to know them. As Bradwardine had said in De causa Dei, God's perfection is of his essence and not

---

[1] Fo. 54r^a–r^b. Scientia dei qua scit hoc existere est eadem cum scientia qua scit hoc esse, sed contingenter est deum scire hoc existere, quamvis sit necessario deum scire hoc esse.

[2] Fo. 54r^b. Nullum enim intelligere dei terminatur ad existenciam creature principaliter sed ad eius ydeam a qua habet esse, et primum scire rei secundum esse intelligibile vocatur scientia simplicis intelligencie, sed secundum vocatur scientia visionis, ut patet per sanctum Thomam, prima parte summe, qu. 14^a art. 5°.

[3] Cf. Lechler, pp. 250 ff.

[4] Fo. 54r^b. Unde patet veritas huius antiqui sophismatis Oxoniensis, deus scit quicquam scivit.

in any way acquired: nothing therefore can be added to his knowledge.[1]

Nor can we attribute degrees of perfection to God's knowledge. Some theologians, Wyclif said, had suggested that we could distinguish three kinds of divine knowledge: that which is God himself and by which he knows everything as intelligible being; relative knowledge, which necessarily knows ideas but only contingently knows the subjects they inform; and purely contingent knowledge.[2] But for him there can be neither distinction nor limitation; for we cannot suppose God to know more or less perfectly or to be moved to a greater or less degree. For this reason, he supposed, Bradwardine had declared in *De causa Dei*, Book I, ch. 19, that the things which God knows can move him only 'metaphorically', that is through their ideas and not through their actual existence. But even this cautious limitation was too lax for Wyclif, since it accepted that in some form, however modified, God was moved by a relation between the idea and himself. For Wyclif nothing whatsoever can move God. Moreover Bradwardine had implicitly rejected his own suggestion by declaring elsewhere, in Book I, ch. 14, that future events and other eternal truths 'eternally begin to be', that is, always exist in God.[3]

---

[1] Fo. 54r^b–v^a. Quis, queso, dubitat si ullo modo est scientia divina que non est deus, quod nullum scitum extra deum est causa divine scientie, specialiter si divina scientia non occasionaliter vel contingenter sit divina scientia, quod est absolute necessarium. Si autem loquamur de relacione que est dei ad scita secundum esse intelligibile, patet quod nulla existencia creature est causa illius scientie, quia omnis talis scientia est absolute necessaria. Et existere temporale et omnis per se causa ut huiusmodi est nedum in ordine nature prius suo causato, sed prius tempore vel esse prima [*sic*], ut tam finalis in intencione dei ordinantis ipsam est eterna et sic prior natura suo causato, quamvis secundum esse existere sit longe posterior tempore suo gradu cuius intenditur, ut patet de beatitudine....

Fo. 54v^b. ...verum igitur dicitur quod deus non capit suam perfectionem, cum nulla perfectio deitatis sit sibi accidentalis; ideo non capit eam sed est sua perfectio a rebus...ut dicit Origenes et exponit Doctor Profundus, libro primo cap. 17, 18 et 19.

Cf. *De causa Dei* (ed. Savile), pp. 219–27.

[2] Fo. 55r^a.

[3] Fo. 55r^a. Ulterius de mocione dei concedit Doctor Profundus, primo libro cap. 19, quod intellecta movent non proprie sed metaphorice intellectum divinum, non secundum esse existere sed secundum esse ydeale quod habuit in deo, et allegat Philosophum, libro 3° De Anima...multis autem videtur proba-

Existing objects, therefore, can never cause a new relation, since he has always known them—a form of cognition radically different, of course, from man's, whose mind acts through being moved by intentions which it did not previously possess. Wyclif found support for his belief in the words of Thomas, whose Aristotelianism led him to argue that nothing is created absolutely *ex nihilo* but is always at least potential. The distinction therefore between intelligible and created being is valid, provided we recognise that both are forms of an undivided being, just as past and future are always present in God.

Inevitably this conviction had the most profound effect on Wyclif's attitude to the topics of contemporary theological controversy, and especially the problem of necessity and contingency; for his metaphysics assumed the eternity of being, and hence the immutability of God's acts. God cannot predestine or reprobate any creature whom he has not always accepted or rejected; and so inflexible is this truth that God cannot even cease to love one predestined to salvation, though he fall into mortal sin. It is noteworthy that the passage from *De causa Dei* cited in support appears to be precisely that which Buckingham so strongly opposed.[1]

Secondly, it is clear that all God's volitions and acts of love are eternal ...and so the Profound Doctor in Book 1, corollary to chapter 23, truly says that God does not love or hate anybody anew, nor moderate nor increase his love or hate, and in the following chapter he replies to objections. And he concedes that God loves one who is predestined to salvation, but who is in mortal sin, just as much during the time he is in sin as when he was in beatitude, for he always wills that he should have the greatest possible good in his time.

But one who is foreknown to reprobation, even if he should have been in the grace and love of God while he lived, but not in the grace

biliter posse dici, quod natura divina sit quantumcunque extensse, loquendo de motu omnino inmobilis, quia si ydee causarent motum in deo, hoc esset potissime generandam relacionem in eo. Sed hoc non habet colorem, tum quia ad relacionem non est motus, ex 7° Phisicorum, cum eciam quia talis relacio est eterna et per consequens non pocius motu adquisita quam generacio filii. Doctor tamen ille ad tantum ampliat verba talia, quod concedit futuricionem et alias veritates eternas eternaliter incipere esse, ut patet primo libro cap. 14.

Cf. *De causa Dei*, pp. 208–14, 225.

[1] *De causa Dei*, p. 241; and see above, pp. 59–60.

of final perseverance, God continues to hate because he wills for him the eternal ill of punishment and also eternally wills that, in his life, he should be in grace.... God therefore loves many creatures to the extent of their having the grace of temporal justification whom he does not love to the extent of eternal beatitude.[1]

Such a declaration raised the grave problem of determinism. Anything that God wills he must will eternally, for 'the judgement of the grace of predestination is eternally written in the hand of God'. What he necessarily knows and has known, Wyclif states, must come to pass at a particular moment; since God's knowledge is absolute and fundamentally the divine essence, a future event must necessarily happen in its due time.[2] God knows contingencies; but this was, of course, a far cry from saying that his knowledge is itself contingent. We can test the truth of this statement, Wyclif says, by positing the opposite opinion, that God knows things only in so far as they exist; if this were so, his knowledge would be variable and incomplete. Yet, he adds, this very point he had conceded in former days when, 'against the teaching of Augustine and the saints' he had 'restricted the meaning of "present" to "this particular moment"'.[3]

---

[1] Fo. 55v[b]. Secundo patet quod quelibet volucio vel dileccio dei est eterna a parte ante...unde Doctor Profundus, primo libro corollarie capituli 23, vere dicit quod deus neminem noviter diligit sive odit nec una vice magis aut minus quam alia, et capitulo sequenti respondet ad obiecta. Concedit itaque quod predestinatum existentem in mortali peccato tante diligit deus pro illo tempore sicut cum fuerit beatus, quia semper vult quod habeat tantum bonum pro tempore suo: prescitum vero, etsi fuerit in gracia vel caritate temporali sed non finaliter perseverancie, continue tante odit, quia vult sibi eternaliter malum pene et eternaliter vult quod habeat illud bonum gracie temporalis...multas igitur diligit deus ad gratiam vel justiciam temporalem quos deus non diligit ad eternam beatitudinem.

Cf. *De causa Dei*, p. 241.

[2] Fo. 56r[a]. Ex isto patent tria: primum quod deus ex inmensitate eternitatis sue existentis [P, fo. 20v, assistentis] omni tempore preterito vel futuro habet eternam scientiam de quocunque....2° patet quod relacio racionis inter scientiam dei et scitum [*sic* P. statum T] non habet fundamentum distinctum a divina essencia; et 3° patet quod omnia futura necesse est contingere in suis temporibus.

[3] Fo. 56r[a]–r[b]. Igitur tam accidentalis deo foret scientia contingencium sicut causancia eorundem, quod quondam concessi quando restrinxi verba de presenti ad unum instans, sed stat quod illud est contra sensum Augustini...ac [contra] alios sanctos, ut sepe allegatum est.

Again and again in the *Summa de Ente* Wyclif returns to the theme of the 'amplification' of present to cover the past and future. In accordance with his teaching on the subject he admits that, since God is eternally omniscient, absolute contradictories must in him be simultaneously true. It does not follow, of course, that if men know one fact, they must also know its opposite, for our knowledge is circumscribed by temporal bounds; but in God both are necessarily present as intelligible being. In fact it is misleading to speak of contradictories at all, since to God they are merely facets of a single truth. One of these is known to us as a temporal reality, but the other is equally true through (to use Anselm's words) 'the presence of eternity in the past and future'. Wyclif admits the conventional division of knowledge into kinds; he himself speaks of the *visio activa*, by which God knows reality, as against the *simplex apprehensio*, in which he knows intelligible concepts. But in reality there is no essential difference between the two kinds, for the superiority of the divine mind lies in its ability to know with equal perfection all that it perceives in whatever form.[1]

On this matter Wyclif took issue with some of the opinions he found in *De causa Dei*. He accused Bradwardine of diverging on occasion from the rules of established logic and admitting that God at times forgot what he previously knew, that in certain circumstances he might know nothing outside himself, and that since truth and falsehood relate to contingent things, what is true or false now may not always be so.[2] For Wyclif this was to fall into the double error of questioning God's omniscience and of supposing that his knowledge is divided and particular. But just

---

[1] Fo. 58v^b. In hoc igitur est supereminencia divine scientie supra nostram, quod omne cognitum a deo scientia simplicis noticie potest cognosci ab eo intuitive vel noticia visionis; creatura autem cognoscit quamlibet in esse intelligibili quorum [*sic*] nullum potest intueri vel cognoscere in esse actuali.

[2] Fo. 57r^b. [Sentencia Doctoris] discrepat in tribus a recte [*sic*] logica antiquorum: primo in hoc quod dicit deum multa nescire existere que quondam [*MS.* quoddam] scivit existere, ut quod scivit Christum pati; [*P*, fo. 23v: et nunc ut dicit nescit Christum pati;] secundo in hoc quod ponit deum nihil preter seipsum scire existere, posito quod destruatur tota universitas creata; et tercio in hoc quod ponit propositiones contradictorias alterari de veritate in falsitatem et econtra, ipsis significantibus pro significabili contingenti.

as we know, he says, that a river exists, though part of its flow has passed from our sight, so whilst things slip from our memory God knows and remembers all. Wyclif in fact suspected the 'Doctor Profundus' of believing that the past, present and future are separate. For instance, he commented, Bradwardine had said that God knows the stages of the Passion as distinct acts (which are first future, then present, and finally past), arguing that to vary the tense is to vary the subject of the sentence, and that the truth of a contingent proposition is altered by a variation in the subject to which it refers. Indeed unless the tenses are varied, he had said, there is no reason why one should not be the other. This is, of course, precisely Wyclif's own proposition, that ultimately they are the same. But he excuses Bradwardine; the 'Doctor Profundus' had really meant to suggest that time was distinct not in its essence, but only in its predication of particular events.[1] However, Bradwardine also seemed to have made a false distinction between the powers of God by dividing his knowledge into simple and complex (which could not, in the second case, be completely self-sufficient). The answer, replied Wyclif, is that all divine knowledge is simple; and though we speak loosely of his knowing things 'complexly', it is in reality our knowledge of him—*signa nostrorum artificialium*—not his of us, which is complex.[2]

In truth God's mind cannot be really said to act at all, at least not after the manner of the human mind, for any such acts would make his knowledge complex. So whilst the simplicity of divine

[1] Fo. 59rᵃ–rᵇ. Sed illam sentenciam inpugnat [MS. inpignat] Doctor dupliciter, primo per hoc quod diversitas parcium orationis diversitatem enunciabilium causat; 2° quia iuxta illud sequitur quod propositio semel vera maneret continue sic vera, quod est contra Aristotelem sic ponentem proposicionem veram contingentem mutari a veritate in falsitatem propter mutacionem rei extra. . . . Patet autem utraque illarum deduccionum sic, nisi foret distinccio signatorum huiusmodi proporcionum de presenti, preterito et futuro, non esset ratio quare una foret huiusmodi vera [MS. verum] quin per idem quelibet. . . . Et quoad discrepanciam Doctoris, videtur quod Doctor Profundus intelligit illa tria que distinguntur secundum rationem non distingui essencialiter sed in predicacione secundum essenciam esse naturam divinam, et illa sentencia est vera, ut patet ex dictis.

Bradwardine in fact states an almost identical view of the 'eternal present', *De causa Dei*, Book I, ch. 14 (corollary), pp. 209–14.

[2] Fo. 64rᵇ.

knowledge ensures that he cannot be moved by any relation, its eternity bars him from being moved by creatures. For if we, who are the objects of his knowledge, could cause him to know us, we would be capable of causing his preordinance, though ourselves the subject of it; in this way, for example, we could elicit grace by showing merit.[1] In fact, Wyclif declares, God's powers are eternal and therefore necessarily prior to their temporal effects. So there is no contradiction between the eternity of his power to preordain and the actual preordinance caused by existing objects of his knowledge, occurring in time; for what is to men a future event is to him a present reality.[2] Though temporally the end follows the means, the end has been eternally ordained by God; and hence his knowledge of existing things is contingent, but none the less perfect for that.

III

If Wyclif continually asserts that God's knowledge is perfect and absolute, he is more cautious in asserting the absoluteness of his power. This question he treats in the final tract of the *Summa*, Book II, tract 6, *De potencia Dei productiva ad extra*.[3] It has long been recognised that this tract contains an important discussion of annihilation; but the chapters printed by Dziewicki are not alone in the *Summa de Ente* in mentioning this problem, and his edition, made without reference to the contents of the rest of the treatise, sheds a slightly misleading light on their significance. For Wyclif's principal subject is rather the extent and limits of God's power,

---

[1] Fo. 60rᵃ.

[2] Fo. 60rᵇ. Ulterius conceditur quamlibet creaturam incipere causare scienciam dei quando incipit esse verum, cum causacio dei quecunque divine sciencie est eterna [*MS.* eterne]. Unde sicut preordinancia dei est eterna et preordinacio creature est temporalis, cum incipit esse cum creatura, sic causancia creature respectu divine sciencie est temporalis et causacio sciencie est eterna; nec pocius sequitur, illa sciencia nunc causatur ab illa creatura existere, igitur illa nunc existit. Deus enim eternaliter scit omnem creaturam existere tempore suo, cum sequitur, si existet, existit.

[3] The only complete text known to us is in MS. Trinity Coll. Camb. B. 16. 2, fos. 123vᵇ–141rᵃ. Chapters 12–14 (fos. 135rᵇ–138vᵇ) have been printed as *Fragmentum de annihilatione* in Dziewicki, ed., *De Ente*, pp. 287–315; see also the editor's comments, *ibid.* pp. lv–lx, and above, pp. 122, 132. Some short passages from chapters 12–14 are printed in *FZ*, introduction, pp. lvi–lx.

and only secondarily the particular problem of his power to annihilate substance. For if God cannot annihilate, must there not be other restraints on his activity?[1]

God's power, he declares, using the classic scholastic distinction, is either absolute or ordinate: the first refers to everything which is absolutely possible of intelligible being; the second to possible things in so far as they actually exist. Ordinate power is contingent because tied to existence, but is not thereby made accidental to God, since it is inseparable from him.[2] But if God has absolute power, must this not mean that he can do anything—create a vacuum, for instance, or annihilate substance? If we follow Anselm's definition, says Wyclif, that every act depends on a previous volition, we must conclude that he may do whatsoever he can be conceived of as willing. But was this not the absolute liberty which the radical Ockhamists were ready to attribute to the divine will? At any rate Wyclif refused to accept so loose a construction, which would even allow God, should he so wish, to terminate his own power. In treating this problem of the ultimate limits of divine power a number of theologians, he noted, including Scotus and Bradwardine, had taken up the question of so-called 'impossible propositions', and had asked whether God could not simultaneously cause things to be and not to be, and so forth. At the opposite extreme stood Henry of Ghent, who had said flatly that God cannot perform the impossible. But in fact, Wyclif declared, Henry's opinion is not irreconcilable with the doctrine of God's supreme power, for it is he himself who is the cause of the necessary impossibility of an act; God freely wills his own limitation.[3] Of course, he continued, a pagan philosopher

[1] On the limitations of divine power in Wyclif's system, see Lechler, p. 251.

[2] Fos. 123 v^b–124 r^a. Potencia absoluta est que terminatur ad possibilia in esse intelligibili et absolute possibili; potencia autem ordinata est que terminatur ad possibilia secundum suum esse existere pro alico tempore, et illa potencia ordinata vocatur contingens sed non accidentalis deo, cum non potest talem ordinatam adquirere vel deperdere.

[3] Fo. 124 r^b. Possunt ex dicta deduccione equivocacionis divine potencie concordare doctores qui diffuse discutiunt si iam deus non potest facere illud simul esse et non esse, quia illud non potest fieri et econtra...quam materiam tractat Doctor Subtilis, super 1° Sentenciarum, dist. qu. (?), et Doctor Profundus, libro primo, cap. 13. Doctor autem Solempnis, Quodl. suo 6°, qu. tercia,

would deny that there could be any restriction of the divine power. If God is omnipotent, he would say, he can do whatever he pleases.[1]

Here, it appears, Wyclif was referring not to an imaginary opponent but to a particular group of philosophers. Shortly before this last remark, whilst discussing the scope of divine power, he had attacked those who had used the theory of the double truth to assert that 'philosophically' speaking we can deny catholic doctrine and confirm self-contradictory propositions.[2] This was an attack on those who had attempted to free themselves from the bonds of theology by postulating a suspect metaphysical argument. Yet the Averroist heresy of the double truth had from the first been condemned by the Church and there would seem to be little point in Wyclif adding his voice to orthodox opinion. But who were these philosophers whom he was so anxious to refute? As he made clear, they were the *infideles philosophi* who had declared that there were no limits to God's power, and had sought protection for their argument in the distinction between 'philosophical' and 'theological' truth. Such independent 'philosophical' truth (which included the principle, so repugnant to Wyclif, of God's supreme power to annihilate), they had tried to base upon Aristotle. Some philosophers, he states, through a too exclusive reliance on Aristotle had fallen into error on the subject of creation. But many catholics believe on philosophical grounds that God's existence is absolutely necessary, and yet are prepared

dicit quod omne impossibile ideo est impossibile quia deus non potest illud facere; et Quodl. 8°, qu. tercia, dicit quod deus non potest tale facere quod illud non potest fieri. Que dicta in nullo contradicunt quia illa veritas, que est 'impossibile est tale fieri', est causa potencie relative terminate ad illam. Econtra autem potencia qua deus causat inpossibilitatem illam, id est causa quare necessarium est quod inpossibile est sic esse.

Cf. *De causa Dei*, pp. 205–8.

[1] Fo. 125 v^b.

[2] Fo. 125 r^a. Ideo, ut alias dixi, notabiliter decipiunt [*sic*], qui ponunt philosophicum esse negare articulos fidei vel aliquam veritatem, quia consequenter habent dicere quod philosophicum esset concedere quantumlibet conclusionem naturalem contradicere sibi ipsi; ut theologus, asserens philosophice negandum esse quod deus est trinus et unus, quod deus est creativus etcetera, eo quod repugnant principiis philosophie, habet consequenter concedere quod quelibet particula philosophie repugnat eciam sibi ipsi.

to assert that there are some acts with which he cannot possibly be associated. On the other side stand those who believe that God is capable of any conceivable act, including annihilation. Yet there is nothing incongruous, Wyclif says, in affirming that there are things which God cannot do. His opponents mistakenly believe that Aristotle must always be right; there is, they say, such a thing as pure philosophical truth—*puri philosophi non est theologizare.* Wyclif retorted that Grosseteste had already shown, in his *Hexameron*, how vain and foolish were the arguments of those so besotted with the Philosopher or their own cleverness, that they thought all Aristotle's statements could be reconciled with Christian doctrine.[1]

From this outburst we can identify these Modern Averroists as the radical 'possibilist' theologians, who were prepared to attribute any act to God. It is true that contemporary radicals were exploring the extent of 'possibility' in many other fields besides that of annihilation; we have just mentioned the question of simultaneously existing contradictories. But it was this above all which obsessed Wyclif. In his eyes, to admit that God might possibly annihilate substance was to mark one as openly heterodox, and to deny its possibility the strongest proof of orthodoxy. One was refusing to attribute the ridiculous and the scandalous to God. Wyclif's identification of radicalism with the possibility of annihilation is strikingly illustrated in Chapter 12 of *De potencia Dei.* In a reference to the condemnation of its impossibility

---

[1] Fo. 127v^a. Et nedum philosophi sed multi catholici verisimiliter credunt philosophice deum esse tamquam absolute necessarium, et tamen aliqui attribuunt sibi quasdam passiones huiusmodi tamquam impossibiles absolute; et indubie altera pars opinatur inpossibile et negat necessarium simpliciter, ut aliqui theologi concedunt ut absolute necessarium quod deus est adnichilativus, infiniti vacui creativus, cuiuscunque nature create ypothetice susceptivus, cuiuslibet corporis dimencionaliter multiplicativus, et sic de huiusmodi infinitis que concernunt divinam potenciam. Alius autem econtra dicit quodlibet tale inpossibile, unde non est inconveniens philosophos quoscunque, v[ar]iantes preter unum, concedere in casu absolute necessarium negare ut inpossibile. Unde vane solicitantur aliqui palliando vel glosando dicta Aristotelis...ideo dicit Lincolniensis in suo Exameron cap. 10°, contra tales inordinate affectos Aristoteli vel sibi ipsis inaniter iactando, quod sciunt glosare patrem philosophie Aristotelem concordando omnia dicta sua cum theologia, quod studium huiusmodi est inane.

which, as has been noted, can hardly refer to anything but Archbishop Langham's censure of Uthred of Boldon in 1368, he couples the 'many condemnations' of this thesis with the 'general testimony of the Moderns'[1] (a term which invariably refers, in Wyclif's works, to Ockhamists). And the Moderns defended the power to annihilate as a part of God's omnipotence. But, though he held a high doctrine of divine power, Wyclif was not prepared to say that it was absolutely unlimited. The irony of his position was, of course, that he utilised a metaphysical principle, which he thought of as a guard against heretical opinions, but by which he was himself being inexorably driven into open heresy. For his denial of transubstantiation was the consequence of his belief that God cannot annihilate matter.

Not that he wished in any way to detract from God's power. On the contrary he followed his attack on the Moderns with an affirmation of the uniqueness of his power to create, *creancia*, which cannot be transferred to any other being. Wyclif's refusal to admit God's power to annihilate was founded not on theological radicalism but on purely metaphysical assumptions; it was incompatible with his doctrine of the eternity of being. If one could annihilate substance, he says, one would destroy also its past and future, since it would have lost the *esse rei* which is its eternal being.[2] Similarly in *De Universalibus* he had declared that the continuity of being precluded its annihilation, because 'is' and 'was' cannot affect the existence of 'will be'; time can individuate being as known to us but not its indestructible essence.[3] Wyclif

---

[1] Dziewicki, ed., *De Ente*, p. 287. Secundo confirmatur ex eo quod aliter videtur derogari potencie divine, ut patet ex multis dampnacionibus posicionum negancium possibilitatem adnichilacionis, et communi testimonio loquencium modernorum, qui omnes dicunt concorditer quod deus non esset plenus dominus creature, nisi ipsam possit adnichilare. Ymmo, negare a deo possibilitatem adnichilacionis esset tollere eius omnipotenciam.

On Uthred's censure see above, p. 109.

[2] Dziewicki, ed., *De Ente*, pp. 291–2.

[3] *De Universalibus*, ch. 13, fo. 32r[b]. Multa accidencia mundi deus non potest adnichilare; ergo nec eorum subiecta... et assumptum patet de tempore, motu et ceteris accidentibus successive individuatis ab istis, que deus de potencia sua absoluta non potest destruere ante finem sue naturalis periodi, ut alais ostendi.

believed that nothing can cease to be as long as its essence remains in God; and so extreme was his realism that the destruction of a single substance, as he thought, would bring the whole realm of being to an end. His belief had important implications for the working of divine power. Has not God absolute power to conserve or destroy what he has created? Wyclif replies that God certainly has liberty of contradiction and cannot be bound by anything outside himself. But he is free in that he may act or not act; he cannot bring to an end a course of action once begun.[1] So when he has created a substance he cannot deprive it of its eternal being. It is true, Wyclif says, that he freely wills beatitude to creatures, but once made acceptable to him they cannot be reprobated. In this way the principles of his metaphysics led Wyclif to censure those who put no bounds to the possible extent of divine activity, and to declare that God of his own free will limits the operation of his power.

We are so accustomed to think of him as inflexible on the matter of annihilation that it is worth noting the few occasions on which he is less than absolute. As is well known the early treatise *De actibus anime* shows him undecided on the problem;[2] and in *De potencia dei*, which gives his mature opinion, he makes a curious retreat. After an explicit denial of the proposition that God could but would not annihilate, he appears to quote with approval Richard FitzRalph's assertion of this very point, that his omnipotence is fully protected by allowing that God could annihilate, if he so wished. In *De Universalibus* also he makes a show of moderation more apparent perhaps than real:

Because it seems to many philosophers that omnipotence of God would require his capacity to annihilate, and so that I should not sustain incorrect conclusions and weary of the discipline of truth, I now make this caution. Neither Scripture nor reason makes it certain that God can annihilate; and because it would be most dangerous to assert and concede what, if it should be false, would be impossible and heretical,

---

[1] Fo. 31vª. Libertas contradiccionis consistit in posse libere facere vel non facere, non autem in posse facere atque desistere; ut deus libere contradictorie facit me fuisse et tamen non potest desistere ab huiusmodi factione.

[2] *Miscellanea Philosophica*, ed. Dziewicki (*WS*, 1902), I, 49, 127.

I shall not admit that he can until I have greater evidence in which I can believe, which will not come before we shall have heard at the Last Trump the voice of the Archangel.[1]

Despite the considerable attention he devotes to the question of annihilation in the last tract of the *Summa de Ente*, Wyclif has remarkably little to say about its relation to the problem of transubstantiation, and this is further evidence for giving a comparatively early date to the treatise. We know that in the years 1370–2 his views on transubstantiation were undergoing rapid change, and that he was unwilling to give in public any fixed definition of the nature of the consecrated host. In *De potencia Dei* as elsewhere Wyclif states that in the eucharist the substance of the bread cannot be annihilated if the accidents remain. And if the accidents remain, how much more does the quiddity of the subject remain undestroyed?[2] It is hardly surprising that this opinion had been attacked by 'a certain doctor' (how one despairs of the anonymity of the schools), who had turned Wyclif's own logic against him. Reading between the lines we can sense that the doctor was pulling his opponent's leg:

And from this consideration a certain doctor says that God could not by his absolute power more exalt something than by annihilating it; for just as that object would be utterly identified with God, so it could not be more impoverished than by its creation because made more distinct from him.[3]

So could the tenets of ultrarealism be turned against their author.

It is most unfortunate that Wyclif is not more specific here or elsewhere in the *Summa* in his statements on the eucharistic ques-

---

[1] Fo. 31vᵃ. Unde quia multis philosophis videtur quod tenderet ad dei omnipotenciam posse adnichilare...ideo ne suscitem conclusiones inutiles et tardem a disciplina veritatum utilium, utor hodie hac cautela: ecce non est michi certum ex racione vel scriptura sacra quod adnichilacio potest deo competere; ideo cum periculosum sit illud asserere vel admittere, si sit falsum, quia tunc esset impossibile et summe hereticum, ideo non admittam illud propter periculum sine evidenciis facientibus mihi fidem, et credo quod hoc non fiet antequam audiverimus in tuba novissima vocem archangeli.

Also Dziewicki, ed., *De Ente*, pp. 300–1.

[2] Dziewicki, ed., *De Ente*, pp. 289–90.

[3] *Ibid.* p. 291. Perhaps the doctor was Kenningham, who knew Wyclif's weakness in this quarter; cf. Gwynn, *Austin Friars*, p. 229, citing *FZ*, pp. 11, 67.

tion, since it is the only subject for which we can with certainty trace the development of his thought at the time he was reading the *Sentences*. Our knowledge of the successive changes in his views at this time comes to us from William Wodeford, who included in his great defence of transubstantiation against the Lollards, *De sacramento altaris*, two autobiographical passages describing his relations with Wyclif.

The name of Wodeford[1] is familiar to all students of Wyclif, though his works have not yet received the attention their considerable bulk deserves. They fall into two classes: the apologetic treatises, attacking Wyclif's doctrinal errors and opinions on lordship, and countering the anti-mendicant tracts of Wyclif and FitzRalph; and scriptural studies. He wrote commentaries on Ezechiel, Ecclesiastes, the Epistle to the Romans, Luke and Matthew.[2] Certainly his heart seems to have been in biblical study. His interest as a controversialist lies in the fact that he was not only a critic but a long-standing friend of Wyclif. The close alliance of Wyclif and the friars,[3] which continued surprisingly far into the 1370's, when he had long become suspect to the other regulars and to the hierarchy, has often been noticed. In the autumn of 1376 John of Gaunt had no difficulty in finding a doctor from each of the four Orders of friars to defend Wyclif at St Paul's. The Austin friars seem to have been particularly loth to attack his view on dominion by grace, and they countenanced, if they could not have supported, his eucharistic teaching up to its actual condemnation in 1381. It is significant that as late as 1396 Wodeford admitted that Wyclif's opinions still had several defenders.[4] His friendly acquaintance with the Austin friar, Thomas Winterton, a contemporary in the school of theology,

---

[1] *DNB*, *s.v.* Woodford; *FZ*, pp. xv, 517; Workman, I, 185–90; A. G. Little, *The Grey Friars at Oxford*, OHS, xx (1891), 81, 246–9; Gwynn, *Austin Friars*, pp. 227 ff.; also references cited below.

[2] *DNB*; Conrad Walmsley, 'Two Long Lost Works of William Woodford and Robert of Leicester', *AFH*, xlvi (1953), 459.

[3] The rest of this paragraph depends upon Gwynn, *Austin Friars*, pp. 227 ff.

[4] Gwynn, p. 235, citing Wodeford's 'De causis condempnacionis articulorum 18 dampnatorum Johannis Wyclif', in E. Brown, *Fasciculus rerum expetendarum et fugiendarum* (London, 1690), I, 250.

also endured until the breaking point in 1380-1. The tone of his *Absolutio*, one of the several replies induced by the *Confessio* of 1380, is 'courteous and respectful' in its refusal to brand Wyclif as a formal heretic.

But the friendship, and friendly disagreement, with Wodeford is the most striking. Their discussions when reading the Lombard (described below) were, of course, private. As early as 1374 the *Determinatio* on lordship had earned Wodeford's opposition;[1] but even in 1376-7 Wyclif could still thank his protagonist in unmistakably warm terms for criticism and advice at the time of their incepting acts:

doctor meus reverendus magister Willelmus Wadford [*sic*]...et revera obligor eo amplius huic doctori meo, quo in diversis gradibus ac actibus scholasticis didici ex eius exercitacione modesta multas michi notabiles veritates.[2]

Wodeford's is likely to be the most balanced judgement on Wyclif, and his changing arguments, that we shall find. The two men, as bachelors of theology, had read the *Sentences* 'concurrently'; in this way each could respond in his own lectures to the arguments of the other.[3] Wyclif was accustomed to lend Wodeford his notebook so that the latter could study his opinions and add his comments at leisure; and when the Franciscan wrote in 1381 he was able to be so precise because he had to hand the autograph of Wyclif's argument, composed at the time of their reading the Lombard. One would give a great deal for those hurriedly scribbled notes.

The references to transubstantiation in the *Summa de Ente* are too brief to enable us to test the suggestion already advanced that the theological treatises in Book II are based on Wyclif's *Commentary on the Sentences*. The sacraments were customarily treated

---

[1] Loserth, ed., *Opera Minora* (*WS*, 1913), pp. 415-16.

[2] J. Loserth, ed., *De civili dominio* (*WS*, 1902), III, 351.

[3] The story of the exchanged notebooks has often been given; see Little, *Grey Friars*, p. 81 and n. 6; Workman, II, 34; Gwynn, pp. 227-8; *DNB*. A partial version of the first passage from Wodeford's *De sacramento altaris*, given below, is printed by Shirley in *FZ*, p. xv n. 4, from MS. Bodley 703 (transl. Workman, II, 34). A part of the second passage is quoted by Little, *op. cit.* p. 81 n. 5, citing Twyne MS. xxi, 502.

in the fourth Book, and the tracts edited in the *Summa* seem rather to correspond to Book 1. But even if this theory is dismissed, Wyclif's opinions at the time of his inception in theology are intimately connected with the matter of the *Summa de Ente*; and William Wodeford's recollections of the *Doctor Evangelicus* at the crossroads are invaluable. Moreover the note of deep personal acquaintance and respect which informs them, and which is missing in Kenningham's tracts, increases our confidence in his fidelity and judgement. The passages run as follows:[1]

The 14th truth is that like a wavering man this master many times changed his opinion on the subject of the accidents in the sacraments. This is clear from the fact that when he first read the *Sentences* at Oxford he asserted that their subject was a *corpus mathematicum*. After many arguments put to him he said that their subject was not the bread but a *corpus mixtum*. Afterwards when he was a responding bachelor he publicly held, in his replies in the schools of theology, that the accidents did have a subject, although he did not know what it was. After, when he had become a doctor, he held that the bread which the priest blesses remains after the blessing, and the sacrament is the Body of Christ and also the subject of the accidents as before.

Now lately, after leaving the university, writing to a knight who had argued against him, and moved by fear as I think, he has said that in the sacrament is the Body of Christ in the form of bread, but has also asserted that he did not explain whether that form is the material substance of bread or an accident without a subject as, so he says, heretics declare. And so in turn he has many times changed his opinion as a reed dipping in every direction; and likewise, as it seems to me, little store need be set by his opinions.[2]

[1] To the five MSS. of *De sacramento altaris* listed in the *DNB* can be added Cambridge University Library, MS. Add. 3571 (formerly MS. Phillipps 9730), fos. 3r–65r; described in C. Walmsley, 'Two Long Lost Works of William Woodford and Robert of Leicester', *AFH*, XLVI (1953), 458–70. The text here given is that of British Museum, MS. Royal 7. B. III, fos. 4v–65v.

[2] MS. cit. fo. 45r. 14[a] veritas est quod, sicut homo instabilis, in suis Sententiis multotiens iste Magister mutavit sententiam suam de subiecto sacramentalium accidentium. Patet hec, nam primo, quando legit Sententias Oxonie, asseruit quod subiectum illorum fuit corpus mathematicum; post multa argumenta sibi facta dixit quod subiectum illorum non fuit panis sed corpus mixtum; post, quando fuit Bacalarius Responsalis, tenuit publice respondendo in scolis theologie, quod habuerunt subiectum, sed nescivit quid

And later in the same question of *De sacramento altaris* Wodeford continues:

The 18th truth is that just as he varied his opinions on the subject of the accidents of the sacraments, so he varied his opinions on transubstantiation. This is clear; for when I was reading the *Sentences* concurrently with him at Oxford, speaking of transubstantiation he asserted and long held that it was a mathematical replacement [*successio multiplicativa*] of the Body that was present, in an equivalent of the Body which ceases to be. And he then explicitly posited that when the bread is transubstantiated into the Body of Christ it is then annihilated—and I have his own words in his own hand beside me now.

For it was his custom to write his replies to the arguments which I made to him in a notebook which I sent him with my points, and he would return the notebook. But now he says that transubstantiation does not require the annihilation of the bread; but that just as a sinner converted to righteousness is still the same man as before (and yet the unrighteous has been converted into the righteous), so when the bread is converted into the Body of Christ it remains the same bread as before, and yet is converted into Christ's Body. And so he has changed his opinion. But I then deduced and to this day hold true, that no particle of that description is necessarily required for transubstantiation, and that such a description does not amount to transubstantiation, as is clear from many arguments I made when reading the *Sentences*.[1]

Since Wodeford tells us that he disputed publicly with Wyclif,

fuit subiectum illorum. Postquam fuit Doctor, tenuit quod panis quem sacerdos benedicit manet post benediccionem. Et est sacramentum corpus [*MS.* corporis] Christi, et est subiectum accidencium sicut prius. Iam tarde, postquam recessit de universitate, scribens ad unum militem qui contra eum se posuit, timore ut credo ductus, dixit quod in sacramento est corpus Christi sub forma panis, sed asserit se non explicasse an illa forma sit substancia panis materialis vel accidens sine subiecto sicut, inquit, dicunt heretici. Et sic successive multociens mutavit sententiam suam, velut arundo mutabilis ad omnem partem; et ideo, ut mihi apparet, de opinionibus suis modicum est curandum.

[1] MS. cit. fo. 46r. 18ma veritas est quod, sicut variavit opiniones suas circa subiectum sacramentalium accidencium, ita etiam variavit opiniones suas circa transubstanciacionem. Patet hec: quia quando concurrebam cum eo Oxonie in lectura Sententiarum, describens transubstanciacionem asseruit et tenuit diu, quod ipsa est successio multiplicativa corporis quod prefuit loco adequato corporis desinentis esse. Et tunc posuit expresse quod, quando panis transubstantiatur in corpus Christi, quod tunc desinit esse; sicut de manu sua propria adhuc mecum habeo. Habuit enim de consuetudine scribere responsiones ad argumenta per me sibi facta in quaterno, quem sibi misi cum argumentis, et

it is very possible that he is the 'certain doctor' of whom the latter complained in *De potencia dei*. Wodeford is a thoroughly reliable witness; his words reveal that in the first year in which Wyclif read the *Sentences*—that is, most probably in the year 1370-1—his eucharistic views were unexceptional, if somewhat curious. For there is no doubt that Wyclif's concept of the *corpus mathematicum* accepted transubstantiation, as he clearly explained in Book III of *De logica*.[1] Under questioning (no doubt from Wodeford as well as from others), he was forced further into the open; and in the next year, 1371-2, as a Responding Bachelor, he was prepared to say that the sensible accidents of the bread did have a subject, though he managed to avoid saying that this was the bread itself by the lame excuse that he did not know exactly what it was. And it was only after he had incepted as doctor that he boldly claimed that consecration of the Host left its substance unchanged. It is wise to resist the temptation to antedate as much as possible this final intransigent position, to place it at the moment of his taking the doctorate. For we must compare Wodeford's words with the very cautious statement of Wyclif's eucharistic doctrine given in *De incarnacione Verbi*,[2] a treatise all scholars date to *c.* 1374.

William Wodeford was writing in 1381, when Wyclif had just been expelled from Oxford, and under the shock had tried to prevaricate. Transubstantiation, he suggested, does follow consecration and yet the Body of Our Lord is present in the *form* of bread. It seems a little uncharitable of Wodeford (and this is unusual in him) to say that only fear had driven Wyclif to this statement. Nevertheless he was justified in saying that his old colleague had changed his opinion on the question too often to be

remittere quaternum. Nunc dicit quod ad transubstanciacionem non requiritur quod panis desinat esse; sed sicut quando peccator convertitur ad iusticiam manet idem homo qui prius, et tamen iniustus convertitur in iustum, sic quando panis convertitur in corpus Christi manet idem panis qui prius, et tamen panis convertitur in corpus Christi; et sic mutavit opinionem. Verumptamen tunc deduxi et adhuc reputo verum, quod nulla particula illius descripcionis requiritur ad transubstanciacionem necessario, et quod posita tota descripcione adhuc non ponitur transubstantiatio, sicut patet per multa argumenta que feci in lectura Sententiarum.

[1] Ed. Dziewicki (*WS*, 1899), III, 137.
[2] E. Harris, ed., *De benedicta incarnacione* (*WS*, 1886), p. 190.

fully trusted even to keep to his present position. Yet for a period in the early 1370's Wyclif appears to have held to a position not unlike Luther's doctrine of consubstantiation.

Though we may lament the loss of the notebooks which the bachelors exchanged, the lesson of Wodeford's words is clear enough. Wyclif's metaphysical opinions had hardened into rigidity many years before he incepted in theology; and his earliest discussions of the problem of annihilation barely mention its relevance to the nature of the eucharist—or at any rate treat it as quite secondary. But the long course of acts which an incepting bachelor had to perform, with its lectures and disputations spread over two years, compelled Wyclif to face the consequences of his metaphysical principles. When the clash did come between his preconception of the eternity of being and accepted catholic doctrine there could be no question which path he would choose. But surely Wyclif himself did not realise how stark was his choice? Until the decisive moment was reached, and especially during his earliest years as master in theology, he tried desperately to produce at least a verbal formula, which would reconcile his metaphysics with eucharistic orthodoxy. In the perspective of history Wyclif's intellectual progress has about it an air of the inevitable; we see each presupposition leading remorselessly to its conclusion. But it is a false perspective. Wodeford's words indicate that the discovery that his dispute concerning annihilation and the eucharist was no mere trifle, but was leading him towards a complete breach with catholic Christianity, came to Wyclif as a severe shock. His fluctuating and sometimes disingenuous replies to Wodeford and others bear the mark not of arrogant heterodoxy but of an urgent attempt at a late hour to adjust his beliefs to the necessities, the hitherto unrecognised necessities, of doctrine. He possessed, of course, supreme self-confidence; ultimately it was not he but the Church which must give way. But the years in which he read the *Sentences* were for Wyclif a time of intellectual crisis, of which his prevarications about transubstantiation were a symptom.

CHAPTER VIII

WYCLIF AND
CURRENT THEOLOGICAL DISPUTES

I

THE standpoint from which Wyclif viewed the theological controversies of his day will now be apparent; and such interest as this chapter has will derive from a comparison of his 'metaphysical' approach with that of the 'pure' theologians like Bradwardine and FitzRalph. The topics of dispute had not changed, but we see them in a different light—through the eyes of one who had long been master of arts.

This is particularly true of Wyclif's discussion of divine foreknowledge and free will, developed especially in the third treatise of Book II of the *Summa*, *De volucione Dei*,[1] and in Chapter 14 of *De Universalibus*. He starts from the conviction that God, who is outside time, has an eternal foreknowledge of all that was, and is, and will be.[2] To say that he 'foreknows' is in fact an inadequate and misleading description of the power of him, for whom there is neither before nor after, but only eternal present. Everything that God wills, he wills in perpetuity. What then can we do? There is no virtue, Wyclif replies, in praying that his will be done, for that is inevitable; we can only assent to the fact of its being done.[3] God has placed on us an inescapable obligation to love him. But can this obligation necessitate our will and negative its freedom? In *De Universalibus* Wyclif makes the customary distinction between absolute and conditional necessity (*necessitas ex suppositione*): the one completely binding, the other contingent because depending on an antecedent fact. It is true that he defined antecedent very rigorously as being also eternal.[4] But this did not in itself make antecedent necessity irrevocable, since the antecedent

---

[1] Dziewicki, ed., *De Ente*, pp. 113–286. [2] Cf. Lechler, pp. 255, 262.
[3] Dziewicki, ed., *De Ente*, p. 116. [4] Fo. 33r[b].

though eternal remained contingent. The logician can therefore admit without a blush, says Wyclif, that the most contingent of things are necessary, and that the necessary and the contingent partake one of the other.[1] Both derive their sanction from God, and events are contingent because he has so willed them. Yet, as has been noted before, his metaphysical presuppositions barred Wyclif from assuming too voluntarist a stand. For God cannot will the existence of a new fact, or the cessation of an old one, since both have eternal being. He can will a future event to occur at a particular moment, but cannot annul the future which already exists as past and present. However, these necessary consequences, he states, do not abrogate free will, since every human act depends on a specific volition that only the will can elicit. By abandoning God, man can certainly subject himself to his own desires or to some necessitating power outside himself, but this is a voluntary act.[2] Whilst innate causes may bind men by natural necessity, all individual acts that follow from our willing them are either contingently free or at least only conditionally necessary.[3]

But Wyclif's definition of freedom is itself limited. He defines free will not as complete freedom of choice but as the power to seek the just and shun the unjust.[4] We are all subject to the moral law, and to the conditions of human nature; and we cannot therefore possess absolute 'liberty of contradiction', since all creatures

---

[1] Fo. 33 vᵃ. Veritas connectionis est absolute necessaria, sed veritas antecedentis causantis est contingens; et illam vocant doctores et Aristoteles, in 2° Phisicorum commento, necessitatem ex suppositione; et patet quod logicus non debet erubescere concedendo quod contingentissimum est necessarium.

[2] Fo. 33 vᵇ. ...nec repungnat [sic] talis necessitacio libertati, cum libertas creata requirit necessitatem superioris regule sed excutit omnem necessitatem cause secunde; unde licet cause secunde inclinare possunt voluntatem creatam ad actum proprium, tamen nec ipse nec deus possunt immediate cogere eundem quia, cum proprius actus voluntatis sit volucio, patet quod claudit contradiccionem ut aliquis ipsum eliciat nisi volens. Verumptamen deus necessitat ad benevolendum et permittit hominem necessitare seipsum et subicere se creature inferiori, unde abstractus a deo et illectus in temptatorem necessario malevolet.

[3] Fo. 34rᵃ.

[4] Dziewicki, ed., De Ente, pp. 136–7. 'Est autem liberum arbitrium potencia arbitrandi vel iudicandi bonum, iustum prosequendi et iniustum dimittendi.' For the editor's discussion of the argument at this point see Dziewicki, introduction, pp. xxxvi ff.

tend to some appointed end, and to that extent their freedom is restricted. Certainly freedom to sin is no freedom at all, but its absence: 'non libertas sed illibertas'. He develops this argument in an interesting criticism of the 'Doctor Profundus'. Both Wyclif and Bradwardine were fundamentally determinists (and both protested that they were not); and there is some value in noting where they part company. In *De volucione Dei* Wyclif seizes on Bradwardine's definition of liberty of contradiction as the free choice of alternatives.[1] The ground for this statement, he says, is Aristotle's description of freedom as that which is capable of opposite acts. But this was too loose a construction. Our liberty is not absolute because we tend toward an ordained end, which is not the less determined because, through sin, we may not attain it. Moreover, he declared (and we can agree), such indeterminism is incompatible with the theme of *De causa Dei*, that God's will can never be impeded and that every human act is necessitated in some form. He pointed out that in Bradwardine's system there was no room for contingency at all.[2] We should therefore rather interpret Aristotle's axiom as 'any potency *which is free* is equally and contradictorily free'.[3]

But Wyclif's treatment of Bradwardine, with whose general position he was obviously in sympathy, had its vagaries. He was even at times quite prepared to censure him for excessive determinism. For example, in *De Universalibus*, chapter 14, he piously protests against Bradwardine's declaration that, since God necessitates every act, we are impotent to defy his will. Such an admission, he states, would altogether destroy free will because no man would any longer be master of his own free acts,[4] and because merit and demerit would cease to have independent value. Yet it was Wyclif's fundamental belief that divine acts are eternal. He therefore sought to combine the contingency of par-

---

[1] Dziewicki, ed., *De Ente*, pp. 152–3.   [2] *Ibid.* pp. 156, 158.
[3] *Ibid.* p. 159.
[4] *De Universalibus*, fo. 34r^a. Hic videtur Doctorem Profundum dicere, quod in omni vero contingenti est par necessitas quoad deum necessitantem et par impotencia impediendi quemquam effectum quoad singulas creaturas, sed cum hoc stat summa contingencia quoad deum. Sed videtur ex hoc tolli libertas arbitrii, cum nemo foret sic dominus suorum actuum.

ticular events with the reality of God's eternal volitions by declaring that, whilst he has always known things in their intelligible being, their actual occurrence is caused by a relation between himself and the act, that men perform or not as they choose. It is here that Wyclif finds a place for contingency in his metaphysical system.[1] God's will is thus both free and necessary; free in that even the objective causes of his volitions have always been known to him, and necessary in that he is bound by conditional necessity to reward or punish the elect and those foreknown to damnation. But no volition of ours can directly necessitate God; and when men appear to do so, it is really he who, freely and graciously obliging himself, chooses to be moved through his creatures.[2]

II

Wyclif's opinions on the relation of necessity and contingency were written with two works in mind, De causa Dei and De questionibus Armenorum. We have seen that Bradwardine and Fitz-Ralph tried to solve this relation along very different lines. But in discussing their solutions we should bear in mind how questionable it is to conclude that any argument directly causes any man to reject or embrace predestinarianism; temperament and religious experience are at least as likely to control what is later rationalised as a theological statement. Such an experience came to Bradwardine when he was still a student of Arts; it was then that the Pauline doctrine of grace was revealed to him; it was then that he became a predestinarian. Nevertheless he developed a systematic

[1] Fo. 34r[a]. Hic videtur michi posse dici quod multi effectus sunt in libera potestate contradictionis rationalis creature, sic quod potest facere ipsos fore et potest facere quod non erunt, quia aliter tolleretur meritum atque demeritum; et sic est in potestate hominis facere de quotlibet volucionibus eternis in deo quod nulla earum erit, et sic de non volucionibus et econtra. Pro quo notandum [est] quod volucio dei respectu existentie creature potest intelligi secundum habitudinem relativam, ut est res rationis fundata in deo volente rem esse secundum esse intelligibile, quod est absolute necessarium, et terminata ad existenciam creature in proprio genere; et talis habitudo dependet ab utroque extremo, cum ad hoc quod deus vult Petrum vel aliud factibile esse, requiritur ipsum esse; et ita existencia creature, licet sit temporalis, causat in deo relacionem rationis eternam.

[2] Dziewicki, ed., De Ente, pp. 148, 176.

theology to support his belief. The *De causa Dei* reduces all
activity, human and divine, to aspects of the working of God's
will, into which are subsumed all individual and secondary volitions in men. Since his will is untrammelled, it informs and
directs every particular volition of ours and, since his will is
absolute, it is also absolutely necessitating. In Bradwardine, therefore, contingency is not a variable that can influence, much less
negate, the divine will; it is itself directly willed by God. Fitz-
Ralph also underwent a profound religious experience, but one
that concerned not a single issue of doctrine but his attitude to
theological speculation as a whole. We have tried to show that
FitzRalph was a passionate anti-predestinarian long before he
experienced his 'conversion', and that his defence of free will in
De questionibus Armenorum reveals the same intensity, and is sometimes composed in the same terms, as he had shown when reading
the *Sentences* some fifteen years before. Scholastic theology is
syllogistic theology, and so his defence of free will is by logical
demonstration. Still his belief was surely prior to any systematic
exposition, and neither the *Sentences* nor the *Armenian Questions*
are systematic in quite the same sense in which Bradwardine's
work clearly is. We feel that FitzRalph's arguments are brought
forward to defend convictions which do not themselves depend
upon argument; for example, his new-found belief in the infallibility of Scripture is merely used as a fresh proof of the existence
of free will.

Wyclif may be the most unsystematic of writers, the greater
part of his works tracts thrown off to meet an occasion; but his
determinism is certainly based upon a system. He arrived at his
conclusions in a way that was neither Bradwardine's[1] nor Fitz-

---

[1] Here we cannot follow Laun in making Wyclif's predestinarianism directly
dependent on Bradwardine; cf. J. F. Laun, 'Thomas von Bradwardin, der
Schüler Augustins und Lehrer Wiclifs', *Zeit. f. Kirchengesch.* XLVII (1928),
353–5; *idem*, 'Recherches sur Thomas de Bradwardin, précurseur de Wyclif',
Revue d'histoire et de philosophie religieuses, IX (1929), 229–31. He fails to give
due weight to the realistic basis of Wyclif's determinism. The question is also
discussed by Lechler, pp. 64–70, 262 ff.; Workman, I, 120–5; Thomson,
'Philosophical Basis', *Journal of Religion*, XI (1931), 113–16; Dziewicki, ed.,
De Ente, introduction, pp. xxxiv–xxxvi, xli ff. H. A. Oberman, *Archbishop*

Ralph's. Like 'Ardmachanus', he formulated his beliefs on the relation of divine to human acts before any sudden 'conversion'; and unlike the 'Doctor Profundus', the system from which he deduced his predestinarianism was not theological but metaphysical. If he was ever converted, it was in his early student days, when he perceived the meaning of the eternity of intelligible being. So when we consider his criticisms of FitzRalph on necessity and contingency, we see the strictures of one who was instinctively drawn to determinism upon one who instinctively recoiled from it. When, on the other hand, Wyclif criticises Bradwardine (with the tenor of whose work he sympathised), it is a criticism of the working of his system and of its particular arguments. Both Wyclif and Bradwardine are determinists; but each in his exposition emphasises a different divine capacity. In the *De causa Dei* God's purpose is determined through the working of his ineluctable *will*; in the *Summa de Ente* all things are predestined through the presence of indestructible being in his *knowledge*.

These issues are discussed in detail in Wyclif's analysis of future contingents, of which there is a full treatment in the final section (chapters 10–12) of *De scientia Dei*. Can we hope to reconcile God's foreknowledge with the contingency of future events? Most philosophers, he declares, agree that he cannot know anything indeterminately and that his knowledge is eternal. Indeed it is so because, through the amplification of time, whatever is future is known to him in a single act of knowledge, which is eternally present.[1] Future events known to God will therefore take place at the appointed time. Moreover the future is both

---

Thomas Bradwardine, pp. 198–204, correctly notices the different systems on which Bradwardine and Wyclif base their argument; but the reader should note an important thesis of his book (not fully sustained, in our opinion) that the 'Doctor Profundus' is not a determinist.

[1] *De scientia Dei*, fo. 66v[b]. Item omnis noticia dei est eterna a parte ante et a parte post...assumptum patet ex hoc quod sequitur, si aliquid fuit futurum ipsum erit, sed postquam futurum fuerit preteritum...illa deduccio, sicut condicionales apparentes inpossibiles, habent manifestum colorem penes eos qui ampliant verba de presenti, modo quo dictum est superius; et ideo dicit sanctus Thomas...quod determinacio sciencie dei respectu futurorum contingencium est ex hoc quod simplex eternitas dei assistit cum tempore futuro et preterito.

determined and contingent in God, for, though acts may be contingent in that they occur in time, the passage of time cannot affect the determinacy of divine knowledge.[1] Wyclif believed that to admit that God acted contingently, in the sense that he might or might not cause an event, was to render him indifferent to events and impotent to cause them.[2] But being the universal cause, God can never act contingently, in the mundane sense of the word, nor can his purpose be defied; not because he is omnipotent (though he certainly is), but because he is omniscient. It is true, Wyclif says, that Bradwardine has asserted that it is God's will that necessitates future contingents; but it is rather his knowledge, naturally preceding his volitions, that is their cause.[3]

Some criticisms of doctrines attributed to Scotus are noteworthy, since Wyclif believed the 'Doctor Subtilis' to have employed the theory of ideas to prove that, in some way, God did act contingently. In his *Sentences*, he states, Scotus had truly declared that, by knowing the ideas of things, God knows not only the essence but the habits and qualities of their subjects. But

---

[1] Fo. 67r[a]. Item secundum communem [*MS.* communicabilem] sentenciam philosophorum multa sunt futura contingencia determinate vera, ut quod sol orietur cras quia cras erit etc., sed omnia contingencia futura sunt eque contingencia quoad deum, igitur omnia contingencia futura sunt determinate vera ...cum deus eque determinate sciet aliquid, tam determinate semper scit illud; sequitur semper eque determinate deus scit B sicut A et econtra, nam lapsis illis in preteritum eque determinate sciret deus utrumque. Sed nulla successio temporis facit variacionem ad determinacionem divine sciencie, igitur etc.

[2] Fo. 67r[b]. 3° confirmatur per hoc quod, si deus esset indifferens ad utramque partem illius contradiccionis de futuro, cum inpossibile sit ex contingencia equali causanciam procedere, ut patet 2° Phisicorum commento, sequitur quod neutram partem contradiccionis deus causaret, quod est inpossibile.

[3] Fo. 67r[b]. Igitur supposito prius stanti, quod omnis sciencia dei sit determinata, restat videre modum quo deus determinat se respectu futurorum contingencium. In qua materia sunt multi modi dicendi, de quibus recitat Doctor Profundus 12[cim], libro primo, cap. 18°; omnibus autem satis claret, quod deus se ipso scit determinate esse quod scit...ex qua sequitur, quod determinate scit hoc fore quocunque contingenti assignato, et tenet finaliter [*sc.* Doctor] quod voluntas dei ex qua determinat se ad causandum tale futurum est causa quare determinate scit quodcunque futurum. Sed revera, si est causa danda sciencie dei, est per illud causa danda voluntatis dei, cum eius voluntas sit sicut sua sciencia; et si distinguntur respectu eiusdem, videtur divinam scienciam naturaliter precedere eius voluntatem.

Cf. *De causa Dei*, pp. 220–2.

he also distinguished his knowledge of intelligible being, which is complete and determined, from his knowledge of creatures as they actually exist. Scotus, said Wyclif, had argued that, unless there was a distinction between God's knowledge of ideas and creatures, there could be no place for contingency; moreover ideas naturally precede in the divine essence particular volitions concerning things distinct from him. Secondly he had concluded that, unless such a distinction was made, God must know all future possibilities as ideas, and therefore contingently, since ideas do not represent to him the precise moment at which they are to be effected.[1]

Wyclif replied that this supposed the representation of an idea to God being necessarily followed by a further volition in which he wills himself to know the idea. But God can never know and will complexly or incompletely, nor can he act first generally and then particularly, since the idea contains every aspect of its subject. Scotus seems to agree, he says, that an idea present in God is a future certainty as well as a past fact. For what can the acceptance of divine knowledge through ideas mean other than that God sees the past, the present and the future as a single, and hence deter-

---

[1] Fo. 67r^b–v^a. Recitat autem Doctor Subtilis, super primum Sententiarum dist. 39, tres vias, quarum prima dicit quod propter perfeccionem presentacionis ydearum, que non solum essenciales rerum sed omnes habitudines et raciones earum representant divino intellectui, causatur determinacio divine scientie. Sed constat, si loquamur de sciencia quam deus habet de re secundum esse intelligibile, non oportet tractare de determinacione illius sciencie, quia quelibet talis est absolute necessaria. Si autem loquamur de sciencia dei terminata ad esse existere creature, tunc videtur posicio illa minus sufficiens propter tria. Primo, quod positis sic significantibus, non ex hoc formaliter ponitur futuricio contingencium, quia sic absolute necessario forent talia, sicut absolute necessario ydee representant divino intellectui; quelibet enim ydea est ante communicabilem volucionem rei distincte a deo. 2° sequitur, cum ydee eque naturaliter et perfecte representant intellectui divino possibilia sicut futura, sic [MS. si] representacio talis sit per se completa, cum determinacionis divine scientie [sit] quod omnia possibilia abssolute necessario existent. 3° patet quod ex hoc quod quelibet ydea non plus representat effectum fore in dato instanti quam in quocunque alio, cum omnia sint eque possibilia et eque distincte significata per ydeas.

Cf. Wadding, ed., *Johannis Duns Scoti Opera Omnia* (Lyons, 1639), vol. v, part 2, pp. 1289 ff. The latest examination of Scotus' teaching on predestination is by W. Pannenberg, *Die Prädestinationlehre des Duns Scotus* (Göttingen, 1954), esp. pp. 17–27, 54–68, 90 ff. See also Vignaux, *Justification et prédestination au XIVe siècle*, pp. 23–31.

mined, truth? To this argument Scotus had answered that, if it is
the mingling of eternity with the past and future which is the cause
of determinism, then, since everything known to God is present,
the past and future cease to have any reality.[1] But future and past
do have a real existence, Wyclif replies, in the temporal sphere; for
what is eternally present to God may still be temporally future.

There was another feature of Scotus' realism to which Wyclif
objected. He agreed with Duns' statement that the divine essence
presents to God each of contradictory contingents as intelligible
being. From this Scotus concluded that, at the first moment of
presentation, the divine will is not determined and that both contingencies are equally possible. Once again, in Wyclif's eyes, this
was to fall into the error of separating God's knowledge from his
volition; and whilst cautiously describing Scotus' argument as
'subtle and catholic', he criticises it precisely on the ground of
seeming to suppose that divine volitions and intellections are distinct.[2] This is a further illustration of the way in which Wyclif's
anti-voluntarism followed from his emphasis on the primacy of
God's knowledge.

Nor could he recognise the determinist's dilemma that, if God
once wills an event, he is powerless to annul it. On the contrary,
he declared, it is the assertion of the contingency of things, and
not their necessity, which actually limits God's power by restrict-
ing the completeness of his knowledge; and it is his very indeter-
minateness, his freedom from all limitation, that enables his
knowledge to be determined.[3] Similarly in *De volucione Dei* he

---

[1] Fo. 67vᵃ. ...et sic eternitas coassistit omni tempori preterito vel futuro,
esti labatur tempus quoad nos, et sic deus semper videt omne preteritum cum
sit sibi presens....

[2] Fo. 68rᵃ. Ille autem sensus, licet sit subtilis et catholicus bene intelligentibus,
posset tamen inducere simplices in errorem, credendo quod deus elicit actus
post deliberacionem, et quod potencia voluntaria dei distinguitur ab intellectiva,
quod prius naturaliter determinat voluntas divina ad unam partem contradiccionis quam intellectus illam videt.

[3] Fo. 67vᵇ. Unde Egidius, super primo Sententiarum dist. 38ᵃ questione
ultima, dicit quod tota causa determinacionis divine sciencie est quia deus habet
naturam indistantem ab esse, nam quod hoc est deus 'indeterminatus' et per
consequens extra terminos ipsum limitantes, et sic eternus et per consequens
certissime sciens.

vindicates, on the authority of FitzRalph, the absolute quality of divine volitions.[1] His explanation is, of course, that the source of contingency, as of every caused truth, lies in the supremely free will of God, who is the ultimate cause even of contingency in secondary causes. And there is no greater necessity in freely determinable secondary causes than in the First Cause, where all contingency lies.[2] Necessity and contingency, therefore, exist independently of events because eternal qualities and events do not cease to be contingent when a 'future contingent' become a past fact.[3]

His metaphysical principles guaranteed that Wyclif would reject the anti-predestinarian thesis (maintained by Buckingham and FitzRalph, among others), that, though the present and past are necessitated, the future is not. This he labels the fallacy of the 'Philosophers', who have divided the certain from the contingent in accordance with their own knowledge, whereas certainty and contingency actually stem from God. But the true 'Theologian' will rather abandon his opponents' definition of 'contingens ad utrumlibet', implying that an event is equally likely to happen and not to happen, in favour of the concept of 'determinacio ad utrumlibet'; for God in his grace has ordained that many future acts depending on human free will shall be concealed from men.[4]

[1] Dziewicki, ed., De Ente, p. 166, citing De questionibus Armenorum, Book 16, ch. 18 (ed. cit. fo. 135r).

[2] Fo. 68r^b–v^a. Tercio sequitur quod prima racio contingencie stat in libertate voluntatis divine....Ex isto patet quod nichil est contingens quoad causam secundam nisi quod prius est contingens quoad deum...unde notabiliter errant, qui ponunt maiorem necessitatem in contingentibus quoad causas secundas liberas quam quoad causam primam, in qua est formaliter racio contingencie, cum sit de ordine universitatis.

[3] Fo. 68v^a. Quinto, palam sequitur, quod deum vel mundum fuisse est contingens sicud alia veritas de futuro.

[4] Fo. 69r^a. Theologus igitur debet relinquere verba philosophorum de distinccione contingencium et ponere sensum eorum, quod illud vocant contingens ad utrumlibet (quod eque convenit evenire sicut eius oppositum), ipsis ignorantibus determinacionem ad utramlibet partem, cuiusmodi sunt multe veritates de futuro. Deus enim ex abundancia graciose dispensacionis sue ordinavit eternaliter quosdam actus futuros dependentes a voluntate libera creata latere homines.

For Bradwardine's exposition of 'contingens ad utrumlibet', see De causa Dei, Book III, chs. 3–6, pp. 649–68.

Because contingency lies in the divine will, and is therefore known to God as a future certainty, his purpose cannot be frustrated. But clearly he himself cannot be so bound by his own determinations that he cannot prevent the occurrence of any act. Wyclif therefore employs the distinction between God's absolute and ordained power; what has been done cannot be undone by his ordained power, but by his absolute power he can restrain a future event from coming to pass, as he made the sun to stay in its course at the bidding of Joshua.[1] Yet equally he cannot initiate a new truth in time nor remove the freedom of choice once given to us; for the occurrence of an event in the past does not cause it to cease to be now or in the future (though it may appear to us to be past). So Adam, who could once have refrained from sinning, still possesses now the capacity not *to have* sinned; for unless a sinner continues to be free to reject sin, he cannot justly continue to be punished.[2]

Nothing illustrates more clearly Wyclif's belief that contingency is a part of divine determination than this taking the doctrine of eternal being and eternal knowledge to its logical conclusion. The quality of contingency, therefore, cannot begin to affect a foreknown event at some point in time, but must always have existed in God's foreknowledge; and it is only in this sense that our salvation or reprobation truly remains contingent. Many sinners, Wyclif declares, have renounced the opportunity of repentance through their evil natures, whilst others have shown merit beyond possibility of reprobation; both are consequently ordained, though not by an absolute necessity, to their appointed ends. Is there then no place for contingency in the divine ordinance? True to his metaphysical principles, Wyclif replies that, though God cannot now reprobate one predestined to salvation, it remains utterly contingent in him to have done so in his first knowledge.[3]

[1] Fo. 69v[a].

[2] Fo. 70r[a]. Tenendum est igitur quod deus [potest] omnia que unquam potuit, ut Adam nunc potest non peccasse, quia nunc habet potenciam ex qua potest pro tempore ante temptacionem in quo tempore est satis declinare peccatum, quia aliter indubie non esset peccans continue culpandus, nisi continue posset non peccasse.

[3] Fo. 70r[a]–r[b].

His own position, with the comments on the two Oxonians who were his guides, is best summed up in his own words:

And so Master FitzRalph declares in his *Armenian Questions*, Book 16, chapter 4, that he studied this problem [of contingency] in turns for twenty years; but through failure to amplify present terms to cover the past and future, he left the question unresolved, doubting whether God can reveal in the Word in any way the truth about the future. Because either [God] foresees that Christ did not see such things in the Word or, if Christ did foresee, they must necessarily be in their due time. And clearly this deduction must be granted, since every future must necessarily be, whereby the Blessed see all things in the Word of God; and yet, the things themselves are not necessary, but contingent in every respect, as is any truth about the past or existing things in any time.

And in this Bradwardine agrees, but adds to it a degree of necessity in that every future is inevitable to any creature; in that he says that all Christ's temporal acts are inevitable in their time, as can be deduced from [*De causa Dei*] Book III, chapters 1, 2 and 29. But as will become clear, this is a means of necessitating contingencies.[1]

The statement that FitzRalph erred in ignoring the doctrine of the amplification of time is particularly notable.

III

In the autobiographical passage in *De causa Dei*, Bradwardine spoke of his conversion as a recognition of the fulness of the grace of God 'as it is prevenient both in time and nature to all good works', and his book is largely a treatise on grace. But it was also a *pièce d'occasion*, a rigorist defence of traditional doctrine against the attacks of the Modern Pelagians. The battle with the Pelagians appears to have been over by the 1360's (though echoes of it can be found in the *Summa de Ente*), and the problem of the nature and efficacy of divine grace was no longer an acute issue. In Wyclif's theology it has a secondary, if still important, part.

The fullest discussion in the *Summa* of the relation of grace to merit,[2] the subject so frequently touched on in this study and so

---

[1] Dziewicki, ed., *De Ente*, pp. 184–5. Cf. *De questionibus Armenorum*, ed. cit. fo. 130r: 'et tamen per vices iam viginti annos illud intelligere laboravi'. Also *De causa Dei*, pp. 637–49, 725–44.   [2] Lechler, pp. 283–7.

obviously central to a 'realist theology' like Wyclif's, appears in Book II, tract 2, *De sciencia Dei*, chapters 6–9. Perhaps deliberately choosing to misunderstand his predecessor, he regards Bradwardine as treating the relation as an aspect of divine causation. At least, he declares, the 'Doctor Profundus' loosely refers, in the corollary to Book I, chapter 43, to the cause of grace—*de causancia gracie*. But to suppose a causal relationship was to ignore the fact that what is temporally prior to a created object is not necessarily naturally prior to it; and of this the relation of grace to merit was the outstanding example.[1] This goes to the heart of Wyclif's position, that divine grace and human merit, election and reprobation, have their eternal being in God; there cannot, therefore, be cause and caused where there is neither prior nor posterior. So he declares that the grace by which we are predestined to salvation cannot be elicited by merit,[2] for God naturally justifies men to eternal life before the predestined show merit in this world.

This was, of course, the orthodox position, though Wyclif had arrived at it by a somewhat unusual route. He makes the customary distinction between congruous and condign merit. Merit *de congruo* is shown by one whom the pure and uncaused grace of God has moved so to act that he may fittingly reward him; merit

[1] *De sciencia Dei*, ch. 6, fo. 61rᵇ. In omnibus igitur istis sunt tria que maxime confundunt loquentes in illa materia: primum, quando dicitur deum scire et velle causabile, potest dictum intelligi de relacione scientis ad scitum vel de actu sciendi qui est deus; 2° est difficultas in exer[ci]cio videre que relaciones precedunt naturaliter causando divinam scientiam vel aliud causabile, et que non (ut difficultas est, si causancia creature sit prius naturaliter quam scientia qua deus scit [*MS*. sit] creaturam esse, et certum est quod illa est prior quam est scientia aut volucio relativa terminata ad illam causanciam); 3° est difficultas cognoscere causanciam superadditam essencie vel rei causandi [*sic*], ut non sequitur, A non potest esse sine B sed econtra, igitur B causat A...unde propter confucionem horum trium difficultatum est intelligere doctores, et specialiter Doctorem Profundum, libro I cap. 43 et suo corellario 'de causancia gracie'.
Cf. *De causa Dei*, pp. 408–20.

[2] Fo. 61vᵃ. Ad terciam confirmacionem dicitur quod non est possibile hominem sibi mereri [*MS*. merere] primam graciam vel predestinacionem; pro cuius declaracione notandum quod mereri restrictum ad bonum est creaturam racionalem facere aliquod premiabile, et autonomatice dicitur de premio vite eterne.

de condigno by one who has become acceptable to God through the infusion of grace, and whom God, co-operating in his meritorious acts, will justly reward.[1] This preordinance by which he wills salvation to some, *predestinancia*, and reprobation to others, *prescientia*, is a gracious act of two kinds: the eternal volition of God, innate in himself; and the particular form of grace by which he accepts individual creatures. All who are justified to God have been infused with the form of grace eternally existing in him[2] (and in stating this, Wyclif by implication rejects the Ockhamist conception of grace as a simple relation between God and creatures).[3] His distinction parallels that universally made between created and uncreated grace;[4] and Wyclif makes a similar division in respect of necessity: as it proceeds from God it is eternal and absolutely necessary, but as it inheres in creatures it is only contingent.[5] So no man can act meritoriously without divine grace preceding him in the 'natural' (eternal) order, nor can merit, which is temporal, cause the divine habit, which is eternal.

However suspect other features of Wyclif's theology might be, his doctrine of grace was impeccably orthodox; he was in no danger of falling into the Pelagian error of supposing that we can

---

[1] Fo. 61 vᵃ. Et est duplex meritum, scilicet de congruo et de condigno: de congruo quando aliquis meretur de pura gracia premiantis, ut puta, quando premians prevenit cooperando omne meritum merentis ut bene sibi sit, et non illi premianti aliquid bonitatis inde accrescat, cum nullo tali labore indigeat... de condigno autem dicitur quis mereri, quando meretur de pura iusticia ab alico premiante, quod fuit quando premians non graciose coagit cum illo...vel quando fuit meritum ad indigenciam premiantis, sic hec quod preaccipiat vel simul commune accipiat iuvamen vel premium pro labore.

[2] Fo. 61 vᵃ–vᵇ. Alia est gracia qua deus habet creaturam sibi gratam ad quodcunque bonum creature, et illa non est nisi bona voluntas dei qua diligit creaturam...ille autem gracie distinguntur proporcionaliter ut bona voluta [*sic*], et omnes sunt eterne non potentes incipere vel desinere esse. Gracia autem creature formaliter est creaturam esse gratam deo et ita recipit subdivisionem proporcionaliter secundum bona ad que creatura est grata. De primo genere gracie est deus plenus, cum nulla creatura sit grata deo, nisi deus habeat proporcionaliter graciam eternam in ipso sibi correspondentem.

[3] Cf., for example, Uthred Boldon's opinion (Knowles, 'Censured Opinions', pp. 321, 337; and above, p. 110).

[4] *DTC*, VI, 1557 (article: grace).

[5] Fo. 61 vᵇ.

merit salvation. But we can be more specific; we can point to two passages in which he explicitly condemns the Modernists' fallacious doctrine of grace, associates this error with the misuse of the concept of God's absolute and ordained power, and, using Bradwardine's own terminology, directly labels the proponents of this view the Modern Pelagians. In the first passage, in *De sciencia Dei*, chapter 6, Wyclif attributes the root of Pelagius' error to the belief that grace is a distinct and self-sufficient entity:

Grace is the cause of all men's acts. And so it is clear that Pelagius and others, who denied that grace was necessary for merit, have been mistaken in their notion of the quiddity of grace; just as a minority of theologians in their tracts on knowledge, will, grace and predestination and the like are either mistaken or wastefully complicate the matter....
For Pelagius thought that the grace by which a man is formally acceptable to God is a thing that can exist in its own right...and he undoubtedly declared it to be true that a man can merit without any such grace. Wherefore many of the Moderns are so foolish that they suppose such grace to be required by God's law [*de lege*] but not by his absolute power. But, unless I am mistaken, in the whole of Scripture no such [definition of] grace can be founded.[1]

We have already noted Bradwardine's charge that the Moderns justified their Pelagian views on the necessity of grace by invoking the distinction between God's absolute and ordained powers. Though in strict doctrine, they had argued, the gift of grace is

[1] Fo. 61 v[b]. ...et per consequens multo magis est [*sc.* gracia] causa cuiuslibet operis vel accidentis positivi huius creature. Unde patet quod Penlagius [*sic*] et alii negantes graciam requiri ad meritum errarunt in noticia quiditatis istius gracie, sicut minor pars theologorum in [*sic* P, fo. 33 r. *T* nisi] suis tractatibus de sciencia, voluntate, gracia et predestinantia cum similibus, vel errant vel difficultant, dispendiose tractando, in hoc quod volunt servare ordinem questionum: querendo primo, si res est de qua tractarent, si illam esse sit ambiguum; 2° quid est quod [sit] maxime necessarium; et 3° de passionibus eius, si sint, et essenciam, querendo causam quare subiectum est taliter passionatum. Putavit enim Pelagius, quod gracia qua homo est gratus deo formaliter sit una res que potest per se esse...et indubie verum dixit quod homo potest mereri sine aliqua tali gracia. Unde multi Modernorum ad tantum desipiunt [*sic* P. descipiunt *T*] quod ponunt requiri talem graciam de lege, sed non de potencia dei absoluta. Sed si non fallor, in toto corpore Scripture non potest fundari talem graciam esse dandam.

necessary for man to show merit, yet 'absolutely' we can merit, or he can cause us to merit, through our natural virtues alone. These were the theologians whom Wyclif was rebuking; and fortunately, in a repetition of this criticism in *De volucione Dei*, he directly identifies them as the Modern Pelagians.

Yet it would be heretical and utterly profane to say that in God's co-operation with man through his grace, man's acts are naturally prior to and more important than those of God through grace; but this is what seemed good to the Modern Pelagians to say, that man may possibly act without God's co-operating with him. And concerning this they suggest that grace is an absolute and self-sufficient quality, so that by God's absolute, but not by his ordained [*de lege*] power, man can merit without it. And so they are ridiculously compelled to say that a man naturally performs meritorious acts before God works in him, on the ground that such acts can only be done by that man...and so, according to such people, man could act without the grace of God working in him.[1]

Though Wyclif reaffirms the existence of God's absolute power, by which he can permit men to show merit in any way that he pleases,[2] the condemnation is thorough, and the identity of those censured not in doubt. And he pays Bradwardine his highest compliment in using the name by which the 'Doctor Profundus' always referred to the radical theologians.

Because man cannot merit grace, the reward which we elicit from God for works must be congruous, not condign.[3] On the other hand, his reward for our evil acts is far less than the condign punishment we so richly deserve, for God always rewards our meritorious works beyond, and our sins less than, our deserts.[4]

---

[1] Dziewicki, ed., *De Ente*, p. 195. The 'illos' inserted by Dziewicki between 'Pelagianos' and 'modernos' in his edition of this passage from T (fo. 80v[b]) does not appear in the manuscript. For the distinctive use of the separation of God's absolute and ordained power by a number of theologians, who are almost certainly the Modern Pelagians attacked by the 'Doctor Profundus', see G. Leff, *Bradwardine and the Pelagians*, pp. 130–5.

[2] Dziewicki, ed., *De Ente*, p. 196.

[3] *De sciencia Dei*, fo. 62r[a]. 2° patet quod impossibile est creaturam mereri a deo vel creatura premium quodcunque, nisi a deo mereatur illud premium de congruo, non de condigno.

[4] Fo. 62r[a].

It is true that in relation to our fellow men we can show merit
that elicits a condign reward; but Wyclif refuses to admit, even in
the most attenuated form, that we can merit grace. The very
meaning of *congruum*, he says, is that God in the plenitude of his
power gratuitously ordains creatures, having free will, to merit
reward by freely doing right.[1] Where merit, therefore, becomes
the consequence of grace, and where God is absolutely unmoved,
no merit can be condign. Wyclif hastens to add that he does not
question the value of merit, and was only affirming that man cannot merit acceptance *de condigno*.[2] It is grace not merit that is
condign.

We thus arrive at the full predestinarianism, which is the logical
conclusion of Wyclif's belief that God's knowledge and will are
eternal. We are necessitated to election or reprobation by the free
gift of his grace which, working in the divine order that is outside
time, must naturally be prior to merit or any human cause. So
ineluctable is this predestination that no creature predestined to
salvation can merit eternal punishment, however gravely he may
sin, nor any foreknown to reprobation evade it, however pleasing
he may have been to God in this life. For if we allow temporal
merit to elicit its reward, the reward itself cannot be heavenly but
only temporal.[3] Wyclif attempts to draw a general distinction
between earthly and heavenly reward and punishment. Does
mortal sin always earn eternal punishment? He distinguished sin
that is merely venial, requiring temporal punishment, from mortal
sin. God's reward for this is eternal punishment, but what is

[1] Fo. 62v[a]. Congruum namque est valde quod deus, habens plenum
dominium [*sic P*, fo. 34v. plenitudinem *T*] creature, de gracia sua ordinet
creaturam liberi arbitrii ut propter observanciam liberam rectitudinis mereatur
premium.

[2] Fo. 62v[b]. Wyclif accepted congruous merit only in that it was previously
infused by God. Bradwardine, regarding the contemporary use of *meritum de
congruo* as tending to Pelagianism, rejected it altogether. Cf. Oberman, *Archbishop Thomas Bradwardine*, pp. 149-51; Leff, *Bradwardine and the Pelagians*,
pp. 74-9, 158-9.

[3] Fo. 62v[b]. 4° probabiliter videri poterit ex dictis quod sicut nemo prescitus,
in quantumlibet magna gracia existens secundum presentem iusticiam, meretur
beatitudinem, sic nemo [*sic P. Omits T*] predestinatus, in quantumlibet gravi
peccato positus, meretur penam eternam; nam si meritum [*MS.* mereritum]
tunc eius premium in tempore suo est, eo quod dicuntur relative.

eternal must precede its temporal cause.[1] Venial sin, therefore, is like merit in that neither can elicit acceptance or reprobation; for just as no merit short of final perseverance can earn beatitude, so no sin except the sin against the Holy Spirit can merit eternal punishment. In consequence it is useless to speculate on whether or not we are pleasing to God, whose temporal rewards are neither a sign nor a cause of his eternal will; and since we do not know whether he loves or rejects us, we cannot know in this life if we have merited justification or reprobation. Wyclif deprecates the use of the term 'reward' for God's acts, because it implies recompense for merit or demerit.[2] Is there then no place for merit whatever? He repeats the argument often put forward that, since men are the objective cause of God's predestinating grace, they must in part effect his will towards them. Wyclif accepts the premiss but not its consequence; for we cannot move him to act, though we are the objective cause of grace, because meritorious conduct is only temporal and therefore posterior to the reward.[3] Yet he himself felt it necessary slightly to modify his position. After the gift of first grace, he states, a creature can merit secondary grace; and even if he should fall, he may still with God's prevenient grace regain the latter by his own merit.[4] But at heart he agreed with the rigorism of Bradwardine, and he cites *De causa*

[1] Fo. 62 v[b]. Scio tamen quod multi doctores loquuntur aliter, moti ex hoc quod peccatum mortale ut huiusmodi obligat peccantem de condigno ad penam eternam. In hoc enim differt peccatum veniale a mortali, quod primum obligat ad penam temporalem et secundum ad penam eternam. Nichi[l] autem obligatur ad penam eternam, nisi sit dignum habere penam eternam.

[2] Fo. 63 r[b]. Nam si deus premiat creaturam, eternaliter disposuit ex gracia sua dignitare illam ad tantum premium, et per consequens ipsa nunquam actualiter premietur.

[3] Fo. 63 r[b]. Septimo patet quod omnis gracia, omnis predestinancia, omnis ordinancia eterna in deo, respectu creature formaliter relative incepta, causatur ab illa creatura ad quam principaliter terminatur...ex quo patet quod non sequitur, iste homo causat istam graciam vel predestinanciam, igitur ipse meretur eandem; meritum enim dicitur relative ad premium et connotat primo necessitatem temporis respectu premii.

[4] Fo. 63 v[a]. Fine autem predestinacionis et prime gracie, potest creaturam mereri, cum sit beatitudo subiectiva, et sic potest homo mereri secundam graciam vel augmentum gracie, ymmo postquam exciderit a gracia gratum faciente, potest mereri graciam talem, sed non sine gracia [*sc.* prima] preveniente.

Dei, Book I, chapters 3, 35 and 45, to show that God is not moved by objective causes and that the grace of predestination is not caused by creatures. As Wyclif says, it is on these two principles that the greater part of his book depends.[1]

IV

But if nothing occurs which has not its intelligible being in God, are we to conclude that he is also the cause of sin? This problem, examined in the third tract of Book II, *De volucione Dei,* chapters 9–17,[2] was particularly pressing for one who was both realist and predestinarian, and was constantly tempted to subsume every human act into divine causation. It is true, Wyclif states, that all could accept Augustine's axiom that no substance is inherently evil, and that evil is not substantial but simple privation. With this even Bradwardine had agreed—and was glad, no doubt, so to protect his orthodoxy.[3] But if this provided an explanation of the nature of sin, it was more difficult to account for its cause. Though evil is deprivation, this in itself is neither good nor evil, and hence the cause must lie in human will. But is our will necessitated to evil as well as to good? For that some should sin, he says, seems to be ordained as an integral part of this world, since God has never promised universal salvation. So if we admit that God necessitates creatures, we must conclude that at least sinners, if not sin, are ordained by him.[4]

Wyclif is extremely cautious in this matter. He did not deny (and here he followed accepted teaching) that God was the cause of the fact of sin. For example, Peter Lombard had never denied

---

[1] Fo. 63 vᵃ. Item Doctor Profundus, libro primo cap. 3, probat per multa media quod scita non causant in deo scientiam, et capitulo 35° probat quod generaliter gracia prevenit opera meritorum et quecunque bona virtute creature, et non econtra causantur ab eis; capitulo eciam 45° et infra videtur ostendere, quod gracia predestinacionis non causatur a creatura, et super illo dependet maior pars libri sui.
   Cf. *De causa Dei,* pp. 171, 307–13, 420–7.

[2] Dziewicki, ed., *De ente,* pp. 202–77. On this see Dziewicki, introduction, pp. xlvi–lv; Lechler, pp. 263–7; Workman, I, 140, esp. references at n. 3.

[3] Dziewicki, ed., *De Ente,* p. 204. Cf. *De causa Dei,* Book I, ch. 26, pp. 251–61.

[4] Dziewicki, ed., *De Ente,* pp. 232–3.

that the existence of sin (*esse peccatum*) was present in God as intelligible being, but only that he was the cause of particular sin (*mala fieri*); and Bradwardine was mistaken in supposing him to have denied the former. God wills sin as intelligible and as secondary being, but not the sinful act.[1] All Wyclif will concede is that God is the means by which the statement 'this man sins' is true. But he reveals his hand in his exposition of Bradwardine's arguments on the question. It was a principle of the 'Doctor Profundus', he says, that God's will is absolute and eternal; yet as regards the cause of sin, he qualified this in saying that God does not will sin *simpliciter*, but only in respect of something. Again he had suggested (Book I, chapter 34) that his volitions towards sin are neutral, and that only indirectly and in secondary causes does he will men to sin. But Wyclif was able to show (what the Mertonian himself must finally have conceded), that all such qualifications are merely verbal and that, by Bradwardine's own principles, not only does God will sin, but that he wills it directly and deliberately.[2]

In this context Wyclif's reference to a number of 'errors condemned at Paris' is of much interest. The articles, asserting that God wills men to sin and wills the positive volitions by which they sin, correspond almost exactly to those for which Mirecourt was censured in 1347, and he can hardly be referring to any other occasion. Wyclif treats the censure with a respect that is only slightly qualified. First, the condemnation does not apply to Englishmen; secondly, he himself holds to the 'eighth opinion', that God is the cause of the existence of evil and sin; and finally, in the case of many articles, the censure applied only to the interpretation and not to the thesis as such.[3] He formally denies these

---

[1] *Ibid.* pp. 238-9. Cf. *De causa Dei*, Book I, ch. 34 (esp. pp. 297 ff.).

[2] Dziewicki, ed., *De Ente*, p. 248. Cf. *De causa Dei*, pp. 294-307. It was to Book I, chapter 34 that Buckingham (or the marginal annotator of MS. Merton M. I. 11) had called attention. See above, p. 61.

[3] Dziewicki, ed., *De Ente*, p. 253. The 'fourth' and 'eighth' errors here named correspond to the fourth and eighth articles in Jean de Mirecourt's second apology; the 'fifth' error, and that which is unnumbered, correspond to Mirecourt's ninth and fifth articles respectively. Cf. F. Stegmüller 'Die zwei Apologien', *RTAM*, v (1933), 193-6, and condemnation in Denifle and Chatelain, *Chartularium*, II, 610-14.

determinist conclusions; the *antiqui*, he says, affirm that God and nature intend only what is good and cannot cause evil directly, else we should be necessitated to sin and would become pleasing to God by committing sin.[1]

Yet we may still wonder how far he really differed from Bradwardine. His own opinions, if we accept his words in *De volucione Dei*, had previously gone to both extremes; for he states at one point, that he had once admitted that God wills the primary informing, as well as the secondary being, of sin, and at another, that he had formerly denied that he could even will its punishment.[2] He quotes the classic judgement of Anselm and Augustine, that God foresees his creatures as freely sinning, but that this foreknowledge is not the cause of their sin.[3] This is precisely the distinction made by FitzRalph in his critique of determinism, but for Wyclif any such distinction was incompatible with his belief in the eternity of intelligible being. God, he says, cannot make sin intrinsically good, but he has the power to preordain it; therefore we should rejoice, not in the sinful act, but in the fact that he has permitted it, since God, even if not the cause of every act, always concurs in its taking place.[4] For FitzRalph this was tantamount to saying that he necessitates sin, in which case to resist evil would be to defy his will.[5] Wyclif denies this; all sin is voluntary, because God co-operates in the substance of the act, and not in its sinful essence.

The master who wrote these treatises was no innovating theologian, nor one who had begun to look beyond the lecture halls of Oxford. It is true that we find here convictions, chiefly metaphysical, whose rigour was later to lead him into heterodoxy. And at times, in the curt dismissal of received opinion, in the inability to open his mind afresh to argument, we sense the obstinacy which would later brook no retreat. But the composer

---

[1] Dziewicki, ed., *De Ente*, p. 250.   [2] *Ibid.* pp. 246, 262.
[3] *Ibid.* p. 255.   [4] *Ibid.* pp. 261, 272.
[5] *Ibid.* p. 275. Set quia dominus Ardmacanus contradicit isti sentencie, 17° De questionibus Armenorum, 20°, ideo exponam sentencias, ut veritas magis appareat. Videtur enim primo quod deus necessitat homines ad peccandum. . . .
Cf. *De quest. Armenorum*, ed. cit. fo. 141v.

of the *Summa de Ente* remained a cautious and conservative Oxford don. He explicitly affirms the orthodox position on the authority of a priest in mortal sin[1] (the very reverse of his claim in *De dominio divino*). Nor was he anxious to ventilate theological problems before the common people who, by mistaking their meaning, could fall into heresy.[2] He spoke for his fellow masters and students alone.

[1] Dziewicki, ed., *De Ente*, p. 171.   [2] *Ibid.* p. 131.

CHAPTER IX

THE REACTION AT OXFORD TO WYCLIF'S EARLY PHILOSOPHY

I

In this study we have considered only a part of Wyclif's work, limited both in range and time; and it stops just, perhaps, where it might be thought to become most interesting. The interweaving of Wyclif's polemics with his scholasticism; the use of purely academic (we had almost said abstract) principles to further controversial argument; above all, the fascinating psychology of the don in politics: all these are larger and more exciting issues than those here treated. But their examination would also involve a work much wider (however much more desirable) than anything attempted in this study. Conversely the question considered in this final chapter is also closely limited. The recovery of orthodox teaching at Oxford and the renewed vigour of traditional theology, stimulated by Wycliffite and Lollard criticism, is a fascinating story; and, as has recently been remarked, it was by the 'simple, sound and effective' counter-attacks of orthodox apologetics, rather than by the drastic coercions of church authorities, that Lollardy was successfully combated.[1] But, we repeat, the question here taken is only one aspect of the revival of traditional teaching. It is this: how far did Wyclif's purely philosophical teaching survive at Oxford the general condemnation of his works? Did any masters try to salvage the uncontroversial doctrine in his early work, and how far were they interested or successful in preserving his realist opinions?

It was sufficiently difficult at the time of Wyclif's death to remember that his writings had not been universally condemned; after the censures that followed his end and the anti-Wycliffite

---

[1] Knowles, *Religious Orders*, II, 147.

decrees of the Council of Constance it became almost impossible to do so. Yet the specific censures upon Wyclif in his lifetime touched hardly at all on his purely academic philosophy. This does not imply ecclesiatical approval; it was rightly regarded as secondary to the errors deduced from it and the heretical propositions he later propounded. When Gregory XI issued the first bill of censure in May 1377, he attached a schedule of nineteen erroneous propositions. All are to be found in *De civili dominio* and all deal with dominion and the authority of the church and priesthood.[1] The council of Oxford masters, convoked by the chancellor, William Barton, to answer *De Apostasia*, condemned Wyclif's teaching on the eucharist.[2] The twenty-four articles condemned by the Blackfriars Council in 1382 again deal with the question of dominion and the eucharist.[3] Purely philosophical matters, therefore, virtually escaped formal condemnation (except the rejection of annihilation, at the root of the eucharistic heresy). What then of the fundamental principles assumed in his early works? The *Fasciculi Zizaniorum* lists[4] thirteen propositions—the 'tares to be bundled and burned' of the title-piece—taught by Wyclif up to the time of his doctorate, and generally regarded as heretical. Of these the first seven are purely philosophical and make the following assertions: that being is eternal ('anything that was or will be, is now'); that anything is essentially everything else, and all created together; that God cannot annihilate creatures; that Christ is eternally man in respect of his manhood; and that God by his absolute power cannot reprobate any creature united to Christ. Generally accepted as heretical, and plainly contrary to catholic teaching: but not formally repudiated (except as regards the eucharist) in the great condemnations of Wyclif's lifetime.

[1] The bull of May 1377 in *FZ*, pp. 242–4; the schedule of censured propositions in D. Wilkins, *Concilia Magnae Britanniae et Hiberniae* (1737), III, 123. The most recent examination of the official reaction to Wyclif's errors is J. H. Dahmus, *The Prosecution of John Wyclyf* (New Haven, 1952); for this event see Dahmus, pp. 25, 49–51; Workman, I, 293–9; Lechler, pp. 163–7.

[2] Workman, II, 140–8; Lechler, pp. 369–71; schedule in *FZ*, pp. 105–13.

[3] In Wilkins, *Concilia*, III, 157–8; *FZ*, pp. 277–82, 493–7. See Lechler, pp. 380–5; Workman, II, 266–72, 416–17; Dahmus, *op. cit.* pp. 89–100.

[4] *FZ*, pp. 2–3.

Realism was not attacked (it could hardly be so as long as Augustine remained a doctor of the church). Yet the path of the orthodox realist, the master drawn to Wyclif's ultrarealism without wishing to deduce from it what had been condemned, was almost impossible. With the evidence from Oxford so sparse, we may fairly quote the protest of the masters of Prague in 1410[1] who wished, against the destruction of Wyclif's works ordered by Archbishop Zbynek, to sustain the metaphysical arguments in *De Ydeis* and *De Universalibus*. Procopius of Pilsen complained of the ban on *De Ydeis*, though its 'mere five chapters' simply propounded the reality of ideas as they had been sustained by all the Fathers of the Church.[2] Since Augustine had declared that, 'qui negat ideas est infidelis', their reality had been taught by Denis, Anselm, Bradwardine, Grosseteste, Boethius, Plato and Seneca[3] (note how Wyclif's works had carried the fame of his sources with them into Bohemia). Let our opponents, wrote Procopius, either reject ideas or stop burning *De Ydeis*, for neither realism in general nor this particular treatise has ever been censured. In the same manner *De Universalibus* was defended by Ladislaus of Zwiertzeticz. Because his works contain some manifest heresies, apparently they must all be burned.[4] But Wyclif's realism, he argues, is irrelevant to his heresies, and besides the authorities, so anxious to commit his books to the flames, do not even understand the 'universale reale' they are trying to stamp out.[5] The writer's self-appointed role as the impartial scholar was, however, rather compromised by his passionate defence of the 'Doctor Evangelicus':

quia a Deo accepi gratis omnia que habeo et a magistro Iohanne Wyklef tamquam a Dei instrumento accepi multam scienciam et presertim de universalibus realibus, que sunt cause efficaces, formales et finales individuorum universi....[6]

[1] Printed, from MS. Vienna, Nat. Bibl. 4002, fos. 18–41, by J. Loserth, *Wiclif and Hus* (Engl. edn, 1884), pp. 309–36.
[2] Loserth, *Wiclif und Hus*, p. 324.   [3] *Ibid*. p. 326.
[4] *Ibid*. p. 330.   [5] *Ibid*. p. 331.
[6] *Ibid*. p. 329. His claim (*ibid*.) that *De Universalibus* was still read at Oxford is of interest, though of no independent value as evidence: '...cum tamen in valde solempni universitate Oxoniensi practizatur, legitur et tenetur publice. Que

These were the words of committed men; but the problem they posed was genuine. Nor did ultrarealism inevitably lead to heresy. Realism swept the University of Prague, but the great majority of the Bohemian rebels accepted the Real Presence, and the mass administration of the sacrament was a notable feature in the Hussite armies. *Mutatis mutandis*, the distinction between the condemned error in theology and the arguable proposition in philosophy could be made by Oxford masters also. The existence of ideas; the realist argument on the nature of predestination; the limits placed on the operation of God's *potentia absoluta*: all these theses of the early Wyclif could legitimately be sustained by orthodox masters of the generation that had been so greatly influenced by Wyclif as a teacher of philosophy. But were they? It would be something of a miracle if such opinions could survive the plethora of condemnations and the resurgence of triumphant orthodoxy.

II

During the course of the year 1381, after his eucharistic teaching had been condemned by the chancellor's committee of theologians, Wyclif's position at Oxford became untenable, and towards its close[1] he left the university for his living of Lutterworth in Leicestershire. A stream of vitriolic pamphlets continued to flow from his pen. But in 1382 he was partially paralysed by a stroke, and on 28 December 1384, whilst hearing mass, he suffered a second stroke. He lingered for three days, totally paralysed, and died on the last day of the old year.[2]

The condemnations of 1381–2 were a heavy blow to the university as well as to Wyclif and his immediate supporters. For all the pitiful collapse of the Lollard party at Oxford before the firmness

universitas magistrorum, doctorum, et aliarum personarum excessit numero personarum numerum eorum, qui fuerunt in condempnacionis synodo eciam connumeratis omnibus, qui ad huiusmodi sentenciam nullo modo consenserunt. Cum tamen prefata Oxoniensis solempnis universitas prefatum librum De Universalibus pro katholico legat et teneat. . . .'

[1] Workman, II, 147, says 'on the conclusion of the year, possibly some months earlier at the commencement of the Long Vacation'. We note that British Museum, MS. Royal 10. E. 11 was pledged by Wyclif and others on 23 October 1381 (fo. 340v).   [2] Workman, II, 246–324.

of Archbishop Courtenay,[1] we can easily forget the ties which bound the university to its outstanding master, perhaps because the reassertion of authority was managed with such adroitness by Courtenay (who had been elected by the monks of Canterbury to succeed the butchered Sudbury in July 1381). For the anguish of separation was felt not merely by devoted disciples like John Purvey (and much less by 'incurable ecclesiastical anarchists' like William Swinderby), but also by sound conservative teachers, who had never for an instant wavered in their loyalty to the Church, but who were bound to Wyclif by ties of respect and affection formed over many years. We have already remarked how reluctant were his contemporaries to believe that he had relapsed irredeemably into heresy; William Wodeford, however adamant against the Wycliffites, was anxious as late as 1381 to recall old memories. In 1379 or 1380 Adam Stockton, the Cambridge Austin friar, copied out a determination of Wyclif, which 'we know today as one of the bitterest passages in *De potestate Papae*'; this he annotated 'Hec venerabilis doctor magister Iohannes Wyclyf in quadam sua determinacione anno domini 1379'. Only in the following year, or in 1381, when Wyclif's teaching on transubstantiation had become openly heretical and when he had finally broken with his last allies the friars, did Stockton alter the ascription to 'execrabilis seductor'.[2]

And what of Wyclif himself? Is there not, for all the naïvety of his reproaches to old colleagues who now opposed him, a note of pathos in his recognition that friendships that had once seemed so firm were now lost for ever? And some of these dated back to his earliest days. In *De veritate sacrae scripturae*, published in 1378, he refers to an old friend who had recently argued against him.

For thus I have lately been addressed by a certain doctor, whom I believed to be my particular friend and an outstanding defender of catholic truth, and though I will patiently bear personal injuries in accordance with the rule of Scripture, yet for the honour of God and the profit of the church, I must take from her the scandal I would give

---

[1] Courtenay's role has been championed in particular by K. B. McFarlane, *John Wycliffe*, esp. pp. 105 ff., 187.

[2] Gwynn, *Austin Friars*, pp. 238-9.

if I culpably kept silence; and I must reply to the arguments by which, as it seems to many, the doctor teaches that I and my supporters are heretics and sly traitors to the kingdom of God.[1]

Just another of those who had been compelled to break their friendship with a man hell-bent for heresy? But the 'certain doctor', as a marginal reference tells us,[2] was none other than William Barton. In the following year Barton became chancellor and was the first university official actively to take steps to censure Wyclif's opinions; late in 1380 he summoned a council of twelve masters in theology, who condemned Wyclif's teaching on the eucharist.[3] As for the 'special friendship' between the two doctors, it went back over twenty years, for both had been fellows of Merton and both appear in the bursarial roll for 1356.[4]

Yet Wyclif continued to be read at Oxford and his works continued to impress young men. He had, as we have said, been condemned for heretical articles on the eucharist and the nature of the Church; he had not, except incidentally, been condemned for philosophical errors. Moreover Courtenay, as has recently been pointed out,[5] employed the restraint that goes with the sure exercise of power; he did not attempt to interfere in scholastic arguments, and had he done so the university would have fought him to the last (as it fought Arundel thirty years later). Wyclif's logical premisses, except in so far as they led to theological error, could safely be left to time to justify or refute. We may note again the remarkable admission of Netter. The author of the *Doctrinale* had studied at Oxford *c.* 1390. He was never tempted by the theology or sociology of Lollardy, yet he was swept away by Wycliffian logic.

Whilst at first I thought of this in silence, afterwards in my early years I lent credulous ears to his logical teaching. I was quite astounded by his sweeping assertions, by the authorities cited and by the vehemence

[1] Ed. R. Buddensieg (*WS*, 1905), I, 345.

[2] MS. Peterhouse, Cambridge 223, fo. 230r. This text contains the first twenty-four chapters of *De veritate sacrae scripturae*.

[3] Emden, *Biographical Register*, I, 123–4; Workman, II, 140–8; Gwynn, *Austin Friars*, pp. 258–60, correcting Workman's 'very biased manner'. Narrative and schedule of censured propositions in *FZ*, pp. 105–13.

[4] Emden, *loc. cit.*, and above, p. 11.

[5] McFarlane, *John Wycliffe*, pp. 115–16.

of his reasoning. My faith remained intact, but with his opinions I continued to wrestle. Finally after some time I transferred my studies to sacred books, and it was not long before I discovered him to be an open counterfeiter of Scripture; I found that he twisted it to a meaning opposed to all the sacred commentators; that he confused Scripture which was self-explanatory and concealed simple truths, and that with vain glosses he here modified and there rooted up the sacred words.[1]

Netter's recognition that Wycliffian logic and orthodox theology were incompatible apparently came to him at the same time as it came to Wyclif himself: that is, when he began to read theology, 'when I transferred my studies to sacred books'.

Fortunately we are not entirely dependent on scraps of autobiography for information about Oxford philosophy after Wyclif's condemnation and death. For logic and metaphysics we have a valuable document that throws much light on the attitude to Wyclif of the Arts faculty at the turn of the century. MS. Corpus Christi College, Oxford, 116[2] is a collection of incepting disputations and logical propositions by a miscellany of Oxford Artists of the end of the fourteenth century. It is apparently a haphazard scrapbook, written in several hands; but it has one thread running through it: an interest in Wyclif's logic. The compiler of these notes seems to have been an admirer of Wyclif, but he also included an incepting exercise which is largely a passionate attack upon him. Once (and almost certainly twice) an ascription to Wyclif has been erased. Since, as we shall seek to show,[3] the destruction of his works (and the subterfuges necessary to evade

---

[1] *Doctrinale*, ed. B. Blanciotti (Venice, 1757–9), I, 1. Cum tamen primum haec tacitus cogitarem, postquam in iuvenilibus annis logicalibus eius auscultantes aures indulsi, stupebam ultra modum assertiones eius praegrandes, et authoritatum loca taxata, cum vehementiis rationum. Fides mihi mansit integra; sed cum opinione luctabar. Tandem post tempora ad sacros libros me transtuli et non diu quin publicum eum scripturarum invenirem falsarium, extorquere scripturas ad sensum per omnes sacros expositores adversum, scripturas per se planas involvere, occultare simplices veritates, et cum glosis vanis hinc modificare, hinc radere sacra dicta.

[2] Coxe, *Catalogus*, II, 40 (of separate pagination), 'Disputationes et suppositiones quorundam inceptorum in artibus Oxoniensium in physicis et logicis'.

[3] Below, pp. 240 ff.

this) seems not to have become general at Oxford before 1409–10, we date this collection *c.* 1390–1410.

From a long 'nota de ydeis'[1] it is clear that the compiler was a realist. Ideas, he states, are 'forme exemplares' present in the mind of God by virtue of which things are produced; but they do not depend on the thing nor do they suppose the existence of any other essence but God. Ideas in the mind of God are God himself, and as such are universal before things. But who is the authority for this statement? Alas, his name has been destroyed: 'ut patet per [   ] in capitulo de [   ]'. Two vital words have been erased beyond recovery; but we can easily suspect the identity of the ultrarealist whose name it was necessary to expunge. Yet, as so often, the erasures have not been so complete as entirely to banish Wyclif's name, which appears casually in the text at least four times,[2] and openly in a note 'de intelligibili in communi', which refutes an argument ('opinio Wyclyff' reads a marginal annotation)[3] that even the impossible can only be understood in respect of its reality.

More sympathetic are the extracts[4] from a so-called *Summa* of Wyclif, to which we have referred in an earlier chapter in connection with the compiling of the *Summa de Ente*. The abstracts fill nine paper leaves in a regular but difficult hand. Part of the title has been erased, so that Coxe attributed it to a 'Doctor Anglicus'; but under ultra-violet ray the correct title is plain: 'Quedam abstracta a Summa Doctoris Evangelici Magistri Iohannis Wicliff.' Note has already been made of the difficulty in identifying the treatises in this logical *Summa*, for all the apparent clarity of the references—'Ulteriorem processum illius require in 2° capitulo Predicamentorum Summe Magistri Wicliff'.[5] The citations refer to three works only: the *De materia et forma*; and to *Predicamenta* and a *capitulum de quantitate* in a *Summa* of Wyclif's. The particular treatise may be *De ente praedicamentali* (where

---

[1] Fo. 48r.
[2] Fo. 128r, 'nota capitulus [*sic*] in tractatu Magistri Io. W.'; fo. 131r, 'nota secundum magistrum Io. W. in tractatu suo Predicamentorum, capitulo de tempore'; fo. 171r, 'nota argumenta M. Io. ad probandam quartam opinionem de motu in Summa sua, 2ᵐ argumentum ibi'; fo. 177v, 'ut patet per Wiclyf'.
[3] Fo. 46v.   [4] Fos. 132r–140r; and see above, p. 127.   [5] Fo. 132r.

RW

quantity and quality are discussed in great detail in chapters 6–7 and 19–22)[1] or *De Logica*, but cannot be the *Summa de Ente* as known today. But the Leicester and Durham catalogues clearly show the existence at the end of the fourteenth century of a logical *Summa* that has not survived under that name. The summary of Wyclif's opinions on substance, accidents, quantity and predication appears to be taken from *De Logica* and *De ente praedicamentali*; and the warm references shed a valuable gleam of light on the respect for the Doctor Evangelicus shown by at least one member of the Arts faculty at the close of the century.

Si quemquam delectat istam materiam diffusius videre per tractatum in Summa Doctoris subtilissimi Iohannis W. in fine capituli de quantitate inveniet declaratam.

Tertia opinio cui adereo in hac parte ponit, quod omnis quantitas est modus rei sicut multe qualitates: contra quamlibet istarum arguitur in Summa magistri Iohannis W. per multa media, quorum soluciones in parte fundamentaliter [?] percipies in subscriptis.

Si istam materiam prolixius volueris perscrutari, in Summa magistri Io. Wy. in responsione ad 13^m argumentum contra primam opinionem in capitulo de quantitate profundius invenies pertractatam; sed ista sufficiunt pro presenti.[2]

But the compiler of these extracts was sufficiently interested in Wyclif's thought to include an exercise[3] containing a passionate attack upon him. The opening address to the reverend masters and bachelors, imploring 'the help and kindly forbearance of this distinguished audience', shows it to be a scholastic act by an incepting master of arts. Having announced his theme, the nature of quantity and divisibility, the graduand at once turned to an attack on Wyclif's doctrine of the eternity of being. He opposed those who argued that a subject or a moment in time, far from having a fixed number of parts, may be infinitely divisible. Each moment, they have said, is itself infinite, and in consequence no instant can ever be said to be terminated but has eternal and infinite existence.

---

[1] Ed. Beer (*WS*, 1891), pp. 48–78, 179–219.
[2] Fos. 136v, 137r, 139v.   [3] Fos. 49r–56v.

And this assertion is chiefly made by Master I., the principal supporter of this opinion, in his third tractate in the chapter on temporalities, where he explicitly holds that, when the Prime Mover ceases to move after the Last Day, there will still be, after its own kind, an immediate succession of endless moments, which he calls time that is eternal *a parte post*. And from this it is quite plain that there will be an infinite number of moments, since we cannot posit a final moment.[1]

The 'third treatise' of master I[ohannes], to which the Artist refers, is unquestionably *De Logica*, Book III, chapter 10, 'de proposicionibus temporalibus',[2] in which Wyclif expounds, perhaps for the first time, the theory of the amplification of time to cover the past and future. If there could be any doubt of the identification of master I., it is at once removed by the Artist's account of the secondary proof of his opponent's argument, as given in *De veritate sacrae scripturae*.

And the minor proof is that everything that will be is now, as is stated by the same master I. in *De veritate scripturae*, where he posits six opinions as the six 'armours' by which, he says, a catholic can easily escape the wiles of the disputatious. And of these opinions the principal 'armour' is that which posits the amplification of terms, and from this 'armour' he thinks that he can weld the breastplate of Faith. And therefore those who hold this opinion must say either that this breastplate will not remain intact in respect of all its parts (which for them is manifest heresy), or that everything which will be is now, in which case the opposite of their opinion inevitably follows [because the parts will continue to have an eternal and distinct existence]. But I deny the amplification of terms.[3]

---

[1] Fo. 50v. Assertum patet pro maiori per magistrum I. principalem fautorem huius opinionis in tertio suo tractatu, capitulo de temporalibus, ubi expresse tenet quod, cessante motu primi mobilis post diem ultimum, erit successio modo suo et instantia inmediata sine termino sibi invicem succedencia, quam successionem ipse vocat tempus eternum a parte post; quo habito, patet expresse quod infinita instantia simpliciter erunt, cum non sit dare ultimum.

[2] Ed. Dziewicki (*WS*, 1899), III, 133–227.

[3] Fo. 50v. Et minor videlicet, quia omnia que erunt sunt, patet per eundem magistrum I. in De veritate Scripture, ubi ponit sex opiniones esse sex armaturas quibus poterit, inquit, catholicus versucias disputancium faciliter evitare. Quarum opinionum est opinio ponens verbi ampliacionem principalis seu precipua armatura, ex quibus armaturis ymaginatur ipse unam fidei loricam

The theory of the amplification of time can be refuted, states the Artist. For if 'my non-existence at this moment' is an eternal verity (though I shall exist in the future), so is 'my existence at this moment' when that future point is reached. And the consequence of this is an infinite number of 'eternal' and contradictory truths. Wyclif, of course, had replied to this objection on many occasions, declaring first, that what is contradictory to us is resolved as intelligible being known to God, and secondly that such contradictories, though eternally true, are never simultaneously a present reality. But he could not and did not expect this argument to pass unchallenged.

There was a further adaptation of this theory which was equally repugnant to the incepting master; for just as the principles of ultrarealist metaphysics required subjects to have an infinite existence, so it denied that there could be an infinite subdivision of their existing parts. Moreover, as we have noted before, ultra-realism was hostile to the idea of the absolute and unrestrained exercise of God's power, since it supposed that there were things (such as annihilation or the creation of new substance) that he could not effect. We have suggested that, in taking this stand, Wyclif was running counter to an important section of current opinion, and this is amply confirmed in the words of this disputation. For the unknown master proceeds immediately from the refutation of the eternity of being to an affirmation of divine omnipotence. The great philosophers of the ancient world, he states, and the theologians, especially Scotus and Bradwardine in De causa Dei, assert that God by his infinite power can so illumine the least of creatures as to make him capable of infinite division. But those who follow master John deny the validity of God's absolute power and refuse to draw the inescapable deduction.

And so I finally conclude that all the ancient philosophers specially illumined by the light of nature and magnifying their God, have proved that he is the Prime Mover, himself unmoved, of infinite

parcialiter integrare; ergo oportet sic opinantes dicere quod predicta lorica secundum singulas suas partes non manebit integra (quod est illis manifesta heresis), vel quod omnia que erunt sunt; quo dato, sequitur inevitabiliter oppositum opinionis. Sed negando ampliacionem verbi....

The reference is to R. Buddensieg, ed., De veritate sacrae scripturae (WS, 1905), I, 167–73.

strength and power; and extolling his infinite power, they have described him as an infinite sphere, whose centre is everywhere and circumference nowhere. And examining more deeply this opinion of mature theology, these famous philosophers affirm that God by his universal power can produce an infinite number of worlds more perfect than that which he has now produced and infinitely more men than now exist, and so turning to each creature in turn. But the supporters of that other opinion [that is, the Wycliffites], who, saving their reverence, have reversed the truth, derogating as it seems to me from the divine power, assert that God himself by his absolute power cannot produce a better world than he has produced nor more men than he will produce hereafter. And this opinion is held and declared by master Iohannes their head, in his third treatise 'per magnum processum etc.'[1]

Here we have most interesting evidence of how far the doctrine of the limitlessness of God's absolute power had permeated orthodox theology, and an illustration of how Wyclif's metaphysics necessarily opposed accepted teaching at this point. The citation of Scotus and Bradwardine for the opposite view is also noteworthy —and perhaps piquant.

[1] Fo. 50v. Et ita posuerunt antiqui philosophi, ut Aristoteles princeps philosophorum cum veneranda turba venerabilium peripateticorum, et specialiter theologi, ut Doctor Profundus in Causa Dei contra Pelagium ponit expresse quod in minima creatura relucet potencia dei infinita, ut quod quelibet substancia corporea habet potenciam passivam quoad divisionem simpliciter infinitam; etiam Doctor Subtilis, super Metaphisicam Aristotelis, tenet quod sit procedere in infinitum in effectibus. Ut finaliter concludam, quotquot fuerant antiqui philosophi lumine naturali specialiter illustrati, magnificantes [MS. manificantes] suum deum, probaverunt ipsum esse primum motorem immobilem infiniti vigoris seu potencie; et extollentes ipsius infinitam omnipotenciam, dixerunt ipsum esse speram infinitam, cuius centrum est ubique et circumferencia nusquam. Istam eciam sentenciam maturitatis theologice incliti professores intimius [sic] perscrutantes, affirmant deum de sua cunctipotencia [sic] posse producere infinitos mundos perfecciores mundo iam producto et infinitum [sic] plures homines hominibus iam productis, et sic discurrendo per singulas creaturas. Fautores vero istius opinionis vice versa, salva ipsorum reverencia, ut mihi videtur derogantes divine potencie, asserunt ipsum deum de sua potencia absoluta non posse producere meliorem mundum quam de facto produxit, nec posse producere plures homines quam producet posterius; et istud tenet et declarat Magister I. ipsorum capitaneus in suo tertio tractatu 'per magnum processum etc.'

I have not found this phrase; but the subject is treated in detail in Wyclif's Logic, Book III, chapter 7 (Dziewicki, ed., De Logica, II, 130–5).

Two concluding passages of this act are also of interest. In the first, defending the opinions of Aristotle, the inceptor finds it necessary to refute the words of a certain master who had championed, with the support of Grosseteste, the platonic doctrine of ideas. Lincolniensis, he had said, was more trustworthy than 'the blind and obstinate pagans who lack the kernel of knowledge'. The Artist rejects his views on the rather inadequate and tangential ground that Plato was not to be trusted because he had advocated marital communism.[1] But it is worth noting that there were masters who were still prepared to maintain, in an *actus solemnis*, platonic idealism as taught by Grosseteste. The devotion to Grosseteste, shown by Tyssington[2] and many other opponents of Wyclif, helped perhaps more than any other factor to keep realism respectable at Oxford after the condemnations of Wyclif himself.

The second quotation is of greater importance. It is a passionate and eloquent lament for the decay of Oxford philosophy. How far this is rhetoric, how far sober truth is open to speculation. But it is hardly surprising that the disturbances of thirty years (and the most unfortunate intervention of the authorities in 1409–10), should have taken their toll.

And truly, if I am not mistaken, saving even the reverence of so many who adhere to this opinion (that is, the Wycliffites), it is that exceeding the bounds set by the ancients, which is the complete cause why that subtle and lovely philosophy, which formerly made our mother the university glorious throughout the world, has almost totally been lulled to sleep. For, of old, India gloried in jewels and Arabia in gold, but the University of Oxford rejoiced in the multitude of its subtle

---

[1] Fo. 53 r. Nam ipse Plato erravit in multis, nam in morali materia, sicut recitat Philosophus in libris Ethicorum, tenuit et posuit omnes uxores debere esse communes et propriis non gaudere maritis, et erravit in modo ponendi ydeas. . . .

[2] John Tyssington, O.F.M., was a member of Barton's committee which censured *De Eucharistia*. But compare the eulogy of Grosseteste in his reply to Wyclif's *Confessio* (*FZ*, p. 135). 'Infra hoc tempus floruit Lincolniensis, cujus comparatio ad omnes doctores modernos est velut comparatio solis ad lunam quando eclipsatur.' The words might be Wyclif's own.

logicians and the treasure of its mature philosophy. But now, as it grieves me to say, it is scarce possible to brush away from its face the dust of error and ignorance.[1]

It was only too easy for the generation that followed Wyclif to place upon him and the Lollards the blame for the decline in the intellectual achievement of the university. In truth, the roots of this decline lay far deeper than in the upsets which accompanied Wyclif's condemnation and antedated by many years the rise of Lollardy. Nor was it confined to Oxford: it was a European phenomenon. The Wycliffite excesses provided an explanation of a decline which contemporaries sensed, but for which they could not account.

III

But this is only one side of the story; and in the great mass of pastoral and doctrinal literature produced to combat Wycliffite errors, it is easy to pass over what is perhaps the fullest refutation of Wyclif's philosophical system. This is to be found in the great treatise otherwise devoted precisely to such devotional and doctrinal argument; in the first section of the *Doctrinale antiquitatum fidei ecclesiae catholicae* of Thomas Netter[2] of Walden.

Like so many of the English friars in the van of the resurgence of orthodox theology, Netter was a Carmelite; and like so many Carmelites an East Anglian. A native of Saffron Walden, it is likely that he was born shortly before 1370, since he was ordained priest at the Carmelite house in London in 1396. It seems clear that the 'pater meus et magister devotus frater Guillielmus' of whom he speaks was William Wodeford, the Franciscan, though

---

[1] Fo. 52v. Et revera, si non fallor, salva tamen reverencia tante multitudinis huic opinioni adherencium, ista exorbitacio extra limites antiquorum est completa causa quod illa subtilis logica et pulcherrima philosophia, que matrem nostram universitatem istam per universum orbem terrarum olim reddiderant gloriosam, fere in scolis nostris totaliter sunt sopite. Antiquitus enim gloriabatur gemmis India et auro Arrabia, sed universitas Oxonie subtilium logicorum gaudebat multitudine et maturitatis philosophice thesauro [? precio]sissimo. Sed, quod dolenter refero, vix sufficit modo a sua facie excutere pulveres erroris et ignorancie.

[2] Fullest biographical details in Emden, *Biographical Register*, II, 1343–4. See also *DNB*; Knowles, *Religious Orders*, II, 146–8.

the suggestion that he studied under him and resided at Oxford in 1389–90, is now discounted.[1] But a later experience at Oxford, his imbroglio with Peter Payne of St Edmund Hall, is genuine enough. Netter had a notable career: in his own Order for excellence, and outside it as an ecclesiastical politician. He was a delegate to the councils of Pisa and Constance. He became Provincial of the Carmelites in 1414, and also confessor to Henry VI. It was at the king's request that he began to compose the *Doctrinale* about 1421. The first two parts (on the clergy and the sacraments) were presented to Martin V in 1426; at the Pope's urgent request a third part (on the sacramentals) was composed in the following year. In April 1430 Netter accompanied Henry VI to France, and it was at Rouen on 2 November that he died.

Netter has always figured prominently in the story of the anti-Wycliffite revival—though we must now, it seems, abandon the theory that he was part author of the *Fasciculi Zizaniorum*.[2] His reputation has led a recent historian to describe him as 'perhaps the most distinguished (English) friar of any order between the age of Ockham and the Dissolution'.[3] The *Doctrinale* and Wodeford's *De sacramento altaris* are good examples of that solid academic and pastoral theology which Professor Knowles has also selected as the true sources of the defeat of Wycliffite errors: 'Lollardy, in fact, great as was its moral, its emotional and its social appeal, could not stand up to logical thought and traditional theology clearly expressed.'[4] Netter certainly intended the section on Wyclif's formal scholastic philosophy, with which the *Doctrinale* begins, as a mere preliminary to the main discussion—above all, the defence of orthodox teaching on the eucharist. And it is amusing to find his eighteenth-century editor, Blanciotti,[5] actually apologising for his author's unattractive preoccupation with

[1] Emden, *loc. cit.*

[2] V. H. Galbraith, *Eng. Hist. Rev.* LXXII (1957), 105 (reviewing Knowles, *Religious Orders*, vol. II. Professor Knowles has corrected this point in the second edition of his work (1958)).

[3] Knowles, *Religious Orders*, II, 146.   [4] *Ibid.* p. 147.

[5] All references are to the edition of B. Blanciotti, *Thomae Waldensis Carmelitae Anglici Doctrinale antiquitatum fidei catholicae ecclesiae* (3 vols., Venice, 1757–9), vol. I, article 1.

scholastic niceties. Netter's interest, he explains, was necessary because of Wyclif's own dependence on the philosophical axioms that underlay his subsequent errors.[1] Just so: and we may rejoice that Netter (quite correctly) began his work with a lengthy examination of the primary theses of Wyclif's philosophy. The sources used are interesting. First, in number of citations, stands the *Trialogus*,[2] a great tract of controversial apologetic composed in 1382; but it is closely followed by *De Ydeis*, which is taken as the primary text for illustrating Wyclif's realism. Other quotations of tracts in the *Summa de Ente* are from *De Tempore* (for the argument on 'eternal time') and *De Universalibus* (where the key Chapter 13 on annihilation is cited *in extenso*).[3]

Netter's youthful enthusiasm for Wyclif's teaching has already been noted.[4] He tells us that it was the logical writings that carried him away; that revulsion came when he turned to Scripture; and that he discovered Wyclif to be a shameless falsifier of Scripture. Netter, rather conventionally, founds his faith on the word of God and not on 'vana philosophia et humana sapientia', declaring that he is nourished by the threefold bread of Scripture, the Fathers and reason.[5] More acutely he notes that Wyclif halves our experience of religious verification: the written word of Scripture he proclaims, the common faith of the church he neglects and dismisses.[6] Wyclif's failure was, indeed, that of the intellectual who did not comprehend religious experience, and in this blindness to personal, subjective experience he ran counter to the whole current of his age.

In the prologue to Book I Netter summarises Wyclif's philosophical errors: that everything is identical with God; that being, which faith and the Fathers declare to be transitory and variable, is immutably fixed; that everything was, is and will be. Wyclif limits the infinite omnipotence of God: he can only do what he will do; he cannot have done other than he has done; he cannot

---

[1] *Doctrinale*, vol. I, col. 29.

[2] Ed. J. Lechler (Oxford, 1869); and see Workman, II, 309.

[3] For example, *Doctrinale*, vol. I, cols. 35, 39, 41, 47, 52, 53, 56, 104 (*De Ydeis*); cols. 56, 99 (*De Tempore, De Universalibus*).

[4] Above, p. 223.   [5] *Doctrinale*, vol. I, cols. 6, 9.

[6] *Ibid.* col. 5.

annihilate. God necessitates every creature in all his acts; everything that will happen will necessarily happen; one foreknown to grace cannot be lost unless God necessitates him absolutely to deprivation.[1] All these axioms, as we have seen, appear already developed in the *Summa de Ente*.

Netter's first Article[2] is a critical examination of Wyclif's teaching on the essence, the power and the knowledge of God. Founding himself on logic alone, 'logica tam novella quam nulla', Wyclif could see no theological objection to declaring all *raciones* of creatures to be eternal in God, nor any metaphysical objection to positing an eternal plurality of such exemplars. This identification of essences (*quidlibet est Deus*) was only apparent to one versed in his own logico-metaphysical system—'in suis logicalibus...nutritus', he had said in *De Ydeis*, chapter 2.[3] Netter replies that the answer lies in the very propositions denied by Wyclif at this point (*De Ydeis*, chapters 2–3), that things inhere in God not totally, *simpliciter*, but *secundum quid*; that even Christ (who is essentially divine nature) inheres in God not *simpliciter* but *secundum essentiam*. Wyclif himself admits, says Netter, that the accepted realist terminology of inherence in respect of intelligible or ideal being is not his own, and cannot be identified with inherence *simpliciter*.[4] Nor can he ever justify his own qualification that, though all creatures are God, he is not every creature. If the one follows, replies Netter, so must the converse be true.[5] The correct explanation? All things, in so far as they are in God, are God himself. 'Omnia facta sunt in Deo Deus: sed horrenda blasphemia est concedere quomodocunque, et sic simpliciter, quod omnia facta sunt Deus.'[6]

Wyclif's second fundamental error, states Netter, citing *De Ydeis*, chapter 3, lay in positing ideas as coeternal with God, though created by him—which, in turn, supposed the eternal

---

[1] *Doctrinale*, vol. I, cols. 31–2.   [2] *Ibid.* cols. 33–168.
[3] *Ibid.* cols. 33–4. Cf. MS. Trinity Coll. B. 16. 2, fo. 118vª (*De Ydeis*, ch. 2). Video tam antiquos quam modernos specialiter inaniter laborare in ista materia; nec erit capax ad intelligendum illas equivocaciones sensuum nisi in logicalibus primo prolixius sit nutritos [*sic*].
[4] *Ibid.* cols. 35, 39.   [5] *Ibid.* col. 39.
[6] *Ibid.* col. 37.

existence of created things as intelligible being before creation. But God's eternal knowledge of things, Netter replies, is not their eternal existence, in whatever mode that is presumed.[1] Thus Wyclif, taking Paul's words to the Corinthians (I, xv. 28), 'God is all in all', had inflated them into the crudely realist statement: 'deus est omnes rationes ideales in omnibus creaturis'. But the apostle's words describe a theological and not a metaphysical truth, our final acceptance by God and not our present temporal existence: what Paul had said *in ratione finis* Wyclif had construed *in ratione principii*. And in this distortion of the doctrine of ideas Wyclif had defied the platonists themselves, who condemned such theories of divine immanence, and had exceeded the worst errors of the Manichaeans in confounding God with existence.[2]

Wyclif's third fallacy is that of the amplification of time; and here Netter argues from his opponent's statements in the *Trialogus* 'et in tractatu *De Tempore* passim'. Starting by supposing the coincidence of past, present and future in a *tempus magnum*, Wyclif had extended this from temporalities to the whole field of intelligible being; and the result had been to confound actual, possible and intelligible being by 'amplification'.[3] Netter replies that, though things are eternal, created things have no past or future existentially. For past and future are distinct qualities, and whilst they inhere essentially in created substance, they exist only with respect to the actual existence of creatures in measurable time. The 'being' of substance must be 'present being'.[4]

From analysing these premisses, which are indeed fundamental to Wyclif's system, Netter proceeds to criticise the theological deductions made from them. He attacks first (chapters XI–XVI) the proposition that the omnipotence of God is limited to his actual activity, or in any other way, arguing (quite traditionally) that God's potency extends to many things that he neither does nor ever chooses to do. The fact that his activity stems from his will, which is absolute, shows it to be unlimited: 'Father, if it be

---

[1] *Ibid.* cols. 41–2.
[2] *Ibid.* cols. 47–8 (citing *De Ydeis*, ch. 2), 52–3.
[3] *Ibid.* col. 56, citing also *De Ydeis*, ch. 1.   [4] *Ibid.* cols. 57–8, 60–2.

Thy will', not 'if Thou canst'.[1] And his power is prior to his will, however he may choose to limit the latter.[2] The will of God cannot be confined to its actual willing, nor is he bound by the actual composition of physical matter—and here Netter is able to quote Grosseteste on God's capacity to create an infinity of points.[3]

But more central, of course, was the second axiom that followed from the theory of the eternity of being: the rejection of the possibility of the annihilation of substance (rebutted in chapters XVII–XXI). Like a good prosecuting counsel, Netter takes Wyclif through his statements in De Universalibus, chapter 13:

Suppono primo, quod sicut creatio est productio de puro esse intelligibili, et sic de nihilo in effectu ad esse essentiale extra Deum; sic adnihilatio, si foret, esset cessio creaturae in purum nihil in effectu; sic quod existentia creaturae haberet purum esse intelligibile.[4]

Netter fastens on to the definition of uncreated being as intelligible being external to God. But if we admit being as intelligibile, why not also as possibile or volibile? In other words it is tendentious to describe the whole realm of potential being as 'intelligible', which really presupposes no more than 'possible'. Creation, he says, is either effected formally from nothing, de nihilo (as it would have been better to say in the first place), or essentially from God; and in each case it is plainly impossible to speak of creation from independent intelligible being, formally distinct from God.[5] Wyclif supposed being to exist first 'solum in ente analogo', and afterwards produced in its appropriate species: things exist before creation in an ideal 'intelligible' form independent of God.[6] It is at this concept of ideas that Netter strikes hardest. First he insists that God produces 'a primo nihilo': there is no room for independent ideas. He points out that all the realist Fathers refused to separate ideas from God. There is therefore no place for the intelligible being, which would be unaffected by the destruction of its material substance and to the annihilation of which God's

---

[1] Doctrinale, vol. I, cols. 74, 77, 80.   [2] Ibid. cols. 81–2, 91.
[3] Ibid. col. 89, citing Post. An. IV, ch. I.
[4] Ibid. col. 99. Cf. text in MS. Trinity College, Cambridge, B. 16. 2, fo. 311ª.
[5] Ibid. col. 99.   [6] Ibid. cols. 100, 109.

power cannot extend.[1] And to this metaphysical argument against 'intelligible being' Netter adds a theological objection to the parallel concept of 'eternal being'. It effectively bars predestination. You can only predestine something before it is; you cannot have predestination and the 'eternal now'.[2]

From this basis Netter proceeds (chapters XXI–XXV) to refute Wyclif on the absolute necessity of future events, and God's inability to vary them. Such teaching faces the overwhelming moral implication that the foreknown are eternally condemned, and that God sends men like beasts to the slaughterhouse, necessitating them to a second death. Such opinions make a mockery of his prohibitions and exhortations: predestination is not necessitation.[3] For Netter, of course, the fount of error lies in ascribing to God the doctrine of *absolute* necessitation of futures, in which the human will must concur in causing a corresponding merit or demerit. The Church has always taught, he says, that, though God's foreknowledge is necessary and infallible, future events are not absolutely necessary but contingent and variable. However, in abandoning the absolute necessity of foreknown effects and admitting future contingents, it was not necessary to allow that divine foreknowledge may be contingently false. This was the impossible choice Wyclif had tried to impose on FitzRalph. In the *Trialogus* (from which Netter quotes), as ten years before in *De volucione Dei*, he had seized on the famous admission of Ardmachanus that 'for twenty years' he had wrestled with the problem of Christ's capacity to err, without finding a satisfactory solution. Finally FitzRalph had seemed to admit that, at least as a human, Our Lord could err—for Wyclif a plain impossibility and self-refutation of the doctrine of contingency. But Netter denied any such explicit admission by FitzRalph, and quoted no less a witness than Bradwardine to show that the doctrine of absolute necessity was universally condemned.[4]

---

[1] *Ibid.* cols. 111–14.　　　　　[2] *Ibid.* col. 117.
[3] *Ibid.* cols. 119, 121.
[4] *Ibid.* cols. 124–5. On FitzRalph's views Netter cites *Trialogus*, Book III, ch. IX (ed. Lechler, p. 158); the earlier citation in *De volucione Dei* in Dziewicki, ed., *De Ente*, pp. 184–5; FitzRalph's statement in *De questionibus Armenorum*, Book 16, ch. 4 (ed. cit. fo. 130r). And see above, p. 207.

Though God foresees and preordains, states Netter, he does not compel; and the effects necessarily caused by predestination are neither the sinful nor the meritorious act as such, but the retribution or recompense appropriate to each. To quote Augustine, God foreknows all things of which he is the author but is not the author of all that he foreknows: God does not cause sin.[1] Nor on the other hand could Netter accept the Ciceronian view which preserved his liberty by denying his foreknowledge. Augustine had distinguished the external necessity (the *necessitas fati* of the Stoics), which is outside our control, from the necessity within our power. Again Anselm had distinguished precedent and consequent necessity. Since the former is incompatible with free action in men, Netter describes as very dangerous the views of the important group (*quidam magni viri*) which posited such precedent necessity and declared it to flow from the divine will. In effect he rejects any application of *necessitas absoluta* by God to men's wills.[2]

Thus, like all theologians of his age, he arrives at last at the question of future contingents (chapters XXVI–XXIX). This problem seems to arouse and dismay Netter more than any other in this section; it has done so, he says, since the institution of the Church. And he prefaces his remarks with a more than formal protestation that he may not fall into error, and begs forgiveness of those whose doubt he shall not entirely resolve. It is, he warns, a subject particularly treacherous for the logician, *logicus de signis*.[3] In the first place foreknowledge is not mere precognition (in which it would vary little from ideal knowledge), but is precognition accompanied by acceptance or rejection. Netter discusses the argument of those who wished to exclude future contingents from divine foreknowledge, since what is foreknown is necessitated; and he himself does make such an exclusion, by distinguishing God's foreknowledge of the certain future from His comprehension of the contingent and possible, which He understands rather than foreknows, *intellecta non prescita*. Netter certainly wishes firmly to distinguish the *futurum de certo* from the *futurum de possibili*. His second argument is that God's knowledge

---

[1] *Doctrinale*, vol. I, cols. 128–9.   [2] *Ibid*. cols. 137–9.
[3] *Ibid*. cols. 140–1.

is in any case such that he knows things in their infinite variability:
it is we who know things only as naturally necessitated. His
knowledge is of things and not derived from them: *non a rebus, sed
de rebus.* All divine foreknowledge, therefore, is necessary, but the
future remains either necessary or contingent; and the contingent
future is neither more nor less necessary for being foreknown.[1]

But can we still avoid the charge that God necessitates damnation? *Praescitus,* answers Netter, is he who is foreknown to sin,
and does not wish not to sin. God, who created us free, never
deprives us of the will to merit; he merely knows that the foreknown will not will to change his fate. God is the sun and his
foreknowledge the shaft of sunlight. What he sees is certain, yet
he keeps the power to reform the thing seen through grace; and
his foresight of the reward or punishment, according to merit or
demerit, is a secondary act, variable in the object which it perceives.[2] There is no escape, states Netter, from utter predestinarianism once one admits the absolutely certain foreknowledge
of future acts in God. Thus Wyclif may try to distinguish the
necessitation that comes from God's will from the secondary
necessitation that depends on the mutable acts of creatures. But
in his system are not the acts of creatures themselves necessarily
foreknown?[3] Finally Netter summons up a man-of-straw, *noster
logicus* (a blind predestinarian), to recall once more Richard Fitz-
Ralph and his twenty years' struggle with the problem of free will.
Did not Ardmachanus admit that the only alternative to absolute
predestinarianism was the possibility of divine uncertainty? And
here follows at once a personal invocation to the God of prophecy
and infinite foreknowledge, who hides his mysteries from the
wise and reveals them to little children—that irresistibly recalls
FitzRalph's own autobiographical prayer: but perhaps the echo
is really from Augustine himself.

O magne Deus. Cuius prophetia immensa et praescientia infinita; qui
abscondis mysteria tua a sapientibus et prudentibus, et revelas ea
parvulis: fac me de praescientia tua sic sentire et scribere ut nulla logica
improvisa, non corrupta professio scandalizet vel me, vel per me,

---

[1] *Ibid.* cols. 141–4.   [2] *Ibid.* cols. 145, 147.
[3] *Ibid.* cols. 151–3.

aliquem de pusillis tuis, qui in te credunt. Fateor coram te: mallem suspendi mihi molam asinariam circa collum, et in profundum maris demergi, quam vel semel asserere te posse falli, vel fallere: prophetiam tuam posse esse mendacem; praedestinationem tuam mutabilem, vel praescientiam tuam variabilem et incertam....[1]

Netter's joyful acceptance of God's predestinating love is at least as sure as his dislike of rigid predestinarianism.

IV

These words must date from *c.* 1421.[2] How far do they suppose an active group of philosophers actually propagating Wyclif's purely academic ideas at Oxford? Netter's own words should be treated with some caution, his rhetoric weighed against his factual statements. For instance, it is difficult to take seriously his spoken fear of persecution by Lollards for writing the *Doctrinale*.[3] The boot was too much on the other foot. Nor does he try to distinguish between popular Lollardy and academic dispute in the university. Still the *Doctrinale* does seem to assume some interest in Wyclif's philosophy; and there are puzzling pieces of evidence —information from library catalogues, Wyclif manuscripts copied a generation after his death, the Artist's notebook described above—which support the tacit assumptions of Netter and other apologists that Wyclif's academic philosophical concepts were still entertained—as was still perfectly legitimate. Yet clearly at some point the ban on Wycliffite material became absolute—with the resulting destruction of manuscripts or erasure of evidence of his authorship. To determine the date at which the condemnation of particular errors was transformed into a general prohibition to consult will clarify these problems and provide useful information on the course of debate at Oxford. It can also suitably close this study of Wyclif's early academic philosophy and its place in the history of the Oxford schools.

For there is evidence that he continued to be read, and some-

[1] *Doctrinale*, vol. I, col. 158.
[2] Emden, *Biographical Register*, II, 1344, dates commencement of *Doctrinale* about this time.
[3] *Doctrinale*, vol. I, col. 6.

times in surprising places and by surprising people. We have already noted the presence of his logical *Summa* in two libraries of the 1390's,[1] and those the most unexpected. For the Benedictines were never infected by Wycliffite ideas, and Leicester was such a notorious haunt of Lollardy that we should have expected the canons of the Austin abbey to have been doubly careful about the contents of their library. Surviving manuscripts are also revealing. We may perhaps exclude the collection of Wyclif's logic already discussed in this chapter as a private compilation. But the copy of the *Postilla super totam bibliam*,[2] written at Oxford in 1403, is another matter. It was bought by John Cranewys, monk of Bury St Edmunds, probably for the abbey library, and was read and annotated throughout the fifteenth century, as the many marginalia in hands from the early fifteenth to early sixteenth centuries attest. Other examples can be given of men who, though possessing works of Wyclif, are otherwise known chiefly for their anti-Lollard activities. Nicholas Faux,[3] a Benedictine of Glastonbury (by 1377), was a student at Gloucester College in the late 1380's and incepted in theology by 1396-7. He was the owner of at least a part, and almost certainly the whole, of MS. Oriel College 15 (already cited for FitzRalph's *Sentences*). At some date after 1389 he entered at the end of Robert Holcot's *Sentences* (fo. 210r^b), which form part of this splendid codex, the following words:

Scriptus fuerat iste liber de industria fratris Nicholai Fawkes, monachi Glastonie, anno domini millesimo trecentesimo octogesimo nono, quo tempore plures questiones de opere Holkoth grave fuerat invenire.[4]

The fact that this inscription has been erased (though Holcot had never been condemned), must be taken in conjunction with another erasure at the end of Wyclif's *De incarnacione Verbi*—also

[1] Above, p. 127.
[2] Beryl Smalley, 'John Wyclif's Postilla super totam bibliam', *Bodleian Library Record*, IV (1953), 186–205; and for this MS., p. 204.
[3] Emden, *Biographical Register*, II, 671; S. L. Forte, *A Study of Some Oxford Schoolmen of the Middle of the Fourteenth Century* (Oxford B.Litt. thesis, 1947), I, 68.
[4] L. Minio-Paluello, 'Two Erasures in MS. Oriel College 15', *Bodleian Library Record*, IV (1953), 206.

in this codex. At fo. 243 r^a follow the words, since scratched out but visible under the ultra-violet ray: 'Explicit tractatus magistri Iohannis Wiclefi de incarnacione verbi'.[1] Although it is possible that Faux merely wished to avoid guilt by association, the double erasure surely indicates that he owned the complete codex and, very probably, that he was responsible for the copying of the Wyclif text. The next occasion, therefore, on which we meet Nicholas Faux is a piquant one. For on 19 February 1396/7, as a doctor of divinity, he represented the Chancellor of the university before Archbishop Arundel at the Canterbury Convocation, on the very occasion on which a delegation from Oxford was delating the university authorities for countenancing the propagation of Wycliffite works and doctrines.[2] Perhaps it was after this that Faux made the erasures which so embarrassingly identified him as the owner of the Oriel manuscript.

A Cambridge Wyclif manuscript of slightly later date, and its owner, are also of interest. William Lichfield[3] was admitted fellow of Peterhouse in December 1404; he resigned in 1422, and from 1425 to 1447 was rector of All Hallows the Great, London. He was a pillar of orthodoxy, as only a fellow of Peterhouse, who is said to have left over three thousand sermons, could be. He petitioned for the founding of grammar schools, was associated with William Byngham's plans for the enlargement of God's House, and was one of a group of Cambridge B.D.'s, rectors of City livings, who were active in the campaign for the condemnation of Reynold Pecock.[4] Yet whilst still a fellow of Peterhouse, and before the compilation of the library catalogue in 1418, he had presented his college with a book containing a series of Fitz-Ralph's anti-mendicant treatises and the first twenty-four chapters

---

[1] Minio-Paluello, *loc. cit.* p. 207.

[2] Wilkins, *Concilia*, III, 227–31; Workman, II, 343. Faux had already incurred Arundel's displeasure by publishing (1395) a purported bull of Boniface IX, exempting the university from visitation. He was compelled to repudiate the document.

[3] J. and J. A. Venn, eds., *Alumni Cantabrigienses* (Part I), *s.v.*; A. H. Lloyd, *The Early History of Christ's College* (1934), p. 397.

[4] E. F. Jacob, 'Reynold Pecock, Bishop of Chichester', *Proceedings of British Academy*, XXXVII (1951), 133.

of Wyclif's *De veritate sacrae scripturae*.[1] (It is this manuscript which informs us that William Barton was the 'certain doctor' whose friendship Wyclif so regretted losing.[2]) It was perhaps wise of Lichfield to leave the work acephalous; but the fact remains that he owned this work, whose conclusions had been explicitly condemned, and that the fellows of Peterhouse were glad to have it for their library. Wyclif was highly suspect: but (by some) he was still read.

We return, therefore, to the question: when did the ban on Wyclif's pure metaphysics and theology, plainly effective after the first quarter of the fifteenth century, come to be imposed? We have listed a number of works which can be shown to have been copied or used many years after his condemnation. We have noted some sources which reveal the continued discussion of Wyclif's arguments in the Oxford schools. On the other hand, nearly all these manuscripts contain erasures, made at a later date to conceal their authorship, or are acephalous. The critical years, we suggest, lie between 1408 and 1411, when Archbishop Arundel made his long threatened visitation of the university.

That Wyclif himself had any direct connection with Lollardy is open to doubt; but that a number of Oxford masters lent their support is certain. William Courtenay, by swift and energetic action, had struck at this handful and forced them to recant: and in doing so had cut off Lollardy from such academic roots as it had. For though it is clear that a number of Lollard opinions were being aired at Oxford at the turn of the century, there was no real threat to the orthodoxy of the university. Nor, indeed, did the term 'lollard' at that stage have any precise meaning: as has been remarked, it was a derogatory phrase as vague as 'fascist beast'.[3]

---

[1] MS. Peterhouse 223, fos. 179–281. See M. R. James, *Descriptive Catalogue of the Manuscripts...of Peterhouse* (1899), p. 276; and, for the Old Catalogue, p. 13. James does not identify the work, which corresponds to vols. I–II of the *WS* edition by R. Buddensieg (1905–6). It was identified by S. H. Thomson, 'Unnoticed Manuscripts and Works of Wyclif', *Journal of Theological Studies*, XXXVIII (1937), 32. For another MS., also containing Wycliffite material, from the library of the Benedictines at Durham (MS. Jesus College, Cambridge, 59 (Q. G. 11)), see *ibid.* 32–3.

[2] Above, p. 223.   [3] McFarlane, *John Wycliffe*, p. 100.

Unfortunately Thomas Arundel (who succeeded Courtenay in 1396) seems to have lacked his predecessor's finesse, and imagined that Oxford's faith was in peril. All the opposition he received from the university only served to confirm his suspicions. This was in fact a bad misjudgement, for Oxford was far more concerned to preserve academic liberties from archiepiscopal investigation than to countenance heterodoxy. But Arundel made a more serious mistake: failing to make Courtenay's distinction between heretical opinions on matters of faith and arguable propositions on pure philosophy, he set in train a process which had unhappy consequences.

In November 1407,[1] at a provincial synod at Oxford, and in the following January at a session of convocation at St Paul's, Arundel published a set of constitutions designed to check the spread of erroneous doctrine. The key to the new policy (as far as Oxford was concerned) was contained in the sixth constitution:

Because new ways are frequently more seductive than old, we will and command that no tract or treatise of master John Wyclif or anyone else, composed in his day or since or to be composed in the future, shall be henceforth read in the schools, halls or hospices or any other place within our aforesaid province, unless it shall have been examined by the University of Oxford or Cambridge, or at least by twelve masters, whom the said universities or one of them shall have caused to be elected under the laudable discretion of us and our successors; and having been examined, shall have been expressly approved unanimously by the same, and then by us and our successors. Should anyone have read such tracts or treatises in the schools or have taught contrary to this procedure, let him be punished as a sower of schism and promoter of heresy.[2]

The archbishop's moves against unlicensed preaching were justified, but the provisions which affected the university were less happy. Though the text embodied several safeguards and pre-

[1] Arundel's visitation is described most fully in H. E. Salter, ed., *Snappe's Formulary*, OHS, LXXX (1924), 101–15, who also prints, pp. 115–93, a valuable selection of documents on the question. See also Rashdall, *Medieval Universities* (rev. Powicke and Emden), III, 129–35; Workman, II, 355–72. Professor E. F. Jacob kindly drew my attention to the wording of Arundel's *Constitutions*.

[2] Wilkins, *Concilia*, III, 317; *Snappe's Formulary*, pp. 99, 115.

cluded hasty and independent action, it was—in theory—quite comprehensive. This was not merely the suppression of heretical doctrine: it was a 'blanket' prohibition forbidding the study of all texts which had not passed the board of censorship, a prohibition which included the purely philosophical as well as the overtly polemical. And it must be read in conjunction with Arundel's eleventh constitution,[1] which required all Heads of Houses to conduct a monthly enquiry into the orthodoxy of fellows and residents. Those discovered to be holding heterodox opinions were to have the option of recanting or suspension; those who neglected to carry out this duty faced excommunication.

The university resisted, as it always resisted attempts at interference from outside. At first no quorum could be found in Congregation to appoint the Committee of twelve and, when at last constituted, its work was delayed, as it complained to Arundel,[2] by 'the number of treatises and conclusions of that man, and the multitude of his supporters'. Reading between the lines, we can discern some dogged stonewalling, even by the conservative party. The king sent a warning letter to the university, and the archbishop had to republish his constitutions and threaten those who spoke against them. Among these was John Birch of Oriel, proctor at the time of the visitation, who proposed in Congregation the disbandment of the Committee of Twelve, adding that the Faculty of Arts would continue to dispute arguable propositions (*probabiles opiniones*) as before.[3] But Arundel gained the day; and in August 1411, probably supported by the retainers of his nephew Thomas, earl of Arundel, he made his visitation. Entering Oxford, which was in disorder, the archbishop had begun his examination, when a letter arrived from the king, staying proceedings and ordering both parties to appear before him. Arundel thereupon put St Mary's under interdict and departed. The proctor, John Birch, defiantly entered the church and, on the following Sunday, celebrated mass there. But this was the high peak of university resistance. Within a few weeks

[1] Wilkins, *Concilia*, III, 318; *Snappe's Formulary*, p. 116.
[2] *Snappe's Formulary*, p. 120.
[3] *Ibid.* p. 198; Rashdall, *Medieval Universities*, III, 131.

the proctors were in the Tower, and the university, though defending its officers, was taking steps to be reconciled to king and archbishop.[1]

The cumulative effect of these stresses in the Oxford schools, of which the visitation of 1411 was only the climax, can only have been unfortunate. It is true that the wholesale censorship which Arundel sought to impose could not be enforced, and that the Committee of Twelve was quietly forgotten. But Oxford at the beginning of the fifteenth century was not so rich in intellectual vigour that she could ignore the dampening effect of an attempted official censorship. When Gascoigne's laments at the decline of the schools in the middle of the century are being considered, Arundel's activities deserve to be remembered. At any rate, it seems likely that it was in or around 1411 that steps were taken to conceal Wyclif's name in various manuscripts, and that any efforts to treat his pure philosophy were officially abandoned. Since 1382 his works had lingered on, in however attenuated a form, as an object of philosophical study. Henceforth they move into the province of the historian of ideas.

[1] *Snappe's Formulary*, pp. 110–13; Rashdall, *Medieval Universities*, III, 131–4.

THOMAS BUCKINGHAM AND THE EXETER DISPUTE

In *The English Church in the Fourteenth Century* (1955) W. A. Pantin drew attention (pp. 114–15, 263–6) to a group of *questiones* in the later part of Buckingham's *Questions*. Since the discussion of this work in Chapter II above was chiefly directed to examining Buckingham's criticisms of Bradwardine, it seemed best to postpone comment on this interesting section to an appendix.

The *questiones* are to be found in the two known copies of Buckingham's *Questions*: MS. New College 134, fos. 395 v^a–409 v^a; MS. Merton College M. I. 11, fos. 54 v^a–65 r^b (described above, pp. 46–8). Pantin uses only the New College MS., possibly misled by the error of M. D. Chenu ('Les *Quaestiones* de Thomas Buckingham', *Studia...in honorem R. J. Martin*, p. 231), who states that only the first three sections are to be found in the Merton MS. We do not know the circumstances in which the majority of Buckingham's *Questions* were composed; only that the whole series was collected after he had resigned the chancellorship at Exeter (*c.* 1349): he was 'nuper ecclesie Exoniensis cancellarium' (MS. New College 134, fo. 324 r^a). The particular interest of these *questiones* is precisely that, as Buckingham tells us, they were debated at Exeter—'que Exonie inter quosdam doctores diucius vertebatur' (MS. cit. fo. 395 v^a). And it was as evidence of activity, technically advanced activity, in a cathedral school, that they were noticed by Pantin (who prints the principal article of controversy, and its thirteen subsections, on pp. 263–6). Incidentally the participants in this argument all seem to have been trained theologians: 'quosdam doctores', says Buckingham. The dispute appears to have been within the chapter.

Pantin is undoubtedly correct in stating (p. 114 and n. 2) that the debate took place at Exeter, and not at Oxford. The New

College MS. clearly reads *Exonie* on both occasions (fos. 395 v^a, 409 v^a), though in his list of incipits from this MS. Chenu by mistake prints *Oxonie* (*loc. cit.* p. 238). The Merton scribe, who is erratic, and who almost certainly copied from the New College MS. (see above, p. 47), first reads *Exonie* at fo. 54 v^a but lapses into *Oxonie* at fo. 65 r^b. Since the Merton scribe had already in the incipit of the *Questions* made Buckingham '[ecclesie] Oxoniensis cancellarium', he can on this point be dismissed as simply careless. As this group of *questiones* is distinct in time and place the *reverendus doctor* with whom Buckingham disputed at Exeter is not likely to be the *quidam doctor* of the earlier sections, identified above as Bradwardine. This becomes almost a certainty when examination shows that the opponent at Exeter advanced a proposition which was highly Pelagian (as Buckingham promptly pointed out). But he is equally unlikely to have been Richard FitzRalph, as Pantin (very tentatively) suggested (p. 114). We know that FitzRalph wintered at Exeter with Grandisson in 1347–8, before taking up his duties as archbishop of Armagh; and it would be intriguing to be able to identify Buckingham's old master as the adversary. But neither his *Sentences* nor the *De questionibus Armenorum* appear to contain the opinions attacked by the chancellor. The battle between the two theologians was certainly brisk, each being duly 'amazed' at the blasphemies of the other. 'I would never have dared to impute such things to you', said the doctor. 'Let everybody judge for himself whether they are blasphemies or the truth', remarked Buckingham.[1]

The 'Exeter' *questiones* fill most but not all of one of the sections into which Buckingham's *Questions* naturally fall. On fo. 390 v^b he turns to discuss the nature and consequences of original sin, 'ad instanciam sociorum':[2] that is, we suppose, the

---

[1] MS. New College 134, fo. 405 v^a. Alias respondendo dixi, vere admiror quod tam doctus [MS. doctum] movet tam tenue argumentum.…De hac responsione offensus est doctor et dicit quod pro toto mundo tantam blasphemiam non inposuisset mihi. Sed numquid hec responsio sit blasphemia vel realis qui intelligit iudicet.

[2] Fo. 390 v^b. Hec de originali peccato ad instanciam sociorum petencium intermiscebam, querendo utrum originale peccatum solumodo sit peccatum et culpa sub racione qua est sequela et effectus peccati actualis primi parentis.

fellows of Merton, for there is no mention as yet of Exeter. Original sin, he says, is that absence of original justification which affects children and the once-born through the sin of Adam. But it is an absence of love rather than the positive guilt which we incur through our subsequent sins. It is therefore unfortunate, says Buckingham, that the word 'guilt' is loosely applied to both; he believed that our guilt is greater for our deliberate sins than for that which follows from Adam's sin.[1] It is to these sentiments, as unexceptional as they are unexciting, that he adds as a long appendix (fos. 395 vᵃ–409 vᵃ) his account of the dispute with the unknown doctor at Exeter. Thus:

Quia pretacte materie est annexum de statu primorum sanctorum in limbo usque ad christi adventum sub potestate diaboli detentorum, hic inserere questionem que Exonie inter quosdam doctores diucius vertebatur [curavi], et fuit questio sub hac forma: utrum omnes adulti et parvuli mortui ante christum in culpa mortali et sine presentis iustificacionis et remissionis ac gratificacionis gracia decesserunt ad carenciam visionis divine perpetuam obligati?[2]

This opinion the doctor had supported with arguments 'contrary to the words of the saints and generally unheard of in the schools'; and Buckingham holding 'the contrary position as catholic and faithful', was determined to refute it. However, he prefaces his remarks with a profession of faith which seems to refer to Grandisson: 'omnia dicta mea correccioni ecclesie et prelati mei ex corde submitto'.[3]

The controversy arose principally from the Exeter master's proposition that none of the faithful had been received into the full love of God before the Passion of Our Lord, from which he drew some unusual deductions concerning the efficacy of grace and the remission of sin. Before Christ's death, he had said, the sacraments of the Old Law could not ensure the remission of sin

---

[1] Fo. 392rᵇ.

[2] Fo. 395vᵃ. Printed with other material by Pantin, *The English Church*, pp. 263–6. We note that the missing main verb, for which Pantin very suitably supplies 'curavi', is also absent in the Merton MS.: further evidence that it is a copy of the New College MS.

[3] Fo. 396rᵃ. Cf. Pantin, *The English Church*, p. 114 n. 2.

to those in Limbo; they enjoyed a natural justice, but kept only the hope of divine justification. But those who laboured meritoriously had not died in vain; for, though deprived of temporal grace in their lifetime and at their death, their good works would after the Passion merit the gift of *subsequent* grace, by which they would indeed receive eternal life. But would not the souls in Limbo, whilst still graceless, have to bear the punishment of their guilt? Not so, replies the master. The punishment is taken from them, though the guilt cannot be purged until, at Christ's death, God by his grace justifies those souls and absolves the guilt. For only by the supreme sacrifice of the Son is the curse of Adam redeemed and the power of the devil destroyed.[1] Buckingham was easily able to show that this argument (which may appear muddled rather than heterodox) led to unacceptable conclusions. The Exeter master had distinguished the grace of divine predestination, by which even mortal sinners, if foreknown to God, received the guarantee of future salvation, from the grace of present justification and gratification (from which they were excluded before the Passion).[2] Buckingham regarded this as false and dangerous, because it denied the value of merit which could no longer be rewarded *immediately* with the gift of grace. On the other hand, the good works of those in Limbo would seem (on the master's reasoning) to carry assurance of future grace. If their merit brought justification to those without present grace, the master had come close to Pelagianism, and Buckingham was in the happy position of being able to rebuke him on this count.[3] Did he, we may ask, appreciate the irony of the situation?

The master was open to attack on other counts also. His doctrine of subsequent grace required that the sins of those now in

---

[1] Fos. 395v^a–396r^a, articles 1, 6, 10; printed *ibid.* pp. 264–5.

[2] Article 8, fo. 395v^b, printed *ibid.* p. 265.

[3] Fo. 401r^b–v^a. Similiter contra opinionem Doctoris et pro conclusione mea, ad multa inconveniencia deducebam et dixi, quod evacuat omnia merita antiquorum, quia si omnes patres antiqui in peccato mortali et sine gracia gratum faciente fuerunt, igitur vitam non merebantur eternam nec deum super omnia dilexerunt nec eius precepta debite adimplebant, quia ista in peccato mortali et sine gracia iustificacionis et gratificacionis presentis fieri lex condempnat, et esse Pelagianam heresim manifestat.

Limbo, but destined to future salvation, were remitted, but not their guilt. Buckingham admits that this was not totally impossible, since God's absolute power admits of contradictions; but it is to strain the accepted interpretation of his activity towards man. If the sins of those in Limbo are remitted, so is their guilt.[1] But this was only a secondary error arising from the misuse of the doctrine of subsequent grace. First Buckingham affirms that God's acceptance of merit requires the grace of *present* justification.[2] But what does the *reverendus doctor* say? Anxious to avoid falling into Pelagianism, he states that such meritorious souls are justified by the grace of *predestination*. But the Pelagian error denies the necessity not of predestinating grace but of *supernaturally infused* grace (which is Buckingham's grace of present justification).[3] Correspondingly the Exeter master's emphasis on predestinating grace led him, in Buckingham's opinion, to admit that man can merit eternal life (whether or not he attains it) by his natural good, and that this does not require the *supernatural* habit of grace.[4] Only the identification of his opponent and the recovery of his *questiones*

[1] Fo. 405 vᵃ. Vanis verbis omissis et hec pro inpugnacione verbali dico, quod non est possibile quod tollatur culpa si non pena aliqua deleatur, cum omne peccatum sit per se pena, ut patet 2 Sent. d. 36; est tamen possibile de dei potencia absoluta quod, culpa deleta et data iusticia, illa pena eterna sensus et dampni maneat indeleta.

[2] Fo. 405 vᵃ.

[3] Fo. 406 rᵃ. Pro responsione ad auctoritates sanctorum dicit [reverendus doctor] quod opera antiquorum in vita eorum vite eterne meritoria non fuerunt, nec priusquam accederet gracia per mortem christi ea vivificans; unde addit, 'videant ipsi qui dicunt sanctos patres ante tempus gracie, et sic sine gracia, meruisse vitam eternam': cui ego planissime contradico, quia sine gracia mediatoris postmodum subsecuta nulla fuerunt opera vite eterne meritoria. Et secundam responsionem annectens dicit, 'vel quia non nisi de gracia et caritate predestinacionis divine', per hoc credens vitare Pelagianum errorem. Sed contra hec, Pelagius nunquam dixit quod sine gracia predestinacionis habet aliquis vel meretur vitam eternam, sed de gracia supernaturali infusa, que dicitur gracia temporalis iustificationis presentis, dicit: et per consequens sine illa gracia nullus potest vitam eternam mereri.

[4] Fo. 407 rᵇ. Igitur non ad omne meritum vite eterne est gracia predestinacionis divine eterne necessario requisita, ut dicit Doctor, sed secundum argutum [*sc.* suum] sufficit gracia redamacionis et bonum nature. Similiter secundum istam assercionem Doctoris, ad meritum vite eterne non requiritur habitus infusus supernaturalis et per consequens habitus fidei nec spei, sed ad hec omnia sufficit naturale bonum.

will tell us if Buckingham's accusation was justified. But the implication he saw in the Doctor's thesis—'ad meritum vite eterne non requiritur habitus infusus supernaturalis'—is of the greatest interest. For the doctrine that acceptance by God may possibly not require the infusion of supernatural habits had been put forward by several theologians (Robert Holcot and Adam Woodham, for example),[1] who are very probably to be numbered with those 'Modern Pelagians' whom Bradwardine set out to refute. The Exeter master may well have been affected by the New Way. If Buckingham himself had been influenced by this current, his youthful flights were well past by 1350.

[1] Cf. Leff, *Bradwardine and the Pelagians*, pp. 217 ff., 243 ff.

BIBLIOGRAPHY

I. PRIMARY SOURCES

(i) *Manuscript*

Cambridge, Trinity College B. 16. 2, fos. 1r–141r. Wyclif, *Summa de Ente*.

Cambridge, Gonville and Caius College 139/79. Walter Burley, *De Universalibus*, etc.

Cambridge, Gonville and Caius College 337/565, fos. 1–48. Wyclif, *De Universalibus* and Prologue to *De Tempore*.

Cambridge, Gonville and Caius College 370/592. Thomas Claxton, *Commentary on the Sentences*, Book 1.

Cambridge, Peterhouse 223, fos. 179–280. Wyclif, *De veritate sacrae scripturae*, chapters 1–24.

Cambridge, University Library Additional 3571, fos. 31–65r. Wodeford, *De sacramento altaris*.

Oxford, Bodleian Library, Digby 176. Astronomical Treatises, *c.* 1350.

Oxford, Bodleian Library, lat. theol. e. 33. Thomas Gascoigne, Theological Notebook.

Oxford, Balliol College 64. Peter of Candia, *Commentary on the Sentences*.

Oxford, Merton College M. 1. 11, fos. 1–83. Thomas Buckingham, *Quaestiones*.

Oxford, Merton College O. I. 9. Anon., *Quaestiones*, *c.* 1350.

Oxford, Merton College Record 3690. Bursarial Roll, 1356.

Oxford, Corpus Christi College 116. Incepting Exercises in the Arts Faculty, *c.* 1400.

Oxford, New College 134, fos. 322–441. Thomas Buckingham, *Quaestiones*.

Oxford, Oriel College 15, fos. 4–112. Richard FitzRalph, *Commentary on the Sentences*. *Ibid.* fos. 210–22. Nicholas Aston, *Quaestiones*.

British Museum, Harleian 2178, fos. 107ff. Sharpe, *De Universalibus*.

British Museum, Royal 7. B. iii, fos. 4v–65v. Wodeford, *De sacramento altaris*.

British Museum, Royal 12. B. xix, fos. 14–19. Mylverley, *De superficiali universalium noticia*.

Lincoln Cathedral, Chapter Library C. 1. 15, fos. 293–340. Wyclif, *De Universalibus* and *De Tempore*.

Worcester Cathedral, Chapter Library F 65. Notebook of Oxford student, *c*. 1370.

Florence, Bibl. Naz., Conv. Soppr. A. 3. 508, fos. 1–109. Richard FitzRalph, *Commentary on the Sentences* (on microfilm).

Prague, University Library 1762 (IX. E. 6). Wyclif, *De intellectione Dei, De scientia Dei, De potencia Dei* (chapters 1–2), *De volucione Dei* (on microfilm).

Stockholm, Royal Library 9, fos. 33–52. Wyclif, *De Ydeis* (on microfilm).

Venice, San Marco, Cl. VI. 173 (2625), fos. 1–60. Wyclif, *Dubia super libros phisicorum* (on microfilm).

(ii) *Printed*

John Wyclif, *Trialogus*, ed. G. V. Lechler (Oxford, 1869).

Johannis Wyclif De Ente: librorum duorum excerpta, ed. M. H. Dziewicki (*WS*, 1909).

Johannis Wyclif De Ente: libri primi tractatus primus et secundus, ed. S. H. Thomson (Oxford, 1930).

Johannis Wyclif De ente praedicamentali, ed. R. Beer (*WS*, 1891).

Johannis Wyclif Tractatus de benedicta incarnacione, ed. E. Harris (*WS*, 1886).

Johannis Wyclif Tractatus de logica, ed. M. H. Dziewicki, 3 vols. (*WS*, 1894–9).

Johannis Wyclif De compositione hominis, ed. R. Beer (*WS*, 1884).

Johannis Wyclif Sermones, ed. J. Loserth, 4 vols. (*WS*, 1886–90).

Johannis Wyclif De veritate sacrae scripturae, ed. R. Buddensieg, 3 vols. (*WS*, 1905–7).

Johannis Wyclif Miscellanea Philosophica, ed. M. H. Dziewicki, 2 vols. (*WS*, 1901–2).

Johannis Wyclif Opera Minora, ed. J. Loserth (*WS*, 1913).

Johannis Wyclif De civili dominio, ed. J. Loserth, 3 vols. (*WS*, 1902).

Johannis Wyclif De dominio divino (and Richard FitzRalph, *De pauperie Salvatoris*), ed. R. L. Poole (*WS*, 1890).

Anglia Sacra, ed. Henry Wharton, 2 vols. (London, 1691).

Aristotle, *Metaphysics*, trans. W. D. Ross (Oxford, 1908).

Questiones solertissimi viri Johannis Bokinkam genere anglici in quattuor libros sententiarum (Paris, 1505), that is, the *Commentary* of Thomas Buckingham.

Thomas Bradwardine, *De causa Dei contra Pelagium*, ed. Henry Saville (London, 1618).

Thomas of Bradwardine, his tractatus de proportionibus, ed. and trans. H. L. Crosby (Wisconsin, 1955).

Walter Burley, *De puritate artis logice tractatus longior*, and revised edition of *Tractatus brevior*, ed. P. Boehner, Franciscan Inst. Publ., text ser. 9 (St Bonaventure, New York, 1955).

Calendar of...Papal Letters, ed. W. Bliss, vol. II (1305–42) (London, 1895).

Chartularium Universitatis Parisiensis, ed. H. Denifle and A. Chatelain, 4 vols. (Paris, 1889–97).

Concilia Magnae Britanniae et Hiberniae, ed. David Wilkins, 4 vols. (London, 1737).

Johannis Duns Scoti Oxoniense scriptum in librum primum Sententiarum P. Lombardi (Coimbra, 1609).

Johannis Duns Scoti Opera Omnia, ed. L. Wadding, 12 vols. (Lyons, 1639).

Fasciculi Zizaniorum, ed. W. W. Shirley (Rolls Series, 1858).

Fasciculus rerum expetendarum et fugiendarum, ed. E. Brown, 2 vols. (London, 1690).

Thomas Gascoigne, *Loci e libro veritatum*, ed. J. E. Thorold Rogers (Oxford, 1881).

Henry of Ghent, *Summae questionum ordinariarum*, Franciscan Inst. Publ., text ser. 5 (St Bonaventure, New York, 1953), from 1520 edition.

Register of John de Grandisson, Bishop of Exeter, A.D. 1327–1369, Episcopal Registers, diocese of Exeter, ed. F. C. Hingeston-Randolph, 3 vols. (Exeter, 1894–9).

Hentisberi regulae, videlicet de sensu composito et diviso...item sophismata (Venice, 1494).

Historical Manuscripts Commission, App. to 4th Report (London, 1874).

Roberti Linconiensis Commentaria in libros Posteriorum Aristotelis (Venice, 1494).

Petri Lumbardi libri iv sententiarum, ed. PP. Collegii S. Bonaventurae, 2nd edn, 2 vols. (Quaracchi, 1916).

Guillelmi de Ockham Opera Politica, vol. III, ed. H. S. Offler (Manchester, 1956).

Statuta antiqua universitatis Oxoniensis, ed. Strickland Gibson (Oxford, 1931).

Summa domini Armacani in questionibus Armenorum (Paris, 1512).

Thomae Waldensis Carmeletae anglici Doctrinale antiquitatum fidei catholicae ecclesiae, ed. B. Blanciotti, 3 vols. (Venice, 1757–9).

2. SECONDARY AUTHORITIES

Abbott, T. K. *Catalogue of the Manuscripts...of Trinity College, Dublin* (London, 1900).

Academia Caesarea Vindobonensis, ed. *Tabulae codicum manuscriptorum ...in bibliotheca palatina Vindobonensi*, 7 vols. (Vienna, 1864–75).

Allen, P. S., and Garrod, H. W. *Merton Muniments*, OHS, LXXXVI (1928).

Bale, J. *Scriptorum illustrium maioris Brytanniae...catalogus* (Basle, 1557–9).

Bateson, F. W., et al. *Cambridge Bibliography of English Literature*, vol. 1 (1940).

Bateson, Mary, ed. *Catalogue of the Library of Syon Monastery, Isleworth* (Cambridge, 1898).

Baudry, L. 'Les Rapports de Guillaume d'Occam et de Walter Burleigh', *AHDL*, IX (1934), 155–73.

—— *Le tractatus de principiis theologiae attribué à Guillaume d'Occam*, Études de philosophie médiévale, XXIII (Paris, 1936).

—— *Guillaume d'Occam: sa vie, ses œuvres, ses idées sociales et politiques*, Études de philosophie médiévale, XXXIX (Paris, 1949).

Baur, L. *Die philosophischen Werke des Robert Grosseteste, Bischofs von Lincoln*, Beitr. z. Gesch. der Phil. des Mittelalters, IX (Münster, 1912).

—— *Die Philosophie des Robert Grosseteste, Bischofs von Lincoln*, Beitr. z. Gesch. der Phil. des Mittelalters, XVIII, 4–6 (Münster, 1917).

Bernard, Edward. *Catalogi librorum manuscriptorum Angliae et Hiberniae* (Oxford, 1697).

Boehner, P. 'The Realistic Conceptualism of William Ockham', *Traditio*, IV (1946), 307–35.

—— *Medieval Logic* (Manchester, 1952).

—— *The tractatus de successivis attributed to William Ockham*, Franciscan Inst. Publ., philosophy ser. 1 (St Bonaventure, New York, 1944).

—— 'Ockham's Theory of Signification', *Franciscan Studies*, new ser. VI (1946), 143–70.

—— 'Ockham's theory of Supposition and the Notion of Truth', *ibid.* VI (1946), 261–92.

—— *William Ockham: Summa Logicae pars prima*, Franciscan Inst. Publ., text ser. 2 (St Bonaventure, New York, 1951).

Breck, A. du P. 'The Manuscripts of John Wyclif's *De Trinitate*', *Medievalia et Humanistica*, VII (1952), 56–70.

Brodrick, G. C. *Memorials of Merton College*, OHS, IV (1885).

Callus, D. A. 'The Oxford Career of Robert Grosseteste', *Oxoniensia*, X (1945), 42–72.

——, ed. *Robert Grosseteste, Scholar and Bishop* (Oxford, 1955).

Carré, M. H. *Phases of Thought in England* (Oxford, 1949).

Catálogo de los códices latinos de la real biblioteca del Escorial, 4 vols. (Madrid, 1910–16).

Catalogue of the Harleian Manuscripts in the British Museum, 2 vols. (1808).

Chenu, M. D. 'Les Quaestiones de Thomas de Buckingham', *Studia medievalia...in honorem R. J. Martin* (Bruges, 1948), pp. 229–42.

Chevalier, U. *Répertoire des sources historiques du moyen âge: bio-bibliographie*, new edition, 2 vols. (Paris, 1905–7).

Collier, Jeremy. *An Ecclesiastical History of Great Britain*, ed. T. Lathbury, 9 vols. (London, 1852).

Coxe, H. O. *Catalogus codicum MSS....in collegiis aulisque Oxoniensibus*, 2 vols. (Oxford, 1852).

Cristiani, L. 'Wyclif', *DTC*, XV, 3585–614.

Crombie, A. C. *Robert Grosseteste and the Origins of Experimental Science, 1100–1700* (Oxford, 1953).

Cronin, H. S. 'John Wycliffe, the Reformer, and Canterbury Hall, Oxford', *TRHS*, 3rd ser. VIII (1914), 55–76.

Dahmus, J. H. *The Prosecution of John Wyclyf* (New Haven, 1952).

Denis, M. *Codices manuscripti theologici bibliothecae palatinae Vindobonensis*, 2 vols., in 5 parts (Vienna, 1793–1802).

Doucet, V. 'Commentaires sur les sentences: supplément au répertoire de M. Frédéric Stegmüller', *AFH*, XLVII (1954), 88–177, 400–27.

Dudik, B. *Forschungen in Schweden für Mährens Geschichte* (Brunn, 1852).

Ehrle, F. *Der Sentenzenkommentar Peters von Candia*, Franziskanische Studien, IX (Münster, 1925).

Emden, A. B. *A Biographical Register of the University of Oxford to A.D. 1500*, 3 vols. (Oxford, 1957–9).

Floyer, J. K., and Hamilton, S. G. *Catalogue of Manuscripts...of Worcester Cathedral*, Worc. Hist. Soc. (1906).

Forte, S. L. *A Study of Some Oxford Schoolmen of the Middle of the Fourteenth Century* (Oxford B.Litt., 1947).

Fryde, E. B., and Highfield, J. R. L. 'An Oxfordshire Deed of Balliol College', *Oxoniensia*, XX (1955), 40–5.

Gilpin, W. *The Lives of John Wicliff, and of the Most Eminent of his Disciples, Lord Cobham, John Hus, Jerome of Prague and Zizca* (London, 1765).

Gilson, É. *La Philosophie au moyen âge*, 2nd edn (Paris, 1944).

—— *Jean Duns Scot*, Études de philosophie médiévale, XLII, 2 vols. (Paris, 1952).

—— *History of Christian Philosophy in the Middle Ages* (London, 1955).

Glorieux, P. 'Commentaires sur les sentences', *DTC*, XIV, 1860–84.

Golubovich, G. *Biblioteca bio-bibliografica della Terra Santa e dell'Oriente Franciscano*, IV (Quaracchi, 1923).

Gordon, E. V., ed. *Pearl* (Oxford, 1953).

Guelluy, R. *Philosophie et théologie chez Guillame d'Ockham* (Louvain, Paris, 1947).

Gwynn, A. 'Richard FitzRalph at Avignon', *Studies*, XXII (1933), 591–607.

—— 'Archbishop FitzRalph and the Friars', *Studies*, XXVI (1937), 50–67.

—— 'The Sermon-Diary of Richard FitzRalph', *Proceedings of the Royal Irish Academy*, XLIV (1937), 1–57.

—— *The English Austin Friars in the Time of Wyclif* (Oxford, 1940).

—— 'Two Sermons of Primate Ric. FitzRalph', *Archivia Hibernica*, XIV (1949), 50–65.

Hahn, S. *Thomas Bradwardinus und seine Lehre von der menschlichen Willensfreiheit*, Beitr. z. Gesch. der Phil. des Mittelalters, V (Münster, 1905).

Hammerich, L. L. *The Beginning of the Strife between Richard FitzRalph and the Mendicants, with an edition of his autobiographical prayer and his proposition Unusquisque*, Hist. Fil. Meddel. XXVI, 3 (Copenhagen, 1938).

Hauréau, B. 'Notice sur le numéro 16409 des manuscrits latins de la bibliothèque nationale', *Notices et extraits des manuscrits de la Bibliothèque Nationale*, XXXIV, part II (1895), 319–62.

Hunt, R. W. 'The Library of Robert Grosseteste', *Robert Grosseteste*, ed. D. A. Callus, pp. 121–45.

Jacob, E. F. 'Reynold Pecock, Bishop of Chichester', *Proceedings of the British Academy*, XXXVII (1951), 121–53.

—— *Some Recent Contributions to the Study of the Later Middle Ages* (Oxford, 1951).

James, M. R. *Descriptive Catalogue of the Manuscripts…of Peterhouse* (Cambridge, 1899).

—— *The Western Manuscripts in the Library of Trinity College, Cambridge*, 3 vols. (Cambridge, 1900).

—— *The Western Manuscripts in the Library of Gonville and Caius College, Cambridge*, 2 vols. (Cambridge, 1908).

James, M. R. 'The Catalogue of the Library of the Augustinian Friars at York', *Fasciculus J. W. Clark dicatus* (Cambridge, 1909), pp. 2–96.

—— and Thompson, A. Hamilton. 'A Catalogue of the Library of Leicester Abbey', *Transactions of the Leicestershire Archaeological Society*, XXI (1939–41), 1–88.

Knowles, M. D. *The Religious Orders in England*, 3 vols. (Cambridge, 1948–59).

—— 'The Censured Opinions of Uthred of Boldon', *Proceedings of the British Academy*, XXXVII (1951), 305–42.

Koch, J. 'Neue Aktenstücke zu dem gegen Wilhelm Ockham in Avignon geführten Prozess', *RTAM*, VII (1935), 353–80; VIII (1936), 79–93, 168–97.

Laun, J. F. 'Thomas von Bradwardin, der Schüler Augustins und Lehrer Wiclifs', *Zeitschrift für Kirchengeschichte*, XLVII, new ser. 10 (1928), 333–56.

—— 'Recherches sur Thomas de Bradwardin, précurseur de Wyclif', *Revue d'histoire et de philosophie religieuses*, IX (1929), 217–33.

—— 'Die Prädestination bei Wyclif und Bradwardin', *Imago Dei*, ed. H. Bornkamm (Giessen, 1932), pp. 63–84.

Laurent, M. H., ed. *Urbain V (1362–70)*, *Lettres Communes*, fasc. IV (Paris, 1957).

Lechler, G. *De Thoma Bradwardino Commentatio* (Leipzig, 1862).

—— *Johann von Wicliff und die Vorgeschichte der Reformation*, 2 vols. (Leipzig, 1873). English edition and trans. by P. Lorimer, *John Wycliffe and his English Precursors* (London, 1884).

Leff, G. *Bradwardine and the Pelagians* (Cambridge, 1957).

—— *Medieval Thought* (London, 1958).

Lewis, J. *History of the Life and Sufferings of the Reverend and Learned John Wycliffe, D.D.* (London, 1720; new edition 1820).

Little, A. G. *The Grey Friars at Oxford*, OHS, XX (1891).

Lloyd, A. H. *Early History of Christ's College* (Cambridge, 1934).

Lloyd, M. E. H. 'John Wyclif and the Prebend of Lincoln', *EHR*, LXI (1946), 388–94.

Loserth, J. *Wiclif and Hus* (London, 1884).

—— 'Johann von Wiclif und Robert Grosseteste, Bischof von Lincoln', *Sitz. Akad. der Wissensch. Wien*, phil.-hist. Kl., 186 (1918), fasc. 2, 83 pp.

Madan, F., et al. *Summary Catalogue of the Western Manuscripts in the Bodleian Library*, 9 vols. (Oxford, 1922–53).

McFarlane, K. B. *John Wycliffe and the Beginnings of English Non-Conformity* (London, 1952).

Magrath, J. R. *The Queen's College*, 2 vols. (Oxford, 1921).

Maier, A. 'Zu Walter Burleys Politik-Kommentar', *RTAM*, XIV (1947), 332–6.

—— *Die Vorläufer Galileis im 14. Jahrhundert*, Storia e Letteratura, XXII (Rome, 1949).

—— 'Zu einigen Problemen der Ockhamforschung', *AFH*, XLVI (1953), 161–94.

—— 'Handschriftliches zu Wilhelm Ockham und Walter Burley', *AFH*, XLVIII (1955), 225–51.

Manning, B. L. 'John Wyclif', *Cambridge Medieval History*, VII, 486–507, 900–7.

Marchi, L. de, and Bertolani, G. *Inventario...della R. Biblioteca universitaria di Pavia* (Milan, 1894).

Michalski, C. 'Les Courants philosophiques à Oxford et à Paris pendant le XIVe siècle', *Bulletin international de l'académie polonaise des sciences et des lettres*, classe hist. phil. (Cracow, 1922–4), pp. 59–88.

—— 'Le Criticisme et le scepticisme dans la philosophie du XIVe siècle', *ibid.* (1927), pp. 41–122.

—— 'Les Courants critiques et sceptiques dans la philosophie du XIVe siècle', *ibid.* (1927), 192–244.

—— 'La Physique nouvelle et les différents courants philosophiques au XIVe siècle', *ibid.* (1928), pp. 93–164.

—— 'Le Problème de la volonté à Oxford et à Paris au XIVe siècle', *Studia Philosophica*, II (Lemberg, 1936), 233–365.

Milner, J. *History of the Church of Christ*, new edition, 4 vols. (London, 1847).

Minio-Paluello, L. 'Two Erasures in MS. Oriel 15', *Bodleian Library Record*, IV (1953), 205–7.

Moody, E. A. *The Logic of William of Ockham* (London, 1935).

Mozley, J. F. *John Foxe and his Book* (London, 1940).

Oberman, H. A. *Archbishop Thomas Bradwardine, a Fourteenth-Century Augustinian* (Utrecht, 1957).

Pannenberg, W. *Die Prädestinationlehre des Duns Scotus* (Göttingen, 1954).

Pantin, W. A. 'Catalogue of the Books of Durham College, Oxford, c. 1390–1400', in H. E. Salter, W. A. Pantin, H. G. Richardson, eds., *Formularies which bear on the History of Oxford, c. 1240–1420*, *OHS*, new ser. IV (1942), I, 240–5.

Pantin, W. A. *Canterbury College, Oxford*, vol. III, *OHS*, new ser. VIII (1950).

—— *The English Church in the Fourteenth Century* (Cambridge, 1955).

Paulus, *Henri de Gand. Essai sur les tendances de sa métaphysique*, Études de philosophie médiévale, xxv (Paris, 1938).

Pelzer, A. 'Les 51 Articles de Guillaume Occam censurés, en Avignon, en 1326', *Revue d'histoire ecclésiastique*, XVIII (1922), 240–70.

Powicke, F. M. *The Medieval Books of Merton College* (Oxford, 1931).

Rashdall, H. *The Universities of Europe in the Middle Ages*, 2nd ed., rev. by F. M. Powicke and A. B. Emden, 3 vols. (Oxford, 1936).

Salter, H. E. 'The Stamford Schism', *EHR*, XXXVII (1922), 249–53.

——, ed. *Snappe's Formulary*, *OHS*, LXXX (1924).

Schum, W. *Verzeichnis der Amplonianischen Handschriften zu Erfurt* (1877).

Sharp, D. E. *Franciscan Philosophy at Oxford in the Thirteenth Century* (Oxford, 1930).

Shirley, W. W. *Catalogue of the Original Works of John Wyclif* (Oxford, 1865). 2nd edn rev. by J. Loserth (London, 1924).

Smalley, B. 'John Wyclif's Postilla super totam bibliam', *Bodleian Library Record*, IV (1953), 186–205.

—— 'The Biblical Scholar', *Robert Grosseteste*, ed. D. A. Callus (1955), pp. 70–97.

Stegmüller, F. *Repertorium commentariorum in sententias Petri Lombardi*, 2 vols. (Würzburg, 1947).

—— 'Die zwei Apologien des Jean de Mirecourt', *RTAM*, v (1933), 40–78, 192–204.

Stein, I. H. 'Two Notes on Wyclif', *Speculum*, VI (1931), 465–8.

—— 'Another "Lost" Chapter of Wyclif's *Summa de Ente*', *Speculum*, VIII (1933), 254–5.

Thomson, S. H. 'Some Latin Works Erroneously Ascribed to Wyclif', *Speculum*, III (1928), 382–91.

—— 'A "Lost" Chapter of Wyclif's *Summa de Ente*', *Speculum*, IV (1929), 339–46.

—— 'The Order of Writing of Wyclif's Philosophical Works', *Českou Minulosti*, Essays presented to V. Novotny (Prague, 1929), pp. 146–66.

—— 'The Philosophical Basis of Wyclif's Theology', *Journal of Religion*, XI (1931), 86–116.

—— 'A Gonville and Caius Wyclif Manuscript', *Speculum*, VIII (1933). 197–204.

Thomson, S. H. 'Unnoticed Manuscripts and Works of Wyclif', *Journal of Theological Studies*, XXXVIII (1937), 24–36, 139–48.

—— *The Writings of Robert Grosseteste* (Cambridge, 1940).

—— 'Walter Burley's Commentary on the Politics of Aristotle', *Mélanges Auguste Pelzer* (Louvain, 1947), pp. 557–78.

Trapp, D. 'Augustinian Theology of the Fourteenth Century', *Augustiniana*, VI (1956), 146–274.

—— 'Peter Ceffons of Clairvaux', *RTAM*, XXIV (1957), 101–54.

—— 'Unchristened Nominalism and Wycliffite Realism at Prague in 1381', *RTAM*, XXIV (1957), 320–60.

Truhlar, J. *Catalogus codicum manuscriptorum qui in C.R. bibliotheca...asservantur*, 2 vols. (Prague, 1906).

Twemlow, J. A. 'Wycliffe's Preferments and University Degrees', *EHR*, XV (1900), 529–30.

Ueberweg, F., and Geyer, B. *Grundriss der Geschichte der Philosophie*, vol. II, new edition (Berlin, 1928).

Venn, J. and J. A. *Alumni Cantabrigienses*, 10 vols. (Cambridge, 1922–55).

Vignaux, P. *Justification et prédestination au XIVe siècle*, Bibl. de l'école des hautes études, sc. relig. 48 (Paris, 1934).

—— 'Nominalisme', *DTC*, XI, 717–84.

—— *Nominalisme au XIVe siècle* (Paris–Montreal, 1948).

Vooght, P. de. *Les Sources de la doctrine chrétienne* (Bruges, 1954).

Walmsley, C. 'Two Long Lost Works of William Woodford and Robert of Leicester', *AFH*, XLVI (1953), 458–70.

Warner, G. F., and Gilson, J. P., eds. *Catalogue of the Western Manuscripts in the Old Royal and King's Collections*, 4 vols. (London, 1921).

Weisheipl, J. A. *Early Fourteenth-Century Physics and the Merton 'School'* (Oxford D.Phil., 1957).

——, and Oberman, H. A. 'The *Sermo Epinicius* ascribed to Thomas Bradwardine (1346)', *AHDL*, XXV (1958), 295–329.

Werner, K. *Der Augustinismus in der Scholastik des späteren Mittelalters* (Vienna, 1883).

Wislocki, W. *Catalogus codicum manuscriptorum bibliothecae universitatis Jagellonicae Cracoviensis* (Cracow, 1877–81).

Woolley, R. M. *Catalogue of the Manuscripts of Lincoln Cathedral Chapter Library* (Oxford, 1927).

Workman, H. B. *John Wyclif*, 2 vols. (Oxford, 1926).

INDEX